SIX OF
THE BEST

SIX OF THE BEST

Jimmy Edwards

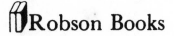

Robson Books

FIRST PUBLISHED IN GREAT BRITAIN IN 1984 BY
ROBSON BOOKS LTD., BOLSOVER HOUSE, 5-6
CLIPSTONE STREET, LONDON W1P 7EB. COPYRIGHT
© 1984 JIMMY EDWARDS

British Library Cataloguing in Publication Data
Edwards, Jimmy
    Six of the best.
    1. Edwards, Jimmy. 2. Comedians—Great Britain—
    Biography
    I. Title
    791'.092'4   PN2598.E/

ISBN 0-86051-236-3

Printed in Great Britain by
The Garden City Press, Letchworth.

Contents

	Introduction	7
1	Cambridge at War	9
2	That Bloody Tower	14
3	Halt! Who Goes There?	19
4	Per Ardua . . .	32
5	Drink Canada Dry — I Did My Best	47
6	Washouts	60
7	Straight and Level	78
8	Coastal Command	110
9	African Fiasco	122
10	Transport Command	145
11	In Action at Last	165
12	Down But Not Out	190
13	You've Done Enough	203
14	What Next?	217
	Postscript	223

Introduction

I embarked on this story a couple of years ago and had spent the advance royalties before I had written many chapters. It's not only that I am idle—I was launched on an extensive tour of the musical *Oliver!*, which took me all round England, and also for two months to Toronto. Any sort of mental application is difficult when you are on your travels. I was about three-quarters of the way through, and had convinced myself that my light-hearted approach to the subject was perfectly in order, when I chanced upon a copy of *Bomber Command*, and it reminded me, very forcibly, that there were many chaps in the RAF who did not have such a happy-go-lucky career. One need only look at the aircrew losses for one night over the Ruhr to realize how fortunate I was. And so I doff my cap to the airmen in other commands whose lifestyle was, perforce, more rigorous than mine. What follows, in fact, is a somewhat haphazard account of the way the war unfolded . . . for me.

I served for six years, flew for four of them, never flew anything that wasn't obsolescent, never dropped a bomb or fired a gun, and finished up with the DFC. How's that for a line-shoot?

And what about this? I was too young for the Battle of Britain, and too old for the film.

'The day war broke out . . .' Who remembers dear old Robb Wilton now? But that was the catch-phrase of the time. Everybody could tell you where he was—the day war broke out. Just as later on everybody had a story about what he was doing 'when the bomb dropped'.

Well—the day war broke out, I was picking potatoes on a farm in Wiltshire.

A number of us undergraduates from Cambridge University had accepted the offer of Rolph Gardner to go down to his estate in Fontmell Magna in the summer vacation for a working holiday. We had done it the year before. We slept in tents, pitched in a circle round a flagpole, on which at dawn Rolph would raise a Union Jack while we jogged round and round in shorts chanting:

> *Morning is come*
> *Night is away.*
> *Rise with the sun*
> *And welcome the day.*

And when the last yawning young man had joined the circle (guess who?) we came to a standstill and faced the flag as it fluttered in the summer breeze. In bare feet, by the way! There's something quite pleasant about bare feet in the early-morning dew—but in the rain it's horrible.

We ate communally in an old barn, and worked in the fields in gangs in the morning. After lunch we had lectures and discussions on agricultural topics. In the evenings there were sing-songs, and on the last night of our stay I put on a skit or two about such romantic things as compost heaps, and did my impression of our host.

Not so much a host, as it happens, as an employer. For our work we got about threepence an hour—not a lot even in those days. The unions wouldn't stand for that sort of thing now.

J.E.

CAMBRIDGE AT WAR

IT WAS A strange time. I went back, as usual, to my old digs in Portugal Place, Cambridge. I carried on singing three times a week in St John's College chapel, and continued to attempt to teach the little swine in the Choir School. I spoke each week in the Union debates, played trombone in the Arimatheans Dance Band, and we of the Footlights Club put together a revue with which we attempted to entertain the troops at local camps. Without much success, I should add. There were frequent shouts of 'Join!' as we manfully ploughed our way through the opening chorus (dressed as folderol clowns!) and it was at one of these shows that I first heard the expression 'Get your knees brown!'

But we were doing our bit. I used to tell a joke—told me by someone else—about climbing a mountain and meeting no one for three days. Then at the top of the mountain I found a hut, and the door was opened by an old man wearing no clothes at all, except a top hat. I said to him, 'Why don't you wear any clothes?' and he replied, 'Nobody ever comes up here.' I asked, 'Then why do you wear the top hat?' He said, 'You never know—they might.' Innocent enough, I thought. But one night a red-faced officer said to me: 'How dare you tell a joke like that?' I replied, 'There were no ladies here, were there?' 'No, but there may well have been some gentlemen.'

Rugger continued. Squash continued. Punting on the Cam continued. But gradually more and more friendly faces disappeared as chaps were called into the Forces. Some of the older ones, who had already been in the OTC or the Air Squadron, had not come back to University, and a great many dons and lecturers were already in uniform. I went, not very enthusiastically, to the OTC myself to see what my prospects were. 'I think I'd like to be in the cavalry,' I said, when asked my preference. I was told very firmly that they weren't going to have cavalry in this war—'It is all going to be tanks.'

My friend IVJ at Selwyn College persuaded me to apply for the Air Squadron, but they were full up, and I knew nothing about aeroplanes anyway. So it was back to the trombone. I believe I attended a few lectures too.

Eventually IVJ managed to persuade me to volunteer for the RAF. My call-up would not come for months, but I began to have a few pangs of conscience about hanging around at Cambridge, and I was also convinced that there was slightly more kudos in being a volunteer than a conscript.

So off to Uxbridge we went. IVJ was full of romantic ideas about flying together. 'Side by side we will claw the Hun out of the sky,' and all that. But it was not to be. My interview with the Selection Board was calamitous. How was I to know that they were all Group Captains? I'd never seen one before in my life.

I wandered in, sat myself down in front of them, and surveyed them with a cynical eye. I was wearing my green corduroy trousers and a very loud spotted bow tie—all the fashion in Cambridge at that time.

'Sit up straight and take your hands out of your pockets,' rapped the older one in the middle.

I pulled myself together reluctantly, and apparently not quickly enough.

'You are at Cambridge University, are you?' he barked.

'Yes.'

'Yes . . . SIR!' he roared. 'Now then. Why do you want to be a pilot?'

That stumped me, because I didn't really. I just wanted to do something.

'Well, sir . . . I suppose it's because I want to be in command.'

'Oh. Want to run the whole show yourself, eh?' he

remarked sarcastically. 'Well, now. You see that wall out there, through that window? How would you calculate its height by trigonometry?'

That was easy. 'I wouldn't,' I replied truthfully. 'I don't do trigonometry.'

He was thunderstruck. 'You're at Cambridge University, and you don't do trigonometry?' he shouted.

'There are other things in the curriculum, sir,' I replied coldly. And that was the end of that.

'You can be an Air Gunner, if you want to. We are very short of them.'

I'd read about that. 'No, thank you sir,' I said, and hurried out of the room. I'd love to have heard what they said to each other.

Back in the Orderly Room I met IVJ.

'How did you get on?' he asked.

'No good. They offered me Air Gunner. How about you?'

'Oh. I got in all right. I'm going to be a pilot. Quite soon, I believe.'

So that was the end of our romantic wartime partnership.

There was one further slap in the face in store. We marched up to the desk and demanded our return train fare to Cambridge. IVJ duly got his, but when I asked for mine, I was told I didn't qualify.

'You signed this form when you came in, didn't you? Well, it says 'ere if you don't get accepted you pays yer own fare home.'

Since then I've never signed anything without reading it carefully.

So back to the Union, the Choir School and the Dance Band. IVJ went off to learn to become a pilot, and I stumbled on in my bumbling way. I didn't really know what the war was all about. I didn't read the papers much, except for 'Varsity', for which I became a film critic for a time. Well, it meant free seats. Then, all unobtrusive, arrived a red-letter day. Until then I had never taken a drink of alcohol in my life. I was disgusted by the behaviour of my brothers, who sometimes when I was at home in Barnes, arrived very late in our attic bedroom and puked out of the window. I was disdainful of my fellow-undergraduates, who drank Audit ale, made in the college, at dinner, and talked in loud voices and laughed inanely. But one night in his rooms a fellow choral scholar produced some bottles of Tollemache Ale, a local brew. I was persuaded to try a glass, and soon finished the bottle. Suddenly I leapt up, grabbed a fruit-cake that was on his table, and threw it against the wall with all my strength. Everyone roared with laughter. Later, I tried a glass of this Audit ale in Hall. 'It's not strong,' they kept telling me. Of course, it's one of the strongest beers you can get. Soon I was dancing on the dining-table, and was warned by the senior porter to behave myself before I got thrown out. I was so happy. All my inhibitions had gone.

I've never looked back.

It is hard to piece together those ragged days. Terms came and went. Vacations were spent mostly on the farm in Wiltshire. Once, waiting at Semley station to return to London, an unexpected train drew up and stopped. It was crammed with soldiers, muddy and weary and looking half-stunned. The doors were locked, so we gave them cups of tea from the buffet. We learned later that they were on their way back from Dunkirk.

Eventually I went to Uxbridge again. This time I sat up straight, and showed due respect, and was put down for a pilot. But when it came to the medical examination, there was a surprise in store for me. I knew I was perfectly fit. Rugger and squash were my favourite sports. But my eyes were lazy. All that reading by a bad light in Portugal Place had apparently weakened the muscles that do the focusing, and I was put in the second category for aircrew. I couldn't back out again, and so I signed on to be trained as an Observer.

I was not to be called up straight away. Back to Cambridge I went yet again. After some time in this seeming vacuum, it got through to me—I don't know how, as I so rarely read the papers—that the RAF was anxious for people who had signed on and been 'deferred' to contact them with a view to being in 'Ground Defence' until their chance for aircrew training came up. 'Well,' I thought, 'at least I'll be in, and all this indecision and hanging about will be over—so I applied. 'Await your call-up' was the answer.

My exams came along, rather unexpectedly. I did a panic read-through of Legouis & Cazamien and passed. But only just. Then it was back to Wiltshire and Gore Farm.

One day I was helping Charlie with a crowbar, making holes for fencing posts, when old Harry came slowly by sitting on the horse-drawn water-tank. 'Mornin' Jim,' he shouted. 'There be a letter for you.' And there it was. 'Report for induction to RAF Blackpool.' I didn't know whether to laugh or cry. But when I got to Blackpool I knew.

I cried.

THAT BLOODY TOWER

WE WERE A strange collection at King's Cross station. All about the same age, but all shapes and sizes, and all sorts of clothes. I was in my green corduroys again, with a jacket with leather at the elbows, and my usual loud bow tie. We had been instructed to bring a small suitcase, so that these trappings of civilian life could be sent home.

The journey was long and tedious. I had never been so far before, and certainly not so far north. I don't think I spoke to anyone. On the platform at Blackpool we lined up uncertainly. A corporal surveyed my attire with disapproval. 'Hey, you! Farmer!' he shouted. 'Come over 'ere!' So much for the Great Thinker and Poet.

The only book I had brought with me was *The Oxford Book of English Verse*, and I browsed through its pages miserably as I sat in the boarding-house I had been sent to a few streets from the promenade. There were half a dozen of us in there, and the landlady ruled us with a rod of iron. I expect that was the first north-country accent I ever heard. In fact, all the accents were quite bewildering. Except the one that came through the loudspeakers when we had all been crammed into the football stadium the next day. We sat in the stands, and a small uniformed figure stood out in midfield with a microphone.

'You have been brought here,' his voice boomed round, in an accent that I was to get to know as 'Senior Officer', 'to be inducted into the Royal Air Force. You will only be here two weeks. In that time you will be kitted out with uniforms, taught to march, and shown how to fire a rifle. That is all we have time for.'

The whole idea of this induction period of two weeks was to try to prepare us for the rigours of Service life. To most of us it was such a complete change from our previous mode of life that we were subjected to some terrible shocks—with the best of intentions, of course. The marching was not too difficult for me. I knew vaguely how to salute, and could polish brass buttons as well as anybody else. And the sketchy lectures on Administration and so on I was able to follow.

But I wasn't prepared for the horrors of the lecture on VD. We were crammed, hundreds of us, into the theatre at the end of the North Pier, and when a good fug had been generated by the smokers, a young medical officer launched into a long list of the dangers of promiscuous sex, and the symptoms of various forms of venereal disease. His intention, quite clearly, was to scare us out of ever wanting to go to bed with a woman, and his methods were a triumphant success with me. I was beginning to feel a little sick of the whole subject when he started to detail the tortures we would suffer if ever we were foolhardy enough to contract gonorrhoea. I shall never forget his graphic simile: 'It's like trying to piss red-hot barbed wire.' But that's the last thing I heard. My next recollection is of waking up stretched out in the fresh air on the pier, with a corporal bending over me smacking my face. 'You'll be all right, son,' he said, loosening my collar. 'You'd better go back to your billet and have a lie down.'

Woolworth's on the front had been taken over as a clothing store, and in we all trooped to be fitted with uniforms. They had practically nothing to fit me, and I wandered about for several days wearing a forage-cap and uniform jacket, with my corduroys still incongruously beneath. There was an even bigger chap for whom they could only find an old-fashioned peaked cap. I pulled his leg about it—so we swopped caps, and we became firm friends. He was a huge man—they took weeks to get him a uniform—and had played rugger for Cambridge, though I had never met him there. Bateman-Champain and I suffered many indignities together before our ways finally parted. At least we had University in common, and this drew us together.

At this time we were all given a Number. This had to be stencilled on to every article of clothing we were given, and as mine was 929629, it was made easy for me. All I had to do was bag a 9 and a 2, and I was in business.

We drilled endlessly on the promenade, carving a swathe through the gawping holiday-makers, who stared at us as if we were a sideshow. Which indeed I suppose we were . . . a change from the pin-ball machines and ice-cream stalls and the Smallest Woman in the World. At least our show was free. And I expect we gave them a few laughs, for drilling as a squad is not as easy as it seems, especially when you've never done it before.

How I hated Blackpool. All the phoney paraphernalia of the seaside resort sickened me. Some evenings, when the tide was out—and it goes out two miles at Blackpool—I would walk across the sands right to the edge of the water just to get as far away as possible from the drabness of the town. Then I would turn round and survey it, and cry out obscenities which no one could hear. I even wrote a long Ode to Blackpool, in my favourite iambic pentameters, full of bitterness and cynicism.

> Earth hath not anything to show more base
> Than this detestable and loathsome place
> Called Blackpool . . . There is not in all the world
> A town at which there can, and should be hurled
> More justified and yet more vile abuse.
> I cannot find one single good excuse
> (Except as a prospective bombing target
> Along with Southend, Brighton, Hove and Margate)
> For the existence of this vice-rid sink,
> At once a den of men and whores and drink.
> It stretches mile on mile and pier on pier
> Offending nose as much as eye and ear.
> And over all . . . the front, the cheap hotels,
> The hooting trams, the crowds, the sewage smells,
> The 'pleasure-haunts', the swarming beach, the din—
> The Tower stands—a Monument to Sin.

Wow! Heavy stuff! I didn't really know what sin was at that stage, but it scanned, and no doubt rhymed conveniently. Years later I was to grow to loathe Blackpool even more fervently. I have done three different summer seasons there, two at the Opera House and one at the Winter Gardens. I was sitting one evening in my dressing-room, morosely chewing a chicken-bone, when a journalist from a Sunday paper now defunct, the *Empire News*, called to see me and introduced his small son so that I could sign an autograph for him. I offered the journalist a beer, and he sat down and said, 'What d'you think of Blackpool, Jim?' I was in the mood to tell him.

'Christ Almighty,' I shouted, 'get me out of this blasted place. I hate it. And d'you know what I hate most of all?' I threw the window open. 'Look! Can you see it? Wherever you go in this damned town you can see it. You can see it from twenty miles away. That Bloody Tower!'

I said a great deal more—and it all appeared the following Sunday in the *Empire News*. What a kerfuffle there was. I was threatened with the sack. The local landladies were in an uproar, and said they would have me marched out of the town. And I had to write an apology in the local paper. A friend in the show went to have a haircut one day, and one of the other customers said, 'How dare that Jimmy Edwards call this place a dump when he's making a living here?' To which one of the other customers replied, 'You know bloody well it is a doomp,' and a great argument ensued.

That was later on in showbusiness, when I learned for the umpteenth time the great motto: 'There's no such thing as a trustworthy newspaperman.'

But in 1940 it was just plain loneliness, and being away from home for an absolutely indeterminate period. One of the things I did to try and cheer myself up was to go and see Arthur Askey and Dickey Murdoch at the Opera House. They were all the rage on the wireless at the time, so I bought a cheap standing-room ticket and watched their antics with a jaundiced eye. Little did I know—not only was I to perform in that same theatre many times, but Arthur was to be in my radio series 'Does the Team Think?' on

17

BBC even later on. Meandering about the beach in 1940 I had absolutely no thoughts of showbusiness.

One action-packed day we were marched down to the depot and crammed into trams which swayed us all to the north of the town where the RAF had made a rifle-range in the sand-dunes. We were shown briefly the main features of the Ross rifle, which had been in use in the First World War, and had presumably been lying in an arms dump ever since, and then we lay down on our stomachs and fired off about fifty rounds at targets which seemed miles away. Then it was the next man's turn. No one told us if we had managed to hit the target, and pretty soon we were on our way back to town for more drilling on the front. That was the only time I ever fired a gun in the whole war.

HALT! WHO GOES THERE?

WE WERE NOW officially 'RAF Ground Defence', and our job was to protect airfields from the airborne attacks which it was assumed were imminent. Dunkirk had come and gone, and invasion was supposed to be just around the corner.

After two weeks at Blackpool we could all march, more or less, without colliding with each other, and we could all fire a Ross rifle. Most of us were 'u/t Aircrew'—in other words, we had signed on to fly, and were officially 'under training'. But, as the Flying Training Scheme had not yet fully wound itself up, we had 'volunteered' to serve in this other, less glamorous role, until our turn came to leap into the air.

There were other, more lowly, chaps among us earmarked solely for defending aerodromes; so to differentiate between us, we wore a piece of white material in the front fold of our forage caps. These 'white flashes' gave us a slight feeling of superiority, but they also brought down upon our heads a great deal of derision from time to time, especially when we made a mess of things.

Thousands and thousands of chaps were shoved through Blackpool in this way, and then hurriedly posted to aerodromes all round the British Isles. Some of them eventually took a terrible hammering when the Germans started bombing the Fighter Command bases in the South, and many of them stayed on to be moulded into the 'RAF Regiment', whose praises I need not sing here. But we, Bateman-Champain and myself, plus a couple of hundred other nondescripts, were sent to a place none of us had ever heard of—Hooton Park. Where the hell is Hooton

Park, we all asked. Not far away from the beaches of Blackpool, as it turned out. Poised on the south bank of the Mersey River, a few miles from the heart of Liverpool, and directly opposite Speke, which nowadays is Liverpool Airport. Over there we could see runways, and big black aeroplanes being uncrated and assembled and flown off, but we were just a grass field, with the Officers' Mess perched on the side of a small hill, and a squadron of twin-engined wood and fabric planes which I learned eventually were called Ansons. I knew nothing about aircraft and flying in those days, and we weren't told what they were being used for or where they went when they lumbered off the ground. In fact, they were carrying out sea-patrols, looking for submarines, but we A/C2s were not supposed to be interested in that. Not that we were all that busy. Once we had settled into our bell-shaped tents, into each of which eight men were crammed, and had located the Airmen's Mess and the NAAFI, our only job was to 'Stand to' every time the siren went, bearing with us our Ross rifles, and wearing our tin helmets. 'Standing to' meant rushing frantically to the nearest slit-trench and then sitting there wondering what on earth we would do if anything happened. As the siren went half a dozen times a night and several times during the day, we were up and down from the tents to the trenches so often that we completely lost interest in the whole exercise. We were under the command of a portly pilot officer, who wore an RAF uniform with an incongruous Sam Browne belt, and a short row of First World War medal ribbons. I am sure that he, too, didn't really know what we were defending the aerodrome from, but there were all sorts of wild rumours about parachutists, and I suppose our job was to pick them out of the sky like a flight of pheasants. How we were going to do that sitting in a slit-trench no one asked.

It was not fun. Life was dreary enough anyway without all these alarums and excursions. For one thing, eight men cannot truly fit into a bell-tent with any degree of comfort. We slept on palliasses, feet in the middle just touching the central pole, heads just touching the canvas. Our clothes were all hung on a crazy metal hoop, with several hooks on it, which was nailed to the wooden pole. From time to time this would break loose and crash to the ground, taking all our uniforms with it, and bringing confusion and vituperation to the darkness. When I add that our rifles were also propped up against the same pole, you will see what a shambles it was.

Late at night when things were quiet, one could hear enormous rats scuttling about on the canvas outside, and I would often lie there, clutching my bayonet, and slashing out wildly with it when I thought one of them was in range. Oh, yes. We had all been issued with an immense bayonet, at least an inch wide, with a not-very-sharp edge, but a needle-sharp point, and I suppose the idea was that we would impale German parachutists on them in great numbers. It's amazing that I didn't kill or maim any of my fellow-airmen when my blood was up against those rats.

The tents had been pitched (by us, and what a time that took—*Three Men In A Boat* had nothing on us!) all higgledy-piggledy between the various wooden huts that made up the normal accommodation. Ours was not far from the Airmen's Mess, so that one could peep through the flap and see just how long the queue was for breakfast. That was something new for me—queueing up—and I resolved at this early stage to have nothing to do with it unless forced. I regarded it as a waste of time and an indignity. As a result, when at last the moment came that I could walk into the Mess 'coolly and calmly, without let or hindrance' there was never anything more than bread and marmalade left for me. There was always the NAAFI, that strange institution which has saved many a serving man from starvation, and for which there can be no valid excuse. After all, I reasoned, if it was part of our deal with HM Government that, in exchange for our time and effort, and possibly our lives, we should be fed and clothed . . . what possible excuse could there be for allowing outsiders to sell us food on the premises? Mind you, they sold beer also—that I found perfectly reasonable. And that's where all my money went.

We were paid two shillings a day—fourteen shillings a week—and this was scarcely enough to keep me in booze

21

during my free time. I was one of the lucky ones—a non-smoker—so I don't know how the others managed. I had managed to get my old bicycle sent up from home, on which I had pedalled daily to school across Wimbledon Common, and which had seen me through many journeys down to Wiltshire and back, and also done me two years' service at Cambridge. But, alas, that had to go. When my boozing money ran out, I was forced to sell it to a richer bloke—for the princely sum of ten shillings—and that was soon gone too. So he very kindly lent me the ten shillings back. And that was the way I existed for months . . . always borrowing the same ten shillings from the same chap. He had a sense of humour, and an insight into my character. Every time I paid him back, he used to put it into a special pocket, saying, 'I'll leave it in here, Edwards. You're bound to want to borrow it again.' I wish I could remember his name. He's probably big in the banking world today.

There were rats everywhere. One day a small party of us were doing something futile—picking up paper, or generally tidying up—under the eyes of a corporal, when the station commander hove into sight on his daily inspection. The corporal brought us to attention, and was just 'slinging one up' (saluting) when a huge, overfed rat came bobbing out of the Mess, and crossed the path in front of me. My reaction was instant. I broke ranks, and with one well-aimed kick—with my left foot—killed it stone dead. I shuffled back into line, as the CO approached with a steely eye. The corporal was about to let loose at me, when Squadron Leader Troop's face broke into a twinkling smile. 'Well done, that man,' he said. 'We'll have to have you in the station soccer team.' He paused, while I blushed and stammered (I hated soccer!). Then he came back a step, 'And left-footed too!' he said, and strode on his way.

Night guard duty was another new experience for me. One of us had to stand guard—tin helmet, gas-mask, rifle, bayonet, and all—outside the station HQ, 24 hours a day. I certainly didn't look forward to my turn at night. It wasn't just the spookiness of the dark—don't forget we had a full blackout over the whole of England in those days—and the listening for approaching footsteps—and the owls—and the sounds of Liverpool in the distance. It was never knowing when that bloody siren was going off. It was situated on the roof of the HQ, not more than thirty feet from my head, and there was never any way of anticipating it. It went off several times every night, and never failed to make me jump out of my skin. When it was at full blast it positively hurt my eardrums, and it lasted a full three minutes, with that rising and falling wail that all of my generation—and millions of filmgoers since—will never forget. The All Clear was almost a relief. The air raid was over, and the siren shrieked with a steady note, so at least this ex-choirboy could shout tunes into it without being heard. I racked my brains to think of some way of getting out of this rut of either rushing to a slit-trench six times a night, or standing guard outside the HQ for four hours on end.

One day I noticed, parked in the Motor Transport yard, a two-ton Ford lorry with a strange modification plonked on top of it. It was a sort of square, concrete box, with wooden panelling on the outside, just big enough to hold two men. Across the top was a heavy bar of wood, and, in the middle of this, mounted on a swivel, was a machine-gun. This was laughably described as an 'armoured car', and I went to investigate.

'Oh, yes . . .' said the corporal in charge of the MT section. 'That's our latest thing. It's an armoured car, and its job is to patrol the perimeter of the aerodrome any time there's an air raid on.'

'What's that gun?' I asked.

'Oh, that's a Lewis machine-gun. You know anything about them?'

I took a chance, just as I had done when I told the corporal at school that I could play the bugle.

'Oh, yes. We had those in the OTC at school.' It was no lie. We did have them at school—but I had never touched one. The corporal was impressed. 'They could probably use you on that,' and the deal was made.

I soon learned how to load and unload the Lewis gun, and a little bit about its many 'stoppages', but there was nowhere for us to actually fire it. Therefore I was never put to the test. There was just room for two of us up there, one on either side of the central wooden bar, and I think if one of us *had* tried to fire it, he would most certainly have killed the other.

Inside the concrete box they had nailed sacking, which had pockets in it, and into these pockets was crammed the most horrendous collection of hand-grenades, and Very pistols with a great variety of coloured cartridges. I never asked what these were for, and I never tried out a hand-grenade. I was told you pulled the pin out, and lobbed it in the general direction of the enemy—if you could see them! But it was a kind of freedom. We sat in the sun in the middle of the MT yard, reading books (I was still on *The Oxford Book of English Verse*) and occasionally making a great play of cleaning the Lewis gun, and when the siren went, instead of rushing to a trench, a driver leaped in and we roared off round the aerodrome, looking for 'we knew not what'.

On the far side, between the grass landing-field and the river, there was an old road, and this was our driver's favourite spot, as it was smoother than the grass. In the dark we would sometimes stop, especially if there was a lull in the anti-aircraft fire and the bombs, but if we heard a bomber getting close, he would start up and crash through the gear-box, trying to gain as much speed as quickly as possible. 'A moving target's more difficult to hit,' he said, with questionable logic, as we lurched and roared through the night.

Most of the raids were at night, but there was the occasional daytime alert. Once we were down on this road at about noon, wondering why on earth the sirens had gone at least an hour earlier, and why nothing had subsequently happened, when we heard machine-gun fire the other side of the aerodrome. We bumped into each other frantically as we tried to get our Lewis loaded, and as we were scrabbling about in confusion a lone German bomber flew over the field. It was then that we realized that he was the one that was doing the firing, and I was the first to bob down out of sight. We never even got 'one up the spout' before he was gone. If we had managed to open

24

fire, he was so low that no doubt we would have riddled our own tents.

The climax to all this futility came one night when we had been performing this pantomime of patrolling the perimeter for several months without any result. There was a lull in the bombing this particular night, and we were just moving forward in bottom gear, peering into the darkness as usual, when a clear, frightfully British voice rang out ahead of us: 'Halt—who goes there?' Our driver slammed on the brakes. Nobody said anything. Then it came again—'Halt—who goes there?' I thought we'd better offer something before we got blasted off the face of the earth, so I called out: 'Halt—who goes there as well?' 'Good Lord,' came the reply, and a khaki-clad figure approached out of the gloom. 'I say. We're guarding this bit,' the subaltern said. 'So are we, sir,' I replied. 'We've been doing it for months.' 'Oh, my God. We only dug in this evening. What a good job you didn't come any further. My chaps were just about ready to fire.'

There was another laughable improvisation parked near the main gates of the station. This consisted of an elderly 32-seater Leyland bus, to which had been affixed enough sheets of heavy iron to protect a battleship. Somewhere there were a few slits through which the driver was supposed to be able to see, and in it, on permanent stand-by, sat about twenty bemused soldiers. When the siren went, the gates of the station were thrown dramatically open, and this 'flying column', as they were called, swept out into the night to deal with any mass landing of paratroopers they might encounter. Once they were out a little longer than usual, and the guard on the gate was changed in their absence. He was a young lad, and suitably nervous, so when they approached he challenged them in a loud voice. Not satisfied with the army's answer, and remembering his recently acquired drill to the letter, he made them all 'advance one by one and lay down their arms'. All the red-faced lieutenant in charge could do was congratulate him.

One autumn evening, as the sun was going down, and totally without warning, formations of German bombers appeared overhead on their way to Liverpool. They were pretty high up and we watched fascinated as our ack-ack attempted to deal with them. There were lot of sarcastic remarks and ribald laughter as the shells exploded above them, below them, beside them, but never near them. In fact, we were quite enjoying this unexpected sideshow, until the first piece of shrapnel fizzed down and hit the ground at our feet. There were loud cries of 'Fuckin' 'ell!'— what else can a chap shout?—as we dived for our tin helmets. One or two cowardly airmen spent that night in the slit-trench, but I couldn't be bothered. I lay in my tent, waiting to hear the canvas rent in twain, and protecting myself feebly with my tin helmet balanced on my face. The others all had theirs lower down.

We had absolutely nothing to do with the flying at Hooton Park, and the idea that I would eventually go up in an aeroplane was very much at the back of my mind. We soon learned to cultivate the Serviceman's dogged attitude to the many frustrations of life. Typical scenario: It's pouring with rain. We haven't any waterproof clothing. An officer gives us a form authorizing the issue of same. We skitter through the mud, trying to dodge the rain, and get to the clothing store. It is locked. We knock on the door. A corporal's voice: 'We're closed. Can't you read the bloody sign on the door?' We read the sign. 'Clothing Issue Hours 1000hr to 1500hr'. 'But, corporal, it's only quarter past three.' 'Piss off and come back tomorrow.' We stay wet— and he goes back to his mug of tea.

I must say I hate to see these swear-words in print, but it is difficult to describe life as an A/C2 without them. We were what was called 'the lowest form of animal life' in the RAF, and anyone who has been in the ranks in any of our armed forces knows that the four-letter word comes into every sentence—usually more than once. It is, in fact, used as a sort of punctuation, and by its frequency you can gauge the gravity of the speech. If a corporal says, 'What are you doing, Edwards?' it is just a mild enquiry, made out of vague interest. If, however, he says, 'What the fucking hell are you fucking doing, Edwards?' you know that, whatever you are doing, you shouldn't be doing it, or you are doing it wrong. The final key to the corporal's state of exasperation is if he prefaces the question with: 'Jesus fucking Christ Al-fucking mighty . . .' then you know you're in trouble. I had learned all the words as a kid in the stables back at Barnes, but had never dared use them except when in the company of the grooms. Now I found they were just part of everyday language, and, although I jibbed at first, I gradually broke down and, in the end, was as foul-mouthed as the rest of them. One of my best childhood quotes comes from that period in the stables. I was only about eight, and an even younger inexperienced child asked me for a spade so that he could help muck-out a pony's stable. My groom friends tell me that I said with great heat, 'You don't need a fucking spade . . . use your fucking hands'. At eight years old! No wonder I still occasionally lapse and upset people on aeroplanes or in posh restaurants.

Miraculously, I have never used the 'magic word' on TV or radio, in spite of doing literally hundreds of live interviews all round the world. However, I did once disgrace myself on the stage. It was in about 1955, and it wasn't exactly on the stage. I was appearing in cabaret at the Chevron Hotel in Melbourne, Australia, a venue which was pretty sleazy even in those days, and is a disco now. I had been booked for a month, and was not doing very well. Not many people came in, and those who did were mostly bookmakers and prostitutes, who didn't pay a lot of attention to the act. Food and drink were served throughout the performance, which is always pretty dispiriting, and people were constantly crossing the dance-floor on their way to or from the lavatories. It was nothing to see a waiter dashing across the room with a flaming shashlik held aloft, and one evening a drunk actually lurched across the stage as he took a bee-line for the loo. Later, as he came back, green-faced, his friend shouted out, 'Just made it, eh, Jack?'

Such was the class of the audience. On the second Friday I was invited to a cocktail party at the Southern Cross

Hotel, then, as now, one of the finest hotels in Australia. Peter Jensen, a local eccentric and PR man, was launching a dog-food which was being advertized as perfectly fit for human consumption, so we picked at plates of this muck as we swigged our champagne. On the way back to the Chevron, Peter jocularly suggested that it would be a good night to wake the audience up by using the forbidden word in the act. I mulled this over as I changed in my bedroom on the first floor, and decided on the one place in the act where the word could be used without causing too much furore. I needn't have worried. That night the crowd was as rowdy as ever, and as I stood contemplating my tuba, I said the line I had always said: 'This is a tuba. I'm going to play it . . . in case you thought I was going to . . . go to bed with it . . .' but, instead, I said 'fuck it'. There was a mild laugh, and I proceeded to play it, as always.

I went through the rest of the act to a wave of total indifference, and came off to the usual desultory and half-sarcastic applause. Up in my bedroom I changed out of my dinner-jacket and gulped some whisky. Another performance notched up. Another few dollars in the pocket. There was a knock at the door, and as I opened it, three burly chaps in civilian clothes inched forward. 'Mr Edwards?' one of them said, in a strong Aussie accent. 'We're from the police. The Vice Squad, you know.' I sensed a practical joke—Jensen is noted for this sort of thing. 'May I see your warrant cards, please?'—brilliant stroke, I thought. Two of them were produced in a flash— so they *were* policemen—but the third man fumbled and couldn't find his. The two with the cards were constables— the idiot who couldn't find his was the sergeant.

'Come in, gentlemen,' I said, well fortified with whisky. 'I'll speak to you two constables, but you'll have to tell the sergeant what I am saying. I cannot address him.' In they came, and as they quaffed generous slugs of my Scotch, they explained that they had been sitting at the back having a free meal, with the object of booking prostitutes, when they overheard my act. 'Did you use the four-letter word?' one of them asked. 'How can I argue,' I replied. 'There's three of you and only one of me.'

Well, they drank a lot more of my whisky, we had a few laughs, and eventually they left, with the assurance, 'You'll hear no more about it, Jim.' An hour later, as I was about to turn in, there was another knock at the door. This time it was a newspaperman accompanied by a cameraman. 'You're in the book, Jim,' I was told. And so I was. The charge—'In that you did use obscene language in a public place, to wit the Celebrity Room in the Chevron Hotel, Melbourne.'

My case was to come up in the police court in the suburb of Prahran, but I had ten days to think about it. The following Saturday I was playing polo at the Lilydale and Yarra Glen Polo Club (such delicious names abound in Australia) and I told my tale to a local millionaire, Hilton Nicolas, who ran the Aspro outfit among other things. 'Make sure you get a good lawyer, Jim,' he said. 'Here's a chap you should call.' And he wrote down the name, Frank Galbally. I duly looked him up and made an appointment. As I stepped out of my taxi I was struck by the elegance of the six-storey building and wondered which floor was his. I needn't have bothered . . . they were *all* his, and when I was ushered into his office and saw the smart grey suit, and heard him call into an intercom, 'Miss Jones, get me a rundown on obscenity in Victoria, please,' I realized that I was in the presence of the Perry Mason of Melbourne.

He agreed to defend me. 'I haven't been in a police court for fifteen years, it'll be a bit of fun'—and I waited for the day to arrive. Well, as we approached the courtroom together, with Mr Galbally nursing a huge bundle of files under one arm, and me trying to look smart in my only suit, there was a crowd of newspapermen on the steps. And when we entered the court, the magistrate took one look at Galbally (noted, I had found out, for getting murderers off the rap)—banged his gavel, and said, 'I call a recess.' For fifteen minutes the police tried to do a deal with my lawyer. I heard a sergeant say, 'We'll drop the charges if you'll promise not to rubbish the police,' and Galbally drew me aside. 'Which way do you want to play it?' he asked. 'I can plead guilty and get you off with a warning, or we can have two days of fun. Remember, the maximum you are up for is a fine of twenty dollars.' I chose the former, and Galbally stood up and made his speech. 'My client,' he said, 'is not only the Queen's favourite comedian, but also a personal polo-playing friend of Prince Philip.' I clutched his elbow . . . 'Steady on, old boy.' 'And he bitterly regrets this indiscretion.' There was a lot more of this, and Galbally sat down. The magistrate cleared his throat. 'Mr Edwards. Would you be upstanding, and give an undertaking that you will not use that word again?' 'No, sir,' I replied. He was stunned. 'Why not, Mr Edwards?' 'Sir,' I replied, 'I will not give an undertaking that I cannot guarantee to keep. After all, if you bang your thumb with a hammer, you don't know what you might say. And when you're in a bearpit, you react like a bear.' Wearily he said, 'Will you say you'll do your best?'—and the case was over.

Outside, I faced a barrage of TV cameras. 'All I can say,' I said, 'is that for the swearingest country in the world, you're a very funny lot.'

I received tremendous publicity in Australia over this incident. In fact, reporters quiz me about it to this day when I go to Sydney and Melbourne . . . but in England it didn't look too good. They only reported the fact that I had been prosecuted for obscene language—the rest of the case was not followed up, so that when I returned, my agent was in despair. 'How can I get you bookings?' he moaned. 'Everyone thinks you've gone blue.'

At Hooton Park I still hung on to my *Oxford Book of English Verse*, and went for long walks in the countryside, sitting on five-barred gates reading until dusk forced me back to that hateful camp. We went on occasional pub-crawls in Chester, and once or twice braved the air-raids in Liverpool, but by and large, it was the NAAFI that claimed our boozing money. The threatened invasion failed to materialize, and the monotony of the whole situation was only made bearable by the knowledge that some time, sooner or later, I would start my training as Aircrew.

Many, many years later, when I was starring in a show at Blackpool, I was invited to commentate on a Battle of

Britain air display at the same aerodrome. I flew in with my own aircraft—an Auster Aiglet, and made a great, showy landing in front of the crowd. It was all entirely different by then. Long runways, a big control tower, modern hangars. I looked in vain for the spot where I had endured so much misery, all cramped up in a canvas tent. When I took off again, to get back to that Bloody Tower for my evening performance, I was advised on the radio to stay below 500 feet, as the Hawker Hunter was about to make a low fly-past at 600 mph. I needed no further warning, and hugged the ground all the way back to Blackpool.

PER ARDUA . . .

AT LONG LAST A/C2 Edwards, J.929629, was summoned to do his bit in the air. But there was a long way to go yet before his feet actually left the ground. First of all he had to go to the Receiving Wing at Babbacombe, and, if you know your geography, that's a hell of a long way from Liverpool. The journey was made, as always in those days, by rail. I was given a travel warrant, and committed myself to the railway system at Liverpool station. I can't remember where we went—I've no doubt Crewe came into it—but I do remember a two-hour wait in a siding at Didcot. It was pitch-dark, the blackout in full force, and the other occupants of the carriage were just voices. We sat, and sat, and occasionally somebody swore. No one knew what was going to happen at Babbacombe, except that we were to be prepared in some mysterious way for our Ground Training, which was to prepare us in an even more mysterious way for our Flying Training. With my months of Ground Defence behind me I felt like an old hand, and derived some small pleasure from the fact that most of the others' numbers began with '100', whereas mine began with '92'. At the age of twenty, I was an old sweat.

Two things remain in my mind from this swift fortnight in Devonshire. The local theatre was in the middle of its summer season, and once a week held an amateur talent competition. By this time I had pieced together some sort of an act on the trombone. I featured the same solo that I had started off in all seriousness at St John's College, Cambridge, when I was a freshman in 1939. By now I had learned how to take advantage of the idiosyncrasies of the

trombone, and had also, naturally, larded the patter with
Service jokes. Basically, it was a lecture on 'trombonology',
a word I had invented, and which stayed with me right up
to my Windmill days in 1946. I was over-confident enough
to put my name down for this contest, and packed the hall
with RAF friends when the great night arrived. All went
well until the voting 'by public acclaim' took place. In spite
of the roars of my friends, I was placed second to a girl
singer who, to my ears, had a very indifferent voice. An
early showbusiness lesson—a girl singer will always do
better than a comic, no matter how much he makes the
audience laugh.

Later that week I learned another lesson, but not from
showbusiness. By now we had all gathered that the next
step from Babbacombe was to go to an ITW (Initial
Training Wing), and there were a number of these dotted
around the country. There was one at Torquay, only a few
miles away, and a lot of chaps thought that would be rather
fun . . . only a short train-ride, and a nice seaside billet.
There was another one at Scarborough, which brought up
visions of bitter cold days drilling on the front, with the
smell of fresh fish in the air. But there was also an ITW at
Cambridge, where a number of colleges had been taken
over, and when I heard this, naturally I thought, 'Edwards,
you are going there!' But how? One evening in a local pub I
got into conversation with a corporal, who turned out to
work in the Orderly Room. 'What do you actually do?' I
asked him. 'Oh,' he said unenthusiastically, 'I have to type
out the lists of names when you chaps go to ITW.'

'Well, bless my soul,' I said. 'Have another pint of beer.
Tell me, would it be easy to be sure I was on the Cambridge
list?' 'No skin off my nose,' he said. 'They're just names to
me.' I gave him my name and number, and lo and behold, I
spent the next three months back at Cambridge. Such is
the power of a pint of beer.

Meeting that corporal was the most enormous piece of
luck, and taught me the valuable lesson that it was just
possible to have some slight control over one's career in the
shambles of this rapidly expanding air force. If I had gone
to Torquay or Scarborough my whole RAF career would

33

have been entirely different, in what way one will never know.

And what fun it was. Suddenly, and quite unexpectedly, there I was back amo. g all my old cronies, drinking in all the old haunts, but with the sparkling difference that I was in uniform. Only an LAC, mind you, but I've no doubt I swanked enormously. My old college had not been taken over, which was a slight disappointment, but . . . well, you can't have everything. I was sent to Selwyn, which had been IVJ's old college, so I knew it well.

There was a further stroke of luck to follow. As soon as I possibly could, I contacted my old friend Donald McWhinnie, a lugubrious but brilliantly fluent pianist with whom I had performed many times in the Footlights Club. I found him down at the ADC Theatre, where they were in the final stages of rehearsal for a Christmas pantomime. They were just reeling from a body-blow: Tony Hampton, another Footlighter, who had a leading role in the panto, had received his call-up papers, and had already left for home. Two days to go, and one comic needed. I immediately applied for an interview with the Commanding Officer. Could I help out? Whoever looks after my destiny was in benign mood that day. 'As it happens, Edwards,' said the wing commander, 'your course has been postponed fourteen days anyway. Good luck with the show.' And I was given carte blanche to come and go as I pleased for the run of the panto.

I can't imagine what the rest of the squad thought, and I know the corporal in charge was livid—but there it was. I was 'that jammy bugger, Edwards', and I loved it. Donald McWhinnie and I played the Robbers, or the Broker's Men, or something—and I only had two days to learn the part— but you can bet the Trombone Act was in there again, somehow or other. And every night, after the show, I tottered back in uniform to Selwyn (quite a totter, if you know your Cambridge), and in the morning I got up and did sporadic work with the telephone in the Orderly Room.

Which was *another* stroke of luck. On our very first parade, before I had even contacted Donald, the corporal in charge had lined us all up in the Selwyn courtyard, and barked out, 'Anyone here use the telephone?' Now everyone who has been in any of the Services knows the hidden trap behind a question of this sort. 'Anyone here play the piano?' 'I do, Corp.' 'Well, get down to the Officer's Mess. It wants shifting into the theatre.' 'Anyone here play chess?' 'Yes, corp.' 'Well, there's a few pieces want moving from Number One hangar.' And so on. So when our corporal shouted, 'Anyone here use the telephone?' there was a crashing silence.

I decided to take a chance, and stepped forward.

'Yes, corp, I know how to use the telephone.'

'Right. In the Orderly Room for you, and take down any messages.'

And there I sat for two weeks, whilst the others tramped the roads and marched and counter-marched. Oh, the glorious injustice of it. Sitting by the phone by day, and larking about in a pantomime by night. What a way to win a war!

That didn't last long. Soon we began 'The Course'. Officially. In the RAF, whenever you had to learn to do something, be it fly an aeroplane or make a bed, you were always sent 'on a course'. There seemed to be a course for everything, and I don't know how many I put up with in the six years I served. All of them had an exam at the end, and you always came out with some sort of rating or classification. Sometimes it was a percentage, sometimes it was 'average', 'above average' and 'excellent'. This, at Cambridge, was an 'Aircrew Initial Training Course' and comprised many subjects, all of which carried an exam at the end. We used to march down to the Union, where I had starred many times in debates, and in the actual debating chamber somebody would give us a lecture on one or other of the many subjects we were supposed to master. Thus, one day it would be 'Administration'—very dull—all about 'Putting an airman on a charge', or 'Comparative ranks in the other Services'. Another day it would be 'Elementary Air Navigation'—very confusing, with 'triangles of velocities' and mercator projections—or 'Meteorology'— 'adiabatic lapse rate', cumulo nimbus, and fracto-stratus— and when we weren't being bombarded with all this confusing information, we did PT in the Corn Exchange, or marching in the public car park.

At just about this time, some Senior Officer, skulking in an air-raid shelter in Kingsway, London, had decided that it might be a good idea if all Aircrew Under Training learned to march at the same rate as the Light Infantry. Heaven knows why. The exact figure I've forgotten—was it 144 paces to the minute?—but you've seen 'em do it outside Buckingham Palace, I expect. I think the Gurkhas do it, but it's easier for them, as they've got such short legs. They go like lightning, and the bugle band sounds as if it's been put on the turntable at the wrong speed.

Well, our squad at Selwyn had been selected as the guinea-pigs for this experiment. There was a great deal of moaning from us but we hammered away at it, and eventually became quite good. What it had to do with flying aeroplanes none of could guess, but this was the sort of conundrum that came up all through our period of training. It was no use asking *why* you did it—you just got on with it. Of course, we tried a little sabotage here and there. It was a long march from Selwyn down to the car park, where we practised this madness, and once or twice, as we left the college and swung right, we all instinctively, without more than a muttered word between us, started to shorten our stride. Not the actual pace, you understand . . . but the amount of ground we actually covered with each stride. At first the corporal didn't notice, but when he did, he was mystified.

'Squad. Halt! Now, what is going on here? You! Edwards! What is this?'

'What, Corporal? Nothing, Corporal.'

'Squad! Quick march!'

And we'd do it again. Marching like hell, but just not getting anywhere.

We all had it in for this particular corporal. He used to take his meals in the Gallery overlooking the Main Hall in College, and when he wanted to make an announcement, he would stand up and bang with a spoon on the balustrade. One day, as soon as he started this, we all picked up spoons and started banging on our tables.

Childish, I suppose, but we had no other way of showing our disapproval of his overbearing manner. After a few pinpricks like this, he decided he must get to the bottom of it. He sent for me in his office. (Why me? But they always seemed to pick on me as the ringleader.)

'Yes, Corporal?'

'Now look 'ere, Edwards. What is going on? What is 'appening? Now, look, Edwards. Forget these—' (he indicated his corporal's stripes) '—all rank aside, and as man to man, what is going on 'ere?'

'Well, Corporal, you're a c—'

He leaped to his feet, pointing at his stripes again.

'Now then, Edwards, don't forget 'oo you're talking to.'

Well, I did try.

He was called our Corporal Admin. We had another little runt who was our Corporal Discip. He was short and dark, and had a little Clark Gable moustache, and had the most marked East-end Cockney accent. Somebody found out he had been a butcher's boy, but he was certainly very smart, with the shiniest boots I'd ever seen. His job was to get us 'fell in' and give us drill, and generally keep us up to the mark. It was a strange job for him, for, while he had complete seniority over us, and we had to jump to his every call, he knew that very soon, if we passed the whole course, we would outrank him. He also knew that most of us had had a much better education than he had, which he occasionally admitted in a funny way. He got us all in the Junior Common Room one morning, and, having called for silence, waved a blue-backed volume in the air.

'Nah,' he shouted. 'Dis mornin' I'm gonner read you King's Regulations, so that you'll know what is going on and whatchoo've got to do and all that.'

He cleared his throat and opened the book.

'Section One. Paragraph one. It is enacted that, subject to reg—... 'Ere, Edwards, you read the bloody thing!' and he threw the book at me.

There was another chap called Edwards in our squad, and this corporal devised a typical cockney way of differentiating between us. We were called, quite simply: 'Edwards wiv whiskers' and 'Edwards wivaht'. Funnily enough, I was the one 'wivaht', having not yet been able to sprout anything on my upper lip which did not cause hilarity.

In a funny way, we quite liked this corporal. Certainly we preferred him to the other squirt.

He lined us up on the gravel in the Selwyn quadrangle one day, and standing on the superb lawn in the middle, brought us to attention, and delivered himself of this gem.

'Nah! There's been a lot of complaints about gobbin' around 'ere.'

We shuddered.

'Nah! If yer must gob, tread on it like wot I do.' And, right in front of us, there on that beautiful grass, he gave us a demonstration.

We persevered with the Light Infantry marching, and eventually gave a demonstration of it to an assembled gaggle of wing commanders, standing alongside the car park like a giant's helping of scrambled egg. We can't have been too bad at it, because afterwards it became the standard pace for all ITWs.

Intermittently, we struggled with the Morse code. I found this difficult—all those Dits and Dahs and Dah-Dits. We were given a little pamphlet which, for each letter, gave you a word which began with the letter and had the rhythm of the Morse. For example, A, which in Morse is Dit-Dah, became 'Again'; F, which is Dit-Dit-Dah-Dit, became 'Fundamental'. Some of them weren't very satisfactory, so I made my own amendments, and I gradually became fluent, but not fast, with the Morsecode key. The trouble is, from those days to this, I have always had to have a two-stage translation in my head. If I hear 'Dit-Dit-Dit-Dit' I think, 'Ah yes, Hocus-pocus—that's H.' And so on. Not fast, but safe.

We had to learn it on the Aldis lamp as well, and this was fun, especially as they sent us up to the roof of St John's College chapel to flash messages to each other. Nobody believed me when I said I had played in a brass quartet up there, but it was true. As an undergraduate and choral scholar I went up there each year on Ascension Day with the choir and played trombone as they sang hymns. I must not forget that at this time I was being prepared to be an Observer, not a Pilot, owing to my eyesight, so that the accent was on navigation rather than airmanship. Once I was finished at Cambridge, provided I passed all the exams, the next step would be an Air Navigation School—no one knew where. But no one really cared.

We were fully occupied during the day, desperately trying to cram into our heads a hodge-podge of facts and figures, and during the evenings there was serious drinking to be done. I was once again a regular at The Volunteer, just near Jesus Lane, where the landlord was an ex-pugilist of terrifying proportions. His nightly routine, when the clock struck ten-thirty, went something like this: 'Members of the University, Time, gentlemen please. Members of the Royal Air Force, Time, gentlemen please. All the rest—PISS OFF!' At this time I was having a Pimms No. 1 kick—well, it was only two shillings a go, and the results were very satisfactory. How did I ever make that walk back to Selwyn? IVJ turned up briefly, looking sheepish with sergeant's stripes and brand new wings— that was another enormous party.

Hanging in one of the classrooms was a huge chart, which not only showed all the badges of rank for all three Services, but also included a colour supplement of all the medals you could win. Lurking in amongst these I noticed the King George V Jubilee Medal.

'Well,' I said to the chaps one day, 'I've got one of those.'

'Oh, go on, Edwards. Whatever did you get it for?'

'Singing in the choir.'

There was much laughter at this. With my gravel voice, no one could ever believe I had been in a choir, let alone at St Paul's Cathedral. But it was true. Not only did I sing there at the ceremony in 1935, but I had been the Head Boy at the time. Everyone who had been connected with the service—the troops who lined the route, the police, the choir—we had all been awarded the Jubilee Medal. In fact, I still have it at home in its little red box. Someone said, 'Go on, Edwards. Put the ribbon up. I dare you.' So I went to one of the many tailor's shops in Cambridge and bought a length of the ribbon. After a good deal of toil with needle

39

and thread provided in my airman's Housewife (an item issued to us all on our first day of service), the ribbon was duly up there on my left breast. The corporal was quick to spot it at the next parade.

'Whatchew got there, Edwards?'

'The Polish DFC, Corp.'

'Don't you come that, Edwards. Whatchew got there?'

I told him, and he couldn't dispute it, and there it stayed for the whole of the war, earning me many laughs and quite a few pints of beer.

In spite of all our feuding with the corporal, and all the time we spent learning to march faster than the others, and in spite of all the manifold distractions which my old University held for me, we finished the course, and were declared ready for Air Navigation School. We still didn't know where we were going, but when we were marched into the Clothing Store and issued with flying clothing, plus khaki tropical uniforms and topees, speculation was, as they say, rife. I suppose it was part of the charm of life in the RAF that nobody ever told you anything, at least, not the things you really wanted to know. But I had quickly developed an easy-going philosophy about the whole huge practical joke that it really was. When, in the billet or the Mess Hall, chaps would interminably chew over the pros and cons—'It's got to be Africa—It could be India—You don't need quilted flying suits in India—My father was trained in Palestine—What about those heavy flying boots?'—I used to let them exhaust all the possibilities, and then chime in with my own languid observation: 'Gentlemen, speculation is fruitless. We shall know the truth soon enough.'

But it was weeks before we knew—for certain.

Our next step was to cram ourselves into a train, destination still unknown, humping our two packed kitbags with us. In the middle of nowhere it stopped at a station marked Hednesford, and the cry went round: 'Grab the nearest two kitbags, and get off as quick as you can.'

We assembled on the platform, formed up, and marched,

still humping two kitbags each, several miles into the bleak open country. Out on the moors we found RAF Station Hednesford, Transit Camp No. 6, and there we started to sort out the kitbags. The corporal's logic was impeccable: if each airman picked up two kitbags, and then you sorted them out at the camp, no one would lose theirs. But of course it didn't quite work out that way. At the conclusion of the sort-out, one airman *was* left bereft. Guess who?

My kitbags had gone trundling on in the train to god knows where, and I never saw them again. So all my kit—right down to that brass thing you used for cleaning your buttons, and including two quilted, zip-up flying suits, and fur-lined flying boots—had to be replaced. I reported to the Clothing Store, and acquainted the corporal with my dilemma.

'Well, you'll 'ave to buy another lot, wontcher?'

'Buy!!??'

'Well, you bloody lost it, dincher? It'll be a Form 774B for you, me lad.'

Every single item was listed on this form, which I duly took to the Accounts Department and signed. It was a lot of money, so they only took five shillings a week off me, and I was still paying it when I was demobbed in 1945.

The only piece of luck was that my trombone was still with me. There were times when I used to stick it into my kitbag and then stuff my clothes all round it, so that the top end of the case was sticking out when you tied up the rope, but on this occasion there had been too much kit, and I had carried the slush-pump separately. Which was just as well, because I certainly could not have afforded to buy a new one.

This particular trombone had quite a history. It was given to me in about 1938 by Dr Douglas Hopkins, who had been assistant organist during my time at St Paul's, and had become quite a friend of the family. He knew that I was not making much headway on the trumpet, and he happened to have an old Conn, made in Pennsylvania, in his possession. I learned on it at Cambridge, carried it with me throughout my six years in the RAF, and did my first radio show with it in 1947. Later on, when I got fairly well known, Hoppy wrote and suggested that I could afford to buy myself a newer instrument, because he had a young student in mind who wanted to learn. So I duly sent it back—and it's probably still being played now.

We weren't at that bleak and dreary spot Hednesford long enough for me to do any amateur dramatics. Soon we were on another train heading 'we knew not where'. But in a few hours, we clambered out on Liverpool docks, and formed up on the quayside under the shadow of an enormous liner, the MV *Georgic*. So we were going overseas for our flying training. This was really exciting. And with those goofy, comical, dated pith-helmets squeezed into our kitbags, it was sure to be Africa. We climbed up the gangway, and I found I had been put into a two-berth second-class cabin, which I was to share with a chap called Barnes. I already knew him and we got on well enough together, and it was quite a bonus to be in a cabin. This liner had been pressed into service as a troop-carrier so recently that they hadn't had time to strip out the normal civilian furnishings, so we slept in comparative luxury. The first snag was that we were well up in the bows of the vessel, which meant a long trek to the dining-rooms. There was another snag, which didn't reveal itself until we had been at sea several days. There was great excitement as more and more airmen came aboard, and we scrambled about exploring the ship, and, as usual, trying to guess whither we were bound. As soon as they had got us all sorted out—there must have been over a thousand of us in all—up came the gangway, and we crowded to the side to see the ropes cast off and marvel at all the activity which is commonplace to sailors.

Slowly we moved away, out into the river. We were off at last! What an exciting moment. But we didn't go far. As darkness fell, we moved into the middle of the Mersey, and dropped anchor! We trickled down below to see what was going on, and soon found that there were lists on the notice-board telling us of our new-style duties. I was to go on watch on the bridge from midnight to four a.m. I wrapped myself up in my greatcoat, and reported for duty. And what an eerie four hours it was. There was a slight mist over the river and the usual total blackout, so there wasn't much to see. But the sounds of the harbour were still there, and I felt very alone and frightened. Every now and again a corporal or an officer would pop up and say, 'Everything all right?' but otherwise I was left alone with my thoughts. At one stage, the ghostly figure of the corporal loomed up and said, 'Keep your eyes skinned. There's a mental patient escaped from the hospital.' That's all I needed. From then on I jumped at every sound, and tried to plan what I would actually do if a gibbering idiot came up and attacked me in the dark. I was nearly gibbering myself by the time someone came to relieve me.

When daylight came, what a sight we saw. All night long we had heard the rattle of immense chains as ship after ship dropped anchor, and now we saw them, in a long line stretching up the Mersey. As we were the nearest to the sea, and the last to weigh anchor, we were treated to a grandstand view of the whole armada, as they steamed slowly past us. I tried desperately to make a note of all the names, but they've gone from me now. But it was a mighty fleet of the finest of our merchant navy, and each one crammed to the hilt with troops. What's more, we all noticed—they were all dressed in khaki. Not just ordinary khaki, but tropical khaki, the same as we had. So we were all off to Africa. From each ship as it passed us came a chorus of jeers, raspberries, and derisive cat-alls—aimed at us, we gradually realized. For, still in our blue uniforms, we were clearly all Air Force, and they were all Army.

And even now The Great Adventure hadn't really started. We sailed out of Liverpool, turned left, and dropped anchor again in a large bay, where we stayed for 24 hours whilst more and more ships were added to our number. This gave me an opportunity to get used to shipboard routine, and I soon regarded myself as an old salt, using phrases like 'going aft' and 'below decks' without being in the least self-conscious. Eventually the giant convoy was completed, and we upped anchor. I was thrilled by the whole procedure. There seemed to be ships everywhere, as far as the eye could see, all shapes and sizes, and I stayed on deck until nightfall, drinking it all in.

And that's all there *was* to drink, for, like all troopships, there was no booze available. Except . . . except . . . the date was 21 March 1941, and my twenty-first birthday was only two days away. Albert Clamp, bless him, landlord of my local, the Market Gardener in Barnes, had pressed into my willing hands a quarter-bottle of something described as 'Fine Champagne', and I was hanging on to this to celebrate my majority. No one knew about it, and no one was jolly well going to know about it, but when the great day arrived I intended to enter the state of maturity in a state of inebriety. But first, another shock. We woke up on the morning after setting sail, cautiously opened the porthole, and . . . all the other ships had gone! The sea was empty, except for one huge battleship. The news gradually filtered through to us—we were off to Halifax, Nova Scotia, and the battleship was accompanying us because it was going to Canada for repairs. We didn't know it, then, but the rest of the convoy had gone off for the invasion of North Africa.

And so we ploughed across the Atlantic. Each morning I woke up and opened the porthole, and there was the great grey hulk of HMS *Something or Other*, always in exactly the same position, heaving up and down, half-hidden by spray, and immensely reassuring. She looked quite near, until you realized you couldn't see anybody moving about on her. She occasionally flashed signals, which we excitedly read with our new-found expertise, but they were always in naval jargon, which was a foreign language to us. I must say I was quite convinced that we would be attacked by submarines, but drew comfort from the fact that they would probably prefer the battleship as a target.

Came the birthday. I suppose many people have had disappointing twenty-firsts, but mine was a complete let-down. I showed Barnes my secret bottle, and told him straightaway he was having none of it. Then I opened it and took a tentative sip. Ugh! What a revolting taste. I had never tried brandy before, and this first experience of it really turned my nose up. I handed it to Barnes. 'Thanks, old boy,' he said, and swigged the lot. I was twenty-one—and sober!

The routine on board ship soon became boring, and the big snag about our cabin soon became apparent. Although comfortable enough, it was situated on the starboard side right up in the bow—or nose, as I would call it—and when those long Atlantic rollers got going the motion was, quite literally, sickening. We went up for what seemed miles—hovering and teetering for what seemed hours, then down we went, slowly and inexorably as if we were never going to come up again. All in slow motion. Of course, this gallant old salt, born, like all Britishers, to be a seaman, soon cracked, and I spent nearly all the time on my back, moaning and cursing and sucking oranges. I couldn't eat anything else, and my one visit to the saloon, where all the chaps were playing cards and smoking, was a complete failure. As was our visit to the stern. Barnes said to me one day: 'You've got to get out of the cabin, old boy. Let's take a stroll down to the other end of the ship.' So off we went, clinging to rails, spiralling down stairways, and lurching along corridors. After getting completely lost a couple of times, we eventually emerged on a small deck immediately above the stern. The greenish sea looked awfully close, and there was spray flying in all directions, and when we got to the crest of a wave the propeller came half out of the water so that the whole ship shuddered and banged. I didn't last long in those conditions. Soon I was heaving over the side again. 'Thank you, Barnes,' I moaned. 'A great idea.' And I staggered back to the cabin, there to lie until the sea calmed down a bit.

Which it eventually did.

We stopped one day—I suppose I should have said 'Hove to'—and the crew chucked into the water a sort of float with a flag on it, and this then moved away from the ship into the middle distance. Know-alls amongst us explained that there was one each side of the ship, and they had wire underneath them a few feet down, and they were supposed to fend off any mines that might be lurking about. Comforting—I don't think.

On the same day two ancient flying-boats, with two pairs of wings apiece, held together with a lot of wire, appeared to escort us, and this was our first glimpse of the

Royal Canadian Air Force. We knew the journey was nearly over, and I, for one, was thankful. I have never, to this day, found the right formula for avoiding seasickness.

DRINK CANADA DRY—I DID MY BEST

WE DIDN'T SEE much of Halifax. It was down the gangway, and straight into a train. And what a train! A huge engine in front, with a bell on top of it, just like the films—great bulging coaches, with seats that turned into very comfortable sleeping berths, and more sleeping berths concealed in the roof—and at the back of the last coach, an 'observation car'—a little verandah, on which you could stand and watch the countryside peel away behind. I didn't know it then, but I was to spend two years in this delightful country, and during that time I did a lot of travelling on those splendid trains. They weren't fast. But there was an inexorability about their progress—and there was so much to do and see. The food was excellent, served with willingness and speed, booze plentiful, but above all, we were *English*—and in 1941 that really meant something. Canada had thrown itself heart and soul into the war (we'll leave Quebec out of this hymn of praise!) and the Commonwealth Air Training Scheme had only just been initiated. We were some of the first RAF to be seen in Canada, and we were treated like Royalty. Of course, we were easy to pick out. 'Say, are you from the Old Country?' became a familiar and oft-repeated question, and it was usually followed by an invitation to take a drink. I was once stopped by a chap in the street, who delved into the huge pockets of his overcoat and produced a crock (40oz) bottle of whisky, *plus* a couple of real glasses to drink it out of.

But on this journey from Halifax to Toronto there were no civilians aboard, except for the staff, so it was a continuous, leisurely party on wheels. We stopped often at small towns, and we would hop off and walk about the unfamiliar streets, have a beer at a cowboy-style bar, and wait for the train-driver to give a couple of blasts on his banshee-siren to summon us back. If you lingered too long over your beer, and he moved off without you, it was a question of either running to catch him up, or getting a car to drive you to the next stop. One LAC, George, was the first to find this out. We all thought we'd seen the last of him when he failed to rejoin the train after one particular stop. We were debating what to do about his kitbags—but at the next station there he was, all smiles.

In case you don't know, LAC stands for Leading Aircraftsman, and it's two steps up from where we had all started. I had laboriously and not very tidily sewn a little blue propeller on my left sleeve, and was not a little proud of it. At least we were no longer the 'lowest form of animal life'. George and I were to see a lot of each other in subsequent months, and I see him quite often these days, as he is a Professor of Something-or-other at Brunel University. But at this stage he was just 'that clot who got left behind'. If he hadn't caught up with us, he would have missed the wonderful welcome in Toronto.

I won't say there were 'wild scenes of enthusiasm', or that the 'streets were strewn with flowers', but the good ladies of that great city certainly did us proud. They came down to the station in large numbers, and plied us with cigarettes, candies, and all sorts of refreshments. All these things, of course, were strictly rationed in England, so to us it was like a dream come true. I have been to Toronto many times since, to appear at the Royal Alexandra Theatre and other places, and nobody has offered me chocolate bars!

At this stage of the journey we still numbered several hundred, but now we were to be split up into smaller groups, all going to different aerodromes. We still didn't know our ultimate destination, but about thirty of us now found ourselves put into a really short train, just an engine, one carriage, and one dining-car—and off we went again.

By this time my spirits had picked up enormously, and

they rose higher as we trundled across Ontario. Forgotten were all the miseries of MV *Georgic*, the seasickness, the nagging fear of some disaster, the lack of booze. Here we were in our own private train, seeing new sights, hearing new sounds, meeting new people, waited on hand and foot, and passing through towns we'd never even heard of.

And finally we saw Goderich written up as we slowed down at a small station, and it was time to disembark. Still a few more miles to go—this time in a bus—and then we were through the gates of our new station, RAF Port Albert, No. 31 ANS, which we knew meant Air Navigation School. It was quite clear, as we lugged our kitbags to our new quarters, that the place was only half finished, with mounds of earth everywhere, and a lot of duck-boarding and mud, but the huts were finished, and pretty splendid compared to what one had been forced to endure at Hooton Park. They were made entirely of wood, and no longer did we see that dismal little stove in the middle of the floor, with its bucket of coke beside it. Each hut had a powerful set of fans which drove warm air through ducts, and into the main room. But it wasn't until the next winter that we realized how essential this heating was. At the moment it was April, and the Great Canadian Thaw had set in, and that was why the bus, as it ground its way along the dirt roads, had been forced to make so many detours round great ponds of thawed ice and sludge. If you got into one of those, it was the end of the journey until help arrived. Here, in these huts, was another novelty—double-tiered bunks, built for two—which later became the title of a song I wrote for a revue:

> *In a double-tiered bunk built for two*
> *It's impossible to bill and coo.*

I decided to share one of these metal monstrosities with Frank George, with whom I'd struck up a friendship. First a fateful decision had to be made. Who was to have the top bunk, and who the bottom one? George was a steady pipe-smoker, so that if he slept in the bottom bunk, the filthy fumes from his tobacco would float up into my nostrils. But, on the other hand, if he took the top one, his ash would scatter itself gently over my head. This was a dilemma I faced on many stations in Canada, and it wasn't until I was promoted to Pilot Officer that I was relieved of having to make such a decision. Later on I learned of the other problem—if you were in the top bunk and came to bed late, and a little drunk, it was a bit of a performance to get into the damned thing without putting your foot into your mate's face. And it was just possible, if you lurched backwards having missed your footing, to pull the whole thing over on top of you. In fact, I once saw a drunken Australian do this, and his bunk cannoned into the next one, and the whole blooming lot went down in what I believe is now called the domino effect. There was some swearing in that hut that night, as sixty airmen suddenly found themselves on the floor in the pitch dark.

The decision having been made that I would occupy the top part, I was mooning about unpacking my kitbag, and distributing my things, including my beloved trombone, into my locker, when an unknown corporal came in.

'You,' he said abruptly, 'are in the station dance band. Officers' Mess tonight. Tomorrow—funeral.' I found out later that my instrument, packed as it usually was in a kitbag, and wedged in with socks and shirts, had been spotted by the station police as we checked in through the Guardroom, and its arrival immediately reported to the flight lieutenant in charge of the dance band. And that was it. No audition, no interview, they were just delighted to have one more instrument in their outfit, however badly it might be played.

What a boon that trombone was to me from that day onwards. I had almost forgotten I had it with me on that troopship. I was certainly in no condition to practise, and I don't think Barnes would have been very pleased if I had tried it out in that tiny cabin. But now I was a member of the Station Dance Band, with all the perks that went with it—late nights, free beer, and occasionally a few dollars in the hand to boost one's meagre pay-packet. As an additional bonus, I actually enjoyed playing, and to be in a band of any sort is always fun.

There was one snag, however. Having learned my music as a choirboy in St Paul's Cathedral, and having learned the trombone from Otto Langey's handbook, I could read music with the greatest ease—but I could not improvise, or play 'by ear'. I told the corporal this straightaway.

'That's all right, Edwards,' he said. 'We've got plenty of published music to play from. No busking.' And this was agreed. As he was very north-country, this came out as 'no boosking'. We played at a dance one night at the British Legion club somewhere, and after we had waded through the first ten or more numbers, and I was looking round for some more parts, they all suddenly launched themselves into another number. I tried frantically to find a few notes on my trombone that fitted, and after a few more bars shouted out above the din, 'What are you playing?' The corporal—a trumpeter—shouted back: 'Oondecided.' To which I replied, 'Well, make up your bloody mind.' Of course today I am very familiar with the famous jazz number 'Undecided', but in 1941 I'd never heard of it. The corporal thought I was pulling his leg.

My first appearance with this particular band, at the Officers' Mess, passed off quite well, but the next day, when we had to play for a full-dress military funeral, was not such a success. One of the station's Ansons had crashed a few days before, and the burial was held in the little town of Goderich. I can only say that the Dead March from Saul has been played better. It gradually got faster and faster, and I believe the chaps in the coffins would have laughed if they could have heard it. Well, after all, we were only a dance band.

As far as Navigation went, we were put straight to work in the lecture rooms, and within a week I was all set for my first flight. I got myself all togged up in my flying kit, took my big bag full of maps and navigation instruments, and went to the Flight to climb aboard an ageing Anson. These were the old originals, with two Cheetah engines, and had been shipped out from the UK and reassembled in Canada. At last, Edwards takes to the air! Well, no.

I stowed all my kit, and strapped myself in beside the pilot. The engines were each started by a member of the groundcrew with a dirty great handle. There was a lot of winding to do, and then, with any luck, there was a burst of smoke from the exhaust, and the metal, fixed-pitch propeller reluctantly began to turn. On this occasion . . . my first flight . . . all went well, both engines responded to a bit of coaxing, and we taxied out to the runway. The pilot seemed to be a nervous sort of chap—hands darting about everywhere, and trembling slightly, constantly adjusting things which he had adjusted only a moment before. But he seemed to be satisfied with the 'run-up', when, with the brakes full on, each engine in turn is revved up to check the magnetoes, and we lined up on the runway. My nerves tightened as he opened the throttles and we trundled down the runway. This is it! I could almost hear the surging music which would have accompanied it if we had been in a film. Then, just as the tail was up and I was mentally preparing grand phrases for my next letter home, his trembling hands grabbed the throttles, and he cut the power completely. As we came to a halt, he switched off both engines, and there was a strange silence. I didn't know enough about flying to gauge what had happened, and he didn't say a word. Soon, a tractor dawdled out from the hangars, and we were dragged unceremoniously into maintenance—backwards. I quote from my Observer's and Air Gunner's Flying Log-book:

> Date. 10.4.41. Hr.1415 Aircraft type and No. Anson L7971. Pilot P/O Appleton. Duty. 2nd Navigator. Remarks. Map reading . . . failed to take off. Flying time 0.05.

Four days later I went on a similar sortie, and this time my log-book reads: 'Map-reading. Turned back owing to faulty oil-pressure. 50 minutes flying.'

It's a good job I'm not given to looking for omens.

Four of us, under the leadership of a chap called Laband, who was slightly older, I felt, than most of the others, decided to pool our resources and buy a car. We were getting much better paid now, with flying pay and Canadian Air Force rates, so we thought a little extravagance would be in order. Laband did the driving, and we would set off on exploratory journeys to nearby towns. The dirt roads meant that high speeds were out of the question, but it didn't take long to get into Goderich, which had several hotels where you could drink all day. There were some very strange rules about this, as indeed there still are in Canada today. You had to sit down at a table, and there could not be more than one drink per person on that table at any one time. Each table was equipped with an enormous salt-cellar, but I never quite got the hang of that. If you poured some salt into your beer, it was supposed to reduce the frothiness, but it also vastly increased your thirst. Perhaps that was the idea. Goderich boasted a modest town square, and the only pastime on a Sunday afternoon, as the pubs were shut, was to cruise endlessly around and round this square in your car honking your horn and waving to passers-by. Farmers came from miles round just to do this. Each town seemed to have its own licensing laws. There was a little place called Kincardine, not many miles north, which was officially 'dry'. This was a great blow when we went there for the first time, but a local resident soon put us right.

'Just go to the cafe called Shaggy Mac's,' he said, 'and ask for coffee.' We did that, and the wicked Mr Shaggy Mac winked and beckoned us into the kitchen. There we hastily swilled down a few shots of hooch out of coffee-cups, and, much refreshed, went on to the dance hall. There was another novelty here, called 'Jitney Dancing'. The whole floor was encircled by a rope barrier, just like the ones I remembered from St Paul's Cathedral, and you were only allowed on to the floor on presentation of a ticket. After each dance the floor was cleared and the barrier replaced. You bought the tickets over the soft-drinks-only bar. After a few of these moments of gay abandon, it was back to Shaggy Mac's for a few more slugs of 'coffee'.

Laband was a suave six-footer with a sexy black moustache, and spent a lot of money going through that barrier, but I've never been very good with my feet, and was content to watch most of the time. All my life I have very rarely been brave enough to dance in public, but with

53

a few slugs of booze inside me I sometimes have a go. There was an occasion, in the mid-fifties, when I really got into the groove. Lady Docker was throwing one of her lavish parties 'for all my *dahrling* friends in show business'. I think it was at Claridges, and the real reason for it all was that, after we had all been softened up with expensive food and drink, Tommy Trinder went on to the floor to announce the cabaret, which turned out to be Lady Docker's son. We sat stolidly through his excruciatingly bad turn, and then got back gratefully to the serious business of drinking champagne.

In the early hours of the morning, when there was only one bored cameraman left, I was sufficiently flown with wine to entice her ladyship on to the dance floor. She was in a pretty good humour, and we jitterbugged away in great style. At one point, I stood with my legs wide apart, and motioned to her to go through them. And her ladyship, in her £2,000-plus skirt, duly went down on her hands and knees and crawled beneath my crutch—not once, but several times. The yawning cameraman leaped to his feet—and the next morning, there we were, on the middle page of the *Daily Mirror*, with Lady Docker caught in the act of crawling between Jim's wide-open legs—rear view! It seems the telephone wires were hot that morning, with her ladyship demanding apologies, and lawyers threatening sue-age, but all that happened was that, on the day after all this fuss, the *Mirror* printed the same picture, this time on the front page, under the caption: 'The picture that upset Lady Docker'.

But in Kincardine the only girls who would dance with me did so because they were intrigued by my uniform. It was twice round the floor, and then, 'Say, are you from the Old Country?' all over again. It certainly wasn't my new moustache that attracted them. Inspired by Laband's success with the girls I was having another attempt at whiskers, but, as can be seen from snapshots taken at the time, they could only just be seen in a good light. I was so disappointed with this particular moustache that I decided to sacrifice it when some wag asked if he could use it to test the capabilities of his newly-purchased electric razor. It must have been a good razor, for in no time my upper lip was bare once again.

The car we had bought was a square-bonneted Chevrolet, with a wooden steering-wheel and other quaint appurtenances, the sort of thing that would be tremendously valuable today as a 'vintage' vehicle. I had never driven before, and so inevitably the day came when I asked Laband to let me have a go. After all, I was paying a quarter of the costs. So we waited until we were on a quiet country road—all dirt and very narrow—and I grasped the wheel. What I didn't grasp was that you must look well ahead, and not just in front of the bonnet. We came to some ruts, I over-corrected, and in no time we were in the ditch at the side of the road. She didn't turn over, or anything dramatic like that, but it was quite impossible to get her out. Laband was calm, but I could see he thought I was an inept idiot. Just as I was considering walking into town for help, a farmer came by with a horse and cart. He also luckily had a length of chain with him, so in a matter of minutes he had pulled us out, and the car was undamaged. There was a unanimous vote from the other three that I should never be allowed to take the wheel again, and, in fact, I subsequently learned to fly before I learned to drive.

The Canadians continued to be extremely kind to us, with invitations almost every weekend to private houses in towns like London, Stratford and Orangeville. These visits were particularly welcome because the food on the camp was so vile. Well, that's not fair. The food was quite good—it was all local, and perfectly wholesome—but the RAF had made the mistake of bringing their own cooks with them, and they could ruin anything that came along, just as they had in England. The fact that there was no rationing didn't deter them from churning out the usual mountains of potatoes, or boiling the cabbage until it had been broken down into sludge. And the tea was, as always, undrinkable.

I suppose the greatest boon was the absence of blackout restrictions, and this was particularly useful on night-flying trips, all the towns being brilliantly illuminated and some of the main roads too.

The most enjoyable trips feature in my log-book as

'Reconnaissance and photography'. These were much more fun than the tiresome navigational exercises. We zoomed down low over some small port on the lakeside, and I had to lean out of the window at the back with an enormous, old-fashioned aerial camera, and try to take photographs of the shipping and dockyards, with the slip-stream tearing at my gloved hands. I never lost a camera, but I didn't get many successful shots.

Here is a brilliant piece of poetry I wrote towards the end of the course:

SONG OF G.R. in two parts, sung with great emotion.

REFRAIN (sung by an odiously keen, bright-eyed, swatting youngster, in his teens)

> *You say this course is driving you mad?*
> *Come now, my dear fellow, it's not that bad.*
> *What's that? You don't like D.R. Nav?*
> *You want some of the enthusiasm that I have.*

DIRGE (sung by a bleary-eyed, dissipated, grizzly oldster who is clearly beyond hope)

> *I feel quite sure I haven't got a hope—*
> *I know just when I can and cannot cope.*
> *I know the definition of a rhumb-line,*
> *But, when I try to draw one, it's a bum line.*
> *I struggle hard with graticules and such,*
> *But words like 'poli-conic' don't mean much.*
> *And as for that rat Mercator,*
> *I am his ardent hater.*
> *The projection gnomonic*
> *Makes life chronic,*
> *And in a navigational emergency,*
> *I'm damned if I'd know how to use convergency.*
> *In the air*

I simply sit and tear my hair,
And wish that I could make a murderous assault on
That menace Dalton.
The CSC
Means Crap, Shit and Corruption to me,
And trying to get a sight on Sirius
Makes me delirious.
After all these things, it's a minor factor
When I find I've lost my Douglas Protractor.
(And though it's no concern of mine . . .
What did that flight lieutenant do with my fine?)

REFRAIN

You say this course is driving you mad?
Come now, my dear fellow, it's not that bad.
What's that? You cannot cope with Met?
It's the easiest subject you've tackled yet.

DIRGE

I try my best, but goodness knows
I'm foxed at one by Highs and Lows.
I think the cold Front
Is just a stunt
To make me weary—
And I've got my own Warm Front theory.
After the Met Man's sessions
About depressions
I'd like to drop-kick
The Chart Synoptic.
The thought of Relative Humidity
Drives me into mad stupidity.
I've done my best, although perhaps late
To understand that wretched Lapse Rate,
But I haven't had a try so far
To fathom the Isobar.
Is this depression Deep or Shallow?
What do you know about Buys Ballot?

How long or short is an Isotherm?
This sort of question makes me squirm.
I've got no time
For rime.
The way the Met Man spells, 'hoar'
Is a frost, nothing more.
And after a lecture, I'm so dazed,
My eyes are the only things that are glazed.
And so, with humble, low apology,
I confess I can't cope with Meteorology.

The course continued right up to the end of June, and we were kept pretty busy. I went flying three or four times a week, each trip averaging about two hours, and there were a few night trips thrown in for good measure. The crew consisted of one pilot (usually an old sweat who was resting after a tour of operations), one wireless-op, very bored, whose job was to keep in touch with base in case there was a recall owing to bad weather, and two navigator-trainees like me, who were supposed to give the pilot all the correct courses for him to steer so that after a pre-arranged triangular journey around Ontario, we would arrive back over Port Albert. When I was in charge, this didn't happen very often. In fact, as a navigator, I was a dud.

Of course, my heart wasn't really in it. My eyesight had now improved so dramatically, thanks to a series of exercises which I had been doing studiously ever since I got to Cambridge, that I had been recategorized A1, and was therefore perfectly fit to be trained as a pilot. But it was too late for that, and I was destined to sit behind with the maps and dividers and protractors. But I was hopeless at it. As soon as the pilot snapped his fingers and said, 'Give a course for base', I panicked. I usually also dropped my dividers down behind the tiny navigating table and couldn't find them again, and as we had to wear thick leather gloves plus silk inners, I couldn't draw a straight line on my maps to save my life. I had not inherited a shred of my father's genius for mathematics, and there was nothing I could do about it. So when the time came for our final exams the dreaded word 'Failed' appeared on mine.

Looking at my results today, I see that in Signals I got nearly a hundred per cent, and in Reconnaissance I was pretty good. But in everything else I was a disaster, and in Practical Work I got less than fifty per cent. My overall marks were as low, so that, in spite of the fact that the RAF was in desperate need of aircrew, they quite rightly didn't think I was capable of navigating a valuable aeroplane that contained a crew of half a dozen other fellow mortals.

WASHOUTS

RCAF TRENTON WAS situated literally on the edge of the waters of Lake Ontario. In fact, it had been used as a sea-plane base, and from the hangar a slipway ran right down into the water. This hangar was to be our home for the next few weeks. It had been crammed with double-tier bunks, and there were thousands of us in there, from all over Canada. We became known as the 'Washout Squadron', because we had all failed some sort of course. There were those who had not managed to solo; those, like George and myself, who had not managed to grasp the intricacies of navigation, and there were even those who had found air gunnery beyond their grasp. And we all had to be 'remustered', that is to say, relegated to some other role in an aircraft. As the wing commander said when he greeted us, 'There is no going *up* the ladder—you can only go down.'

George, whose father had himself been a wing commander, and a pilot, was determined to reverse this progression. 'Stick with me, Edwards,' he said. 'You and I are going to become pilots.' I couldn't see much likelihood of two lowly LACs succeeding in fighting the system, but I agreed to support him. So each time we went in front of the Re-selection Board, we stuck to our guns: 'Pilot or nothing.' And the stupidity of it was that they could not force us to change our minds. As we were volunteers, we could only volunteer to be downgraded. The only alternative, which was made quite clear to us each time we stood to attention in front of them, was to be sent back to England to be discharged from the service. And if that was to happen, obviously we would immediately be conscripted into one of the other Services. We didn't appear together in front of this board, so each time I presented my lonely self before the triumvirate of officers, George would be waiting outside. As I saluted smartly and exited, he would be there to grab my arm and say, 'Did you stick to your guns?'

This farce went on for over two months, because after each interview the matter had to be referred to Head-quarters, and eventually to the Air Ministry back in England. There wasn't much to do to fill in the time. We would be paraded, and perhaps small gangs of us would set about some small task like cleaning out a hangar, or moving things from one place to another. But, all in all, it was an idle and demoralizing time. There was drinking to be done in the small town of Trenton in the evenings, but all too often our money didn't run to that because we had now been deprived of flying pay. From time to time I would ask the Canadian warrant officer if he could find me anything to do, but for weeks nothing came up. Then one day his eyes lit up and he said, 'Tell you what, Edwards. You could become an SP and look after the janker-wallahs.' This would mean putting on an arm-badge and joining the despised ranks of the Service Police, who were of course everybody's enemy. The janker-wallahs were the chaps who had committed some sort of minor crime—insub-ordination, returning to camp late, drunkenness—and had been confined to camp. They had to be paraded and drilled and generally overseen by an SP and it was a job nobody wanted. 'Well, Edwards, what do you say?' said the W/O. I thought—what the hell. At least it will be something to do. 'OK, sir, when do I start?' The arm-band was out of his drawer in a second.

The first time I stood in front of the squad I was exceedingly apprehensive. After all, I had exactly the same rank as all of them, but they were expected to obey my commands. The only thing that increased my status was that wretched arm-band. They eyed me sullenly. Here was one of their comrades who had joined the ranks of the enemy. They would have dearly loved to tear me to pieces, but the W/O was there to put me in charge officially.

'You will march them down to the parade-ground, Edwards,' he barked, 'and drill them for one hour. And not more than one stand-easy every fifteen minutes. And—' (he addressed the squad) '—don't forget that I shall be watching from my office.'

'Well,' I thought, 'at least they won't be able to lynch me.'

I marched them down to the parade-ground. We had practised giving commands as long ago as ITW and I proceeded to give all the drill commands in my repertoire. They were all carrying back-packs, which had been loaded with sand up to a prescribed weight, and the sun was blazing down. The poor devils were really sweating, and I felt sorry for them, but there was no way I could make it easy for them. I knew the W/O's beady eye was there in the Headquarters block. In fact, once, when I brought them to a halt, and gave them a 'stand easy' he came bustling out of his office, made me bring them to attention, and walked down their ranks testing the weight of each pack as he went by. I felt then that the chaps began to realize that I was not the real enemy. Later, during that blistering hour, I found the shade of a convenient tree, and shouted my orders from there. There's a lot of advantages in having a loud voice.

They were a mixed bunch, these janker-wallahs, from all over the commonwealth, and they, in common with me, were feeling the stigma of having failed a course. A few days later, it was my job to march them to a piece of ground that was being cleared for some development, and they were issued with picks and shovels and told to get on with it. I had to wander around and see that nobody slacked. As I passed one of them, he muttered: 'Don't turn your back on me, you bastard, or I'll sink this pick into it!' I noticed his accent was slightly different from the Canadian we had got so used to, so I paused, and asked him where he was from. 'Texas,' he growled—and then I noticed the black cowboy boots he was wearing under his uniform. He had come all the way from the States to get into our war, and found himself breaking up stones under the eye of some jumped-up Limey. I found out then that a lot of Americans were doing this (they had not yet been drawn into the war), so many, in fact, that the local joke was to call it 'The Royal Canadian and Texas Airforce.'

At last our wrangling with the Re-selection Board came to an end, and George and I were told to pack our kitbags, and take the train to Moncton, which was a new holding centre for ingoing and outgoing airmen. From there we would be shipped back home for eventual discharge.

'Well, that's the end of that,' I said to George.

'Oh no it isn't,' he replied. 'We are going to get off the train at Ottawa and go to the Air Ministry.'

'But what about our kitbags,' I moaned. 'They'll be in the guard's van with all the others.'

'Oh. They'll send them back,' said George. 'They'll have to.'

I agreed to this hare-brained scheme, but with great reluctance. George's father had given him the name of some very senior officer in Ottawa, and if we presented ourselves to him we might just get away with it. I was the faintheart in the duo, but George kept telling me to stick to my guns—or rather, his guns. I think he also took a little comfort from the fact that there were two of us. But I am quite sure that, if I had backed out, he would have carried on. Whereas, if he had not suggested this scheme, I would have meekly allowed myself to be shipped home. He was an extraordinary chap, well over six foot tall, and built in such a way that no uniform issued to him could ever look smart. His constant pipe-smoking had turned his scrap of a moustache a blackish-brown, and his pockets always seemed to be bulging with odds and ends. His cheese-cutter cap didn't fit, and his boots seemed to be enormous and never polished. And he marched like a demented robot. But at this moment in our careers he was a decided influence on me.

The great moment arrived, and we 'jumped the train' and changed to one going to Ottawa. At Headquarters we were instructed to go to the RCAF station at Rockliffe, which was right in the city, and on the banks of the river, there to await further instructions. Suddenly we were objects of curiosity, for we were the first real RAF chaps they had seen there. Our papers were in such a mess, and our records so scattered around the world, that if we ran short of money, we just went to pay section and got some more Canadian dollars. As long as we signed for them, everybody seemed quite happy. This money we spent largely in the Chateau Laurier, a splendid, monumental hotel, in the grand style, where we would sit in the lounge, quaffing excellent—and strong—Canadian beer, and revelling in the attention everyone paid to us. In those days English beer had already been well watered down, but we were just beginning to get a taste for the many and varied brews of Canada. Many years later, I revisited Ottawa a couple of times to play in their lovely new theatre, and popped into the Chateau for a drink. This time it was the moustache that they recognized, not the RAF uniform.

To occupy our time while waiting for the Great Decision from the Air Ministry, we were given jobs in the control tower, and this was great fun. We flashed green lights at aircraft for take-off, and spoke on the radio to aircraft on the approach and made ourselves generally useful. Nobody could really make out why we were there, but they were all fascinated by 'that cute English accent', and a whole month passed pleasantly enough. One couldn't say that we were doing a great deal to help the war effort, but we hoped our time for that would come when the wheels of the organization had ground out some sort of decision. The only unpleasant incident came one morning when I spotted what I thought was a log floating down the river, which ran right alongside the control tower. I trained my binoculars on it, and realized with a shudder that it was a dead body. A motor-boat was dispatched, and I tried not to watch as the cadaver was brought to the side, and dragged out of the river with the aid of a long pole and hooks. It turned out to be a tramp who had been missing for some days—and it was the only dead body I saw throughout the entire war.

At last we were sent for, and up at HQ George went into the office of the officer in charge of our case, leaving me outside. It seemed ages before he came out again.

'I think it's going to be all right,' he said, 'but you've got to go in there now. For Christ's sake smarten yourself up and give a decent salute, and don't be cheeky to him.'

I'm as good a crawler as the rest of them when it's needed, and I must have crawled extremely well this time, for in a few minutes George was called in again, and it was announced: 'You are both to be posted immediately to No. 32 Elementary Flying Training School, at Swift Current, in Saskatchewan.' The long wait was over. It was Up, Up and Away for these two gallant airmen. Hurrah! Surging music, rattle of drums, and—lots of Canadian beer! It was just over a year since I had signed on, and I hadn't yet had my hands on the controls of an aircraft. But at least I was an LAC u/t Pilot—so let the Hun beware.

I was such an old sweat by now that I didn't expect it to happen quite like that—and of course, it didn't. We arrived in Swift Current after another glorious train-ride, lugging our kitbags—George had been quite right. They were returned to us from Moncton as soon as we were attached to the RCAF at Rockliffe—and we duly marched in to Squadron Leader Hunter's office. He was thumbing through our records. 'Look here, chaps,' he said, 'we've only been open here for a few weeks, and they still haven't sent me a Navigation Instructor. I see you've been to Nav. School. Well, I'm going to postpone your flying training and make you both Nav. Instructors until the right bloke arrives. It'll only be a couple of weeks.'

'But, sir,' I protested, 'we *failed* the course.'

'Yes, but at least you've been through it, which is more than these chaps have.'

And so arose this bizarre situation, where two failed navigators were instructing a bunch of would-be pilots in the mysteries of the very thing at which they had been so abysmal.

Once I had swallowed my disappointment at still not getting into the air, I quite enjoyed the experience. I had done a bit of teaching at Cambridge, so I was used to standing up in front of a class. And knowing that these chaps knew even less than I did, I became almost confident. One or two of my class were corporals and sergeants who had remustered from other trades, but they had to put up

65

with the indignity of being lectured by a mere LAC. And when the exams came—what a smashing success. An average of 95 per cent for the whole class. The squadron leader was delighted. I am sure he must have guessed the secret. After all, it was I who set the exam paper, it was I who, the day before the exam, said, 'Now I want you to pay particular attention to all the subjects I mention today', and it was I who corrected the papers. I had chalked up my first RAF success.

Then at last George and I were put on a course, and started the real thing. The Nav. Instructor had not yet arrived, but was supposed to be on his way, so we had the strange experience for a week or two of lecturing to the chaps who were learning with us.

Each Flying Instructor was allotted about six pupils, and I had the great good fortune to find myself in the hands of F/O Hairs, a soft-spoken pilot with a handlebar moustache, who had been in the Battle of Britain, and had been sent to Canada for a rest. Well, he didn't get much rest at Swift Current. I still have my log-book, in which we were made to record *tidily* every trip we made. The 'tidily' bit was where I often came unstuck, but at least it's legible, and I have it beside me as I write to remind me of the sequence of events.

F/O Hairs took me into the air thirteen times in the two weeks before I went solo, and he had other pupils to contend with as well. The planes being used here were Tiger Moths, which had been crated out from England and fitted with a perspex canopy over the two pilots, who sat in tandem. The instructor sat in front, so that I could never see his face, unless he turned round to look at me over his shoulder. All those interested in flying will be acquainted with the dear old 'Tiger' as we called it, but those of you with your feet on the ground can see from the picture that it was a pretty ancient machine, even in those days. It could be accurately described as a single-engined bi-plane made of fabric stretched over an iron frame. It got off the ground at about 40 mph, and certainly didn't cruise much above 70 mph. It had two cockpits, and the RAF idea was that the instructor should sit in the front one. Each cockpit had its own control-column and set of foot pedals for the rudder, and the two were linked together by an antediluvian speaking-tube, the mouthpiece of which stuck out of the flying panel in front of you. We all wore leather flying-helmets, and these had earphones in them, so that if you plugged them into the correct hole, the instructor could bawl his criticisms into your ears. They never worked very well, and many's the time old Hair simply turned round and shrieked at me. It was an aircraft that demanded a very light touch—not something I am naturally blessed with—and so I found the whole thing very difficult at first. Taking off was my main bugbear. I soon mastered the business of keeping it straight and doing turns once we were airborne, and I was making some passable landings. But on take-off I was zig-zagging down the runway just as I had done when I turned the Chevrolet into the ditch..

I was almost in despair, and after ten hours' instruction still could not keep it straight down the runway. I knew that after twelve hours, if I hadn't gone solo, it was back to Trenton and the Washout Squadron for me. I didn't seem to be able to feel the rudder-pedals, which is not surprising when you consider that I was wearing a pair of heavy Service boots, with fur-lined flying-boots over the top of them. And the only way to keep a single-engined aircraft straight on take-off is with the use of the rudder. Hairs could see my problem, and one day said to me curtly: 'Edwards, we'll go flying tomorrow morning. Wear your gym-shoes.' I thought he'd gone mad. It was November and temperatures were very low. But I did as I was told, and, suddenly, I found the touch. And so, on 7 November 1941, after nearly eighteen months in the Air Force, I was up in the sky, in an aeroplane, alone. Everybody who has experienced a first solo like this remembers the tremendous feeling of exhilaration—the burst of singing, the cry of 'Yippee!!!'—the surge of confidence. And then, after a few minutes, the sudden grip of fear—'Christ, now I've got to get it down!'

There's an old saying in the RAF: 'It's a good landing if you can walk away from it.' Well, I walked away from this one with a great surge of pride. This first solo lasted exactly ten minutes, but it totally changed my Air Force career, and opened up doors that remained open for thirty years. That afternoon I went up again, and this time spent a whole hour doing take-offs and landings—'circuits and bumps', as it was called. A circuit was an imaginary oblong 1,000 feet up, one side of which was the runway in use. So you took off into wind, climbed steadily straight ahead to a height of about 600 feet, then did a climbing turn of 90 degrees to your left. After a short time, when you had reached 1,000 feet, you did another turn to the left of 90 degrees, so that you were then flying in the opposite direction to the one in which you had taken off, holding the aerodrome just under your left wing. This was called 'the down-wind leg', and you carried on with this until the aerodrome was just a little bit behind you. Then you did yet another 90 degree turn to the left, and began to descend. When you judged you were at about the right spot, you did a further left turn, losing height the while, and hoped to come out of the turn with the runway more or less in front of you. You then had to juggle with the throttle and adjust your rate of descent so that you passed over the aerodrome boundary low enough to make your landing. At all places where light aircraft are flown this system still exists today. We had no radio in these ancient Tigers, so that if we had been several miles away from the aerodrome, when we returned, we automatically 'joined the circuit' at 1,000 feet on the down-wind leg, taking great care to fit in with other chaps who were flying around doing their own thing. Nowadays, you call up the tower when you are a few miles away, and get permission from the controller to 'join the circuit'. Need I say that this is not the way things happen at London Airport? There, and at all other national airports, the jumbos are under ground control from miles out, and make long straight approaches.

I was not the only pupil who went solo that day, and in the evening it was natural that a small celebration should develop in the 'wet canteen'. Toasts were drunk to our aerial accomplishments, and soon, under the influence of Calgary ale, there was more drinking, and the ritual singing of bawdy songs. Next day my hangover was of classic dimensions. I was skulking in the crew-room, hoping to avoid F/O Hairs' keen eyes, but it was no good. He put his head through the hatch from the instructors' room. 'Right, Edwards,' he shouted, 'get ready to go flying.' I thought he wanted me to show him a few landings, but not a bit of it. He climbed us up to about 4,000 feet, and then proceeded to demonstrate all the known aerobatics— loops, rolls, stall-turns, with a bit of spinning thrown in for good measure. Just as I was about to die of airsickness, he took us down. As I tottered away he bawled: 'Perhaps that'll teach you not to mix drinking with flying!' In the years to come, I did my best.

In any case, for the next few weeks I scarcely had time for drinking; there was too much flying to do. Once you have learned the art of getting an aeroplane off the ground and putting it down again, the most important thing is to get more and more flying experience. It's called, quite simply, 'getting the hours in'. The more you fly, the more confidence you get, and that's what you need with flying— confidence. In just over a month my grand total of flying hours was just over 57—and more than half of that was solo. At this stage I was positively looking forward to getting into the air. There was no more apprehension about take-off, and my landings were beginning to be beyond reproach. The bit in between I thoroughly enjoyed. I even got to the stage when I challenged George to see who could do the most turns in a spin, before coming out of it safely.

Early in December the whole school was moved from Swift Current to a new aerodrome in Bowden, Alberta. The only real difference here was that, when you did a loop, you pointed the plane towards the Rocky Mountains, which were some twenty miles away, dived down to gain speed, pulled the nose up, and waited until you saw the Rockies come round again. Bowden was an even smaller village than Swift Current, but the beer was the same, and quantities were consumed when we finished the course just before Christmas. I am happy to say that my final assessment was '77 per cent—Above the Average'. And my thanks are due to Flying Officer Hairs for this.

Thus began a career in flying which continued, off and on, for nearly thirty years, for I was mad enough to go back to it, well after the war was over—and then I had to pay for it all myself. It was around 1954, and I was doing a summer season at the Opera House in Blackpool. By this time I had taken up polo, that most fascinating and exciting game which Cockneys call "orse-'ockey', and I was anxious to play every weekend at one or other of the clubs near London. I took to chartering a plane every Sunday from Denis Westoby, whose father ran the Northern Flying Club based at Squires Gate Airport, set among the sand-dunes on the road to St Anne's.

One Monday morning we were tottering back north-wards in a single-engined Auster Aircraft, when I said to him, 'Do you mind if I have a go?' The weather was fine, and the visibility good, so he said, 'Sure,' and I took over from the right-hand seat. In a few minutes it all came back to me, and I was sitting there happily keeping it on course and maintaining altitude just like the old days. After a time, Denis, who had sat beside scores of would-be pilots in his time as an instructor, said, 'You certainly haven't lost your touch. Why don't you take it up again? It'll only take you five hours to get your private pilot's licence, and it'll save you all this money on chartering.' I took the bait—willingly—and the very next day was doing circuits and bumps. Five hours solo, a cross-country, a couple of written exams, and I was through.

The ability to fly is a skill that never leaves you. You need a little practice to get your take-offs and landings right, but the actual flying of it once you're in the air is a piece of cake. Most people don't realize how stable a well-designed aeroplane is. They see bad movies in which the hero clutches the control-column as if he was driving a lorry. He heaves it back into his stomach if he wants to climb, and shoves it forward to descend. It's not like that at all. A good aeroplane, once you have levelled off at your cruising altitude and speed, can be trimmed to fly 'hands off', or at any rate with the most gentle touch on the controls. To climb, you simply ease the throttles forward to add a little more power, and to go down, you close them. In fact, in ideal conditions, the machine is better off without the pilot. I remember once a pilot in Canada, in far from ideal conditions, struggling through a snow-storm at night in an Anson, who lost his nerve, burst into tears, and shouted, 'I can't go on. We've had it!' The wretched pupil-navigators who were with him knew nothing of flying so just sat there and awaited the inevitable crash. But the old 'Annie' had different ideas. As the pilot sat there sobbing with his head in his hands, she just ploughed on, wallowing through the clouds, until they finally broke out into some clearer air. The pilot pulled himself together, wiped his eyes, and took over again.

There's another perfectly true story of a civilian pilot making a very bad landing in an Auster at Rearsby, near Leicester. He hit the ground so hard that the engine stalled, and after about the fifth bounce they came to a stop, and he thought he would get out and swing the propeller to restart the engine. At the first swing she fired, but he had forgotten to put the brakes on and to tighten the friction nut which holds the throttle-lever in place. As the Auster leaped forward, our gallant pilot threw himself out of the way, and up she went. The aircraft climbed steadily in a gentle right-hand turn to about 7,000 feet, and there was terrible alarm. At one stage the local RAF Auxiliary Squadron thought they would go up and shoot it down, but there was no knowing where it would fall. So in the end the area was cleared of other aircraft, and finally the Auster ran out of fuel, and in a series of perfectly executed left-hand turns, descended—and landed one field short of Rearsby.

Once I had my licence, I looked round for an aeroplane to buy. Up to now, all my flying at Blackpool had been in Austers, of one sort or another, and now it chanced that their test pilot, Ranold Porteous, arrived with a super, aerobatic model called the 'Aiglet', which he showed off at an air display at Squires Gate. It was just like all the other Austers, except that it had a more powerful engine. Ranold took me up in it. I took my 16 mm camera, I remember, but was unable to do much filming because he chucked the plane around the sky so alarmingly. Back in the bar I had to

have several stiff brandies to avoid post-landing airsickness, and then, emboldened by the booze, I bought the
damned thing.

'G-AMMS' was its call-sign; not that I had much in the
way of radio on board. There was just enough to ask
permission to take off from wherever I was, and then ask
permission to land when I thought I had reached my
destination. I did a lot of trips south in this machine, mostly
for polo matches, and seem to have taken Denis Westoby
with me on most occasions, just in case I should
accidentally take a drink or two after the match. In the
whole six months that I owned G-AMMS I don't think I
ever made a decent landing, at least, not one to my
satisfaction, but you know what they say—'A good landing
is one you can walk away from.'

It wasn't long before I got fed up with wrestling with this
Auster, and it was fortunate that at about this time Denis
got himself a franchise for the Cessna range of aircraft. He
took me up in a 172—and what a revelation! It had a
nosewheel. No longer that mad, drooping, swooping,
lurching search for a 'three-pointer'—you just flew it to
within a foot or two of the ground and cut the power.

I kept this machine for about a year, going in and out of
polo grounds, and once, daringly, flying all the way to
Frejus, on the French Riviera, for a brief holiday. Then I
got fed up with its slowness, and graduated to a Cessna
182, which had a bigger engine, a variable-pitch propeller,
and other little refinements, like a decent radio and various
aids to navigation. It was even equipped with an automatic
pilot which kept it on course (you had to watch the altitude
yourself), so I had plenty of time for reading maps and
studying manuals. Its call-sign was G-ASRR, which in the
standard radio language I had to use came out as Golf,
Alpha, Sierra, Romeo, Romeo. Once one had established
contact with a station one was permitted to shorten the
whole thing to the last two letters, so I was simply known
as 'Romeo, Romeo', which was all too easy for airport
controllers to remember. As soon as I piped up, they knew
who I was, and were watching for irregularities, which
occurred all too often. I called up an RAF station once and

identified myself as 'Wherefore art thou'. The controller came back icily, 'Could I have your correct call-sign, please?' All the conversations between controllers and aircraft are supposed to be carried out strictly 'according to procedure', but I often found that rather tiresome, and invented my own jargon. Approaching Manchester Airport once, in very bad weather, I called up the tower and asked for a course to steer. A very broad north-country voice came back: 'Romeo, Romeo, what is your approximate position?'

I replied jocularly, 'If I knew that, I wouldn't be asking for a course to steer.'

There was a short, exasperated silence, and then he told me, very deliberately, the course I had to use to reach the aerodrome. He then added, foolishly, 'Let me know when you have the field in sight.'

'In that unlikely eventuality, you will be the first to know.'

All these exchanges between ground and aircraft are recorded automatically so that they can be used as evidence in case of an accident, so that is why traffic controllers are anxious to stick to the script. They don't want to be found out wasting time with jocularities.

I did a summer season at Southend one year, and flew almost every day across the Thames to Sussex, landing at Goodwood, or on the polo ground at Cowdray, so that I could spend a few hours at home. Each day I timed my return trip so that I flew over the theatre about half an hour before curtain-up, waggled my wings so that the stage-manager knew I had made it, and then turned in to land. Southend, at the time, was being used regularly by four-engined DC Sixes, which took cars across to France all day long. The pilots got to know me, and I got to know that if I landed at the start of the runway I had an awful lot of taxiing to do to reach the hangar. So I got into the habit of passing over the airport boundary quite high up, and then touching down very near the other end of the runway. I was doing this one day, when a voice from a car-ferry waiting to take off came into my ears: 'Romeo, Romeo, the runway's down here.'

I radioed back, 'I buy my own tyres.'

I did a lot of trips for professional engagements, including one to Newcastle, where I appeared for a week in the then very new gambling club, La Dolce Vita. On the Saturday night I had resolved to go to bed as soon as I had finished work—which was pretty late, anyway—because on the Sunday I had to fly to Blackpool to appear in a TV show with The Beatles. My plans went wrong (I wonder why?) so that when I got to Newcastle Airport at nine on Sunday morning I had a prime example of an Edwards hangover. The weather was not good, with low cloud and bad visibility, and as I didn't have an all-weather private pilot's licence, the controller would not give me permission to take off. This put me in a predicament, because there was no way I could do the journey by road in time for the show. I had also promised to play in a polo match against the Duke of Edinburgh at Cheshire that afternoon, so altogether it was a pretty important day. I was in the control tower, wondering what the hell to do, when a voice came over the radio: 'There's a good clear lane at 6,000 feet which would suit Jim.' This was from a Dakota which had taken off half an hour earlier. The controller reluctantly let me go, and soon I was airborne and climbing up to find this magic piece of clear air. And it was there!

I heaved a sigh of relief as I levelled off. Sitting alone in a tiny, single-engined aeroplane, unable to see anything at all except a grey wall of cloud, can be a strain on the nerves. You simply have to keep calm, and believe your instruments. Without my little automatic pilot I would never have made it. I wouldn't even have tried it. I sat back and relaxed—it would only be a forty-minute flight, and waited for the cloud beneath me to disperse, as I had been promised by the Met man it would, so that I could drop into Blackpool without any problems. But when, after half an hour, I did call up Blackpool, the news was not so good. They had a ceiling of only 300 feet, and they were not in those days equipped with radar. All I could get was a 'QDM'—which is a course to steer to reach the field. I dropped down to 3,000 feet, which put me in the cloud once again, and proceeded to ask for QDMs. In order to get one of these, I had to transmit a short message, he would get a bearing on my position, and then give me my course to steer. He was not a very experienced controller. He sent me out over Morecambe Bay in a wide arc, and then brought me back, in an ever-increasing number of QDMs, towards the aerodrome. Finally his north-country voice announced, with a slight hint of triumph, 'Romeo, Romeo, you are now overhead.'

'Fine,' I replied sarcastically, 'I am still at 3,000 feet. What do you want me to do? Jump out?' There was a weary pause.

'Romeo, Romeo. Steer 330 degrees for three minutes. You can lose height over the bay.'

So, round I went again. Eventually, after God knows how many QDMs, I landed safely. As I switched my engine off, Denis Westoby ran out of the clubhouse with a crowd of flying members, and amid great jocularity they pinned a set of gold-embroidered wings onto my jacket. They had been listening to the whole farce on their radio in the bar. I believe I still hold the record for the longest let-down in the history of Blackpool airport. Commercial pilots, whose take-offs and landings had been totally suspended while this civilian menace was saved from self-destruction, were not so amused.

That afternoon, just as I had completed an immaculate short landing on Cheshire Polo ground, in front of an immense crowd, two gormless women started to walk across in front of me licking ice-creams. I stamped on my brakes, and hurriedly switched off the engine. 'At least,' I thought, 'if I do hit them, they won't get their heads chopped off.' Luckily they saw me just in time, and stopped in their tracks, giggling foolishly. Prince Philip was very annoyed. Apparently he had spent a great deal of time cantering up and down, shouting, 'Clear the ground. Jim's going to land.'

Next day one of the London papers carried a splendid picture of myself and the Duke, throwing our heads back and obviously enjoying a huge joke. Underneath was some typically stupid newspaper caption: 'Jester makes Prince laugh . . . what was the joke?' In fact, it was quite the other way round. The Duke had come up to me with his polo helmet. 'Look at this,' he said. 'I put it on the ground to go and have a bit of practice, and some bloody dog's done his business in it.'

Such heady encounters were far from my mind as I struggled to master the art of flying back in 1941.

Then, it was weeks of steep turns, spinning, stalling, side-slipping, steering by compass, aerobatics, instrument flying, forced landings . . . all the things that have to become instinctive before you can say you are a pilot. Sometimes I would go up for as many as five trips a day, but rarely for more than thirty minutes at a time. With each take-off and landing my confidence increased.

And every single trip, even if it only lasted ten minutes, I had to record in my Pilot's Flying Log-book, soon to become my proudest possession. I have it with me now, and as I thumb through it, with its details of every flight I made, every type of aircraft I flew, and every aerodrome I landed at, I can conjure up pictures of my entire flying career.

I had only done about twenty-five hours, when the whole unit was transferred to a new aerodrome at Bowden in Alberta. All the Tiger Moths were flown across by instructors and pupils, but I was not considered experienced enough for this, and, along with many others, made the trip by lorry. When we got to Bowden, only one or two aircraft had arrived, and we soon found out that all the others had run out of fuel and forced-landed in the prairies. But none of them came to any harm. It was simply a question of sending a petrol bowser around the countryside to locate and refuel them, and they were all soon with us at our new home.

Alberta was ideal for a flying school, with the flat prairieland all around, and crisp, clear air. If you thought you were lost, you simply followed the only railway-line until you came to a town, whose name was written large on the grain silos. But there was one snag. Occasionally, a dust-storm would get up with such frightening rapidity that within a few minutes visibility was reduced to almost zero, with strong, gusting winds whipping the sandy soil up to several hundred feet. One of these occurred one morning while I was sitting in the crew-room. We were immediately ordered to dash out onto the aerodrome, with handkerchiefs round our mouths, and help to grab any Tiger that landed and hold it down while the pilot taxied it into the haven of the hangar. After a hectic twenty minutes or so of this, with the dust swirling round us as we attempted to clutch the wing of any lurching, bouncing aircraft that came into view, there was a pause. With no more Tigers in the sky—or so it seemed—we ran back exhausted to the crew-room. After a quick count, it turned out that the only pupil missing was my fellow navigator-washout, Frank George. No one showed any great surprise. 'Good old George—it would be him,' was the general sentiment. He was always the one who seemed to be in some sort of scrape. We hung around, waiting for news to filter through. We didn't have to wait long before the phone rang. I think it was Flying Officer Hairs who answered it.

'Ah—it's you, George. Are you all right? . . . Good, I'm glad to hear that. And the aircraft? . . . Oh, tips of the propeller broken? . . . Well, that's not too bad . . . Under-carriage collapsed? Oh well, we can get that repaired . . . Tail-unit smashed, you say? H'm. Well . . . The aircraft's back seems to be broken? Oh, well, George—as long as you're all right. Yes. Get back as soon as you can.'

It came out later that George had been miles further away from the aerodrome than he should have been, showing off to some girlfriend, so that when the storm came up, he had no hope of finding his way back. He had such a rough time before he managed eventually to plonk the aircraft down, that all he could do was leap out of the cockpit and be violently sick.

STRAIGHT AND LEVEL

THE WIND WHICH blows with some regularity from Calgary to Edmonton is known locally as the 'Chinook', just as the Rhone valley wind is called the 'Mistral'. And the 'Chinook' was also the name of the steam train which was supposed to take us away from Bowden at the end of our course. All thirty of us went down to the station, loaded up as usual with our two kitbags each, and sat about near the track waiting for the arrival of this miracle conveyance. But we waited in vain. The first snow of the winter began to fall, and soon old Edwards was prancing about along the track, blowing his trombone for all he was worth, trying to keep up the spirits of his fellow airmen as darkness fell and no train arrived. At about ten o'clock, when spirits were really low and the supply of Calgary ale had been exhausted, word came through that there would be no train at all that night—so back to camp we went.

Next day thirty hefty hangovers clambered aboard the Chinook, and at Edmonton the connecting train had been held up for several hours, so that we could catch it. The load of jaded Canadian civilians eyed us somewhat balefully at first, but once again, when they realized we were lads from the 'old country', smiles broke out, and crocks of rye whisky were soon on offer. Here our party was split in two. Some went east, but we went west. We were going to fly twin-engined bombers—the others had been selected for fighters, and would be coping with the single-engined Harvard.

An important part of our instructors' task back at Bowden had been to assess our various aptitudes, and decide what sort of flying we were best suited for. Quite clearly it had not taken F/O Hairs long to make up his mind about me. I was the stolid, steady, straight and level pilot, good at flying compass courses, and quite happy to stick to unadventurous, rate one turns. Not the 'split-arse' type, in fact.

The correctness of this assessment was soon borne out at our next station. No. 35 Service Flying Training School was situated at North Battleford, in Saskatchewan, and that's where George and I found ourselves next, under the watchful eye of our new instructor, F/O David Porter.

But first there was a diversion to Saskatoon, where I met my brother Alan for the first time since I had left England. He had somehow managed to wangle himself out of the Metropolitan Police Force, and was training to be a pilot at Carberry, in Manitoba. We reckoned Saskatoon to be about halfway between our two stations, and it was in that snowbound, bleak city that we spent Christmas, 1941. Once again, Canadian hospitality was much in evidence, and we had a splendid Christmas dinner with some kind local people who had advertised their open invitation in our hotel. The rest of the time was spent catching up on family news, and consuming quantities of Calgary ale.

It amazes me sometimes to think of the important part beer has played in my life, and yet today I hardly ever touch the stuff. In 1964 I had a splendid contract with Charrington's Brewery, whereby they actually paid me a substantial sum to advertise their Toby Ale on TV and on posters. Not only did they pay me, they also provided me with all the beer I could drink, both at home and in the theatre. On top of that, at my suggestion, they printed booklets of vouchers, each entitling the holder to one free bottle of Toby Ale. These I distributed graciously in any Charrington's pub I happened to be in . . . and naturally took one for myself. By the middle of summer 1964, when I was in a summer season at Blackpool, I had reached the appalling weight of twenty-one stone. I went to see a local doctor. He looked at me with distaste.

'I don't know why you've come to see me, Mr Edwards,' he said sourly. 'Just remember two things: there were no fat people in Belsen. And there is no substitute for will-power. Twelve guineas, please.'

David Porter was a cool, unhurried, meticulous teacher. I had my first flight with him on 28 December 1941, and we are still friends today. The machine in use at North Battleford was the Oxford, a medium-sized monoplane, with two radial engines, shortish wings, and retractable undercarriage. It would seem very small by today's standards, but it was a great step up from the Tiger Moth. It must have been fairly easy to fly, because I had a mere four and a half hours' dual instruction before I went solo. It had its little vices though . . . most aeroplanes do. Its favourite little surprise trick would happen, sometimes, just after touchdown. Whereas in the Tiger you cut the power and glided in fairly steeply for a landing, in the Oxford you motored in at a far flatter angle, and cut the power just as you landed. Then the tail came down, and it was at this moment the Oxford could sometimes play its merry prank. Sometimes, but not always—that was the devilment of it—just as the tail-wheel touched the runway, and you were just congratulating yourself on yet another smooth arrival, a 'greaser', she would whip round in what is technically known as a 'ground loop', and you found yourself facing in the opposite direction. This was bad for one's nerve—and one's pride—and also very bad for the undercarriage. The whole thing was easily corrected by swift use of the appropriate throttle, but you had to be very wide awake to detect its imminence. Anyone who says he has never once ground-looped an Oxford is simply a liar.

Another happy novelty in this machine was that pupil and instructor sat side by side, so that one was able to conduct a fairly reasonable conversation, although the engines were pretty noisy. David Porter and I got on very well together, and I learned that before he joined the Air Force he had been a variety producer on BBC radio. This meant little to me at the time, but later this chance friendship was to play a large and important part in my showbusiness career. Of course, at North Battleford we only met either in the crew-room, or in the air. He lived in the Officers' Mess—I was still a lowly LAC, sharing a hut with some thirty or forty others. Frank George was also a pupil of David's, and he and I spent a lot of time together either in the NAAFI or the airmen's 'wet canteen'. Horrid phrase—but we used a lot of expressions peculiar to the Royal Canadian Air Force, whose guests we really were.

North Battleford was a good station to be on, even though it was surrounded by prairies, and not very far from the Northwest Territories, which was an area peopled mostly by Red Indians. In fact, a couple of chaps whose engines failed on a cross-country flight, and who managed to crash without getting killed, started their journey home in a canoe. The town itself was very small, and scarcely worth a visit, for we had everything we needed on the station. There was always a miserable cluster of hopeful taxis waiting at the main gate, to whisk us to the bright lights, but I was a rare customer. In any case, we worked pretty hard. There was a lot of flying to do, both by day and by night, and there was also a great deal of ground instruction. There were also exams to be faced at the end of the course.

It was a great thrill to find that there was a station dance band once again. They called themselves the 'Blue Rockets', and were led into battle by a corporal from the maintenance wing, who blew a mean trumpet.

We were so far north that the aurora borealis, or Northern Lights, gave a splendid display from time to time, and I was lucky enough to do my first night-flying with their aid. It was really cheating to call it night-flying—it was light enough to read a map at midnight—but that's how it went into my log-book.

I stayed at North Battleford for nearly five months, and did a total of one hundred hours' flying. And then, at last, on the 24th day of April 1942, I qualified for the Award of Flying badge—in other words, I got my wings. It was almost two years since I had first donned uniform at

Blackpool.

It had been an exciting course, and not without incident. One evening the wing commander had gone up to check the weather, taking a pupil with him. Immediately after take-off he found himself in a heavy snow-storm. Being an old hand, he climbed steadily until he came out of the cloud, and then very coolly proceeded to fly backwards and forwards on steady courses which he presumed would keep him in the vicinity of the aerodrome. He had no radio contact, so we on the ground could only listen for the sound of his engines as he crossed and recrossed the field every twenty minutes or so. Eventually, with his fuel gauges reading almost zero, he told the terrified pupil to bale out, shook him by the hand, and wished him luck. Just as our friend was about to open the door, the wingco spotted a break in the clouds. 'Hang on,' he shouted, and dived down through the gap, located the aerodrome, and made a safe landing.

Another night, two of our mates failed to return from a cross-country exercise. Next day we were all sent up on a search, but all that was found was a large hole bang in the middle of a frozen lake, with the wreckage of the aircraft floating in it. The only plausible explanation for this tragedy was that they had misread their altimeter, mistaken the lake for a cloud, and simply dived straight down into it.

And of course there was LAC Fischer, who in a mad moment, in broad daylight, had zoomed twice across the town as low as he could get. It was the Group Captain himself, down in the town doing a bit of shopping, who had taken the number of his aircraft and phoned it in to the control tower. When Fischer was hauled up in front of the old man (unauthorized low flying, especially over a town, was the most heinous crime), he got the medical officer to say that he had a severe head-cold and his eardrums had begun to hurt so much that all he could think of was to lose altitude so as to relieve the pain.

'Oh,' said the CO. 'But why *twice* across the town?' He then very decently gave poor old Fischer the offer of going for a court martial, or taking fourteen days in the 'cooler', straight away. Need I say which he chose? I used to take books in for him to read. He came out and resumed the course, and passed out with the rest of us.

In one's early days as a pilot, low flying is often a great temptation. The nearer the ground you are, the more sense of speed you get, and it's exciting to see people looking up in amazement, and cattle scattering in all directions. It's just showing off, of course. There was a road bridge over the river not far from North Battleford which one of the daredevils spotted, and one day, for a bet, he decided to fly under it. What he hadn't noticed, however, was that there was an old ferry near at hand, which was attached to a heavy metal cable which was strung across the river very close to the bridge. Having performed his great feat of airmanship, our daredevil pilot returned to collect his winnings.

'Excuse me,' said the flight sergeant, as our friend started to walk towards the crew-room, 'How come there's about six inches sliced off the top of your tail-unit?'

'Must have come off in a steep turn,'—and he got away with it, because no one ever found that missing bit of aeroplane. I hope he realized how lucky he was. Another couple of inches lower, and he would have chopped off the entire rudder, and that would have been the end of him.

Seeing us achieve our wings in such a short time and with so few flying hours must have been a bit galling for the more senior officers, who had no doubt sweated and strained for a great deal longer in their day. But there was a war on, and they were pushing us into the air just as fast as they possibly could. The Commonwealth Air Training Scheme was expanding so fast, that of necessity they had to make instructors out of people with comparatively little experience. Consequently, at the end of each course, a number were kept back in Canada to be trained to teach new personnel to fly at the stations that were now opening up all over the country. After our Wings Parade, at which we were all presented with a brevet by the group captain in an atmosphere of great solemnity, we naturally repaired to the wet canteen for a celebratory booze-up. But not before we had anxiously scanned the list of postings to see the jobs that had been allotted to us. Most were going straight back to the UK to swell the ranks of Bomber Command: some were to do further navigational training in Canada before going into Coastal Command; and a few were to stay behind to become flying instructors. Imagine our surprise when Frank George and I found we were to be in this last category. And the cream of the joke was that the Central Flying School at which we would be taught to teach was situated at Trenton, Ontario, where we had suffered the indignities of the Washout Squadron. The only difference was that whereas George, perhaps because of his somewhat offhand and 'bolshy' manner, had been promoted only to sergeant, old 'Toady' Edwards was to become a Pilot Officer.

This meant that we wouldn't be in the same Mess for the first time since we had met. But it was a short-lived situation, because in less than three weeks I had been washed out yet again!

At Trenton we were expected to fly three different types of aircraft . . . the twin-engined Cessna, which was not unlike the Oxford, and quite easy to handle; the Fleet, a piddling little thing like the Tiger Moth; and the Harvard, which had one roaring great radial engine, and which I didn't like at all. During my short stay on this course I only did about thirty hours flying, and I think my instructor knew right from the start that I was no good for the job. He rather unfairly had fixed a rear-view mirror in his cockpit in the Harvard, and I think that one look at my face in a spin was enough for him. After five months of glorious straight and level in the Oxford, I had lost my relish for aerobatics, but I don't know why I was not allowed to persevere with the Cessna. The wing commander had me up in his office and told me that what I really needed was more single-engined experience, and he had found just the job for me. I was to tow aerial targets at a gunnery school.

George, on the other hand, got on famously on the Harvard, and I left him behind to qualify as an instructor on the type. Subsequently, he spent many long months teaching in the mid-west of Canada, but we lost touch and I did not meet him again until after the war.

It was strange for both of us to be back at the station where we had suffered such humiliation, but luckily the flying field and the Officers' Mess were both the other side of the road from the old sea-plane hangar. We kept a low profile, and very few people recognized us. But the warrant officer who had made me a temporary policeman had the greatest difficulty in throwing me up a salute.

It took some time for me to appreciate what a difference it makes to have a commission. For two years I had been what is called, with the brutal tenderness that only exists in the Services, 'Other Ranks'. There's Officers, there's Non-Commissioned Officers—but every other animal that breathes is just 'Other Ranks'. I had been bawled at and been forced to pay deference to, and salute, and call 'Sir', ninnified nincompoops from inferior universities. I had queued up for cold sausages and bread and jam, queued up to use foul lavatories that had the scrawlings of bestial halfwits on the walls (and a great deal of their excreta as well), queued up to receive my miserable weekly pittance from the hands of a jumped-up, short-sighted bank-clerk—and queued up all too frequently to have my genitalia inspected by some pallid putative pox-doctor. But now that was all over. People saluted *me*, people called *me* sir. And I loved it.

But in a modest sort of way, of course.

One slight sadness, but not a serious one, was that I had to relinquish my number, 929629; now I was 123886, not nearly so easy to remember.

Further east along the shore of Lake Ontario lies Kingston, and here the RAF had No. 31 SFTS, where we taught the pilots of the Fleet Air Arm to fly Harvards. So it was not strictly a gunnery school. But at the end of this course, when they already had their wings, they had to have some practice shooting at moving targets in the air. And my job, for the next four months, was to tow these targets—or 'drogues' as they were called—while the Royal Navy came swooping in to try and pepper them with live ammunition. It was a slavish job, and not without its dangers, but I certainly got in some single-engined flying time—200 hours all told.

The aircraft used for this monotonous task was the Battle, which had been in the forefront of the RAF's efforts in France before Dunkirk. It was described as a bomber, but it only had one engine—a Rolls Royce Merlin—and looked like an overblown, elongated Spitfire. The rear turret had been removed, and in the back sat a quaking airman who operated an electric winch, which was used to let out and drag in the drogue, on about 1,000 yards of wire cable. This drogue was like a fifteen-foot windsock, made of canvas, and the ammunition which our brave matelots fired at us was of the 303 variety, spewed out of an ancient machine-gun mounted in the wing of their Harvard trainer. Each sortie lasted about two hours, during which time half a dozen men would make numerous separate attacks. In order to have some check on who actually hit the target and who didn't, their ammo was coated with different coloured chalks, so that, when the drogue had been dropped and retrieved by the gunnery section, the holes in it—if any—were laboriously counted, the colour noted, and the score relayed to the aspiring Hun-killers. My job was simply to fly up and down the firing range, making nervously steady turns at each end so as not to meet the drogue coming the other way, and then, at the end of the exercise, to go down and drop the target in some specified area. The quaking airman's job was not only to control the drogue and its wire, but also to have a Very pistol ready and loaded with a red cartridge. The moment I thought our gallant student was too directly astern, and therefore likely to hit us rather than the drogue, I would shriek at him over the intercom 'Fire a bloody red'—which he was only too ready to do. When the pupil had exhausted his ammo, the drill was to fly alongside me and waggle his wings to signify he was going back to Kingston. My duty was to waggle mine in return, and then look for the next client. Once I was so blazing with rage and frustration at some particularly inept pilot, that I waggled my wings too furiously and my engine cut out, and there were ageless moments of panic before I got it going again.

But first I had to learn to fly the Battle, lumbering old brute that it was. It must have made an easy target for German gunners in France when it was used to support the BEF, for in those days it would have been carrying a load of bombs, besides the pilot and his air-gunner. There was no way I could be given dual instruction on the type. There were only about six of them on the station, and they had been crated over from the UK without any modifications. So Flight Lieutenant Ellis, a tubby Canadian who commanded the Towing Flight, simply gave me the maker's handbook, and I sat in the cockpit while he stood on the wing and showed me where everything was. All aeroplanes conform to some sort of pattern. The throttle is here, the stick is there, the flaps are operated by this lever, the wheels come up when you pull this—and you can memorize the speeds at which certain things are supposed to happen. But when you get to actually do it, it can all seem suddenly quite different. I was pretty confident as I swung my first Battle onto the runway and gingerly opened the throttle. But, horror of horrors, the moment I did so the nose, which on this aircraft stuck straight up in the air, completely disappeared, and all I could see in front of me was runway. I hung on gamely, and when we reached the correct take-off speed, I pulled the stick back, and hauled the old crate into the air. It seemed a bit heavy, but when we got to about 100 feet, I knew the next thing to do was get the wheels up. I let go the throttle to search quiveringly for the undercart lever, and the engine stopped! Or seemed to. I had forgotten to tighten the throttle friction nut, so the moment I took my hands off it, the throttle closed. I instinctively rammed it open again— there was a great cloud of black smoke from the engine as it picked up again—and it was then that I realized that I had set the aircraft trim so badly that she was desperately nose-heavy. So I was stuck. I couldn't take my left hand off the throttle, and I couldn't let go of the control column in my right hand. What do you do in a situation like this? I'll tell you. You sweat with fear, and remember one of the pilot's basic rules: 'Height means safety.' The more air you've got under you, the more time you have to think.

When I had climbed, in terror, to 1,000 feet, I cautiously gripped the stick between my knees, and then with my right hand swiftly tightened the friction nut. Then all I had to do was adjust the trim, and all was well. When I landed, I was a year older.

A mere three weeks later I was such an old hand at flying the Battle that I nipped out one day in a bit of a hurry and failed to do my pre-take-off check as thoroughly as I should. I was bowling merrily along the taxi track, past a long line of Harvards, when I was hit sideways by a slight gust of wind. I tried to stop the aircraft swerving, and suddenly realized I had no pressure in my brakes. Thank goodness I had the presence of mind to switch off my engine, so that the Harvard I actually hit was not chewed to pieces. My log-book contains an 'endorsement' which puts the accident down to (1) Inexperience on type; (2) Carelessness. Signed, Group Captain D'Arcy-Greig.

I was lucky to get off so lightly, but this particular station commander was a very reasonable man. His great claim to fame was that he had been involved in winning the Schneider Trophy before the war, and he had an easy-going manner, and some liberal ideas. One of his dicta was: 'I don't want to see anyone in uniform after six p.m.' All of the officers were made honorary members of the local Yacht Club, so although I knew little and cared less about yachting, I was down there in the bar almost every evening in my grey flannels and sports jacket. Such freedom had been unheard of since I left Cambridge.

Again there was a fairly competent station dance band, but now that I had been promoted to Pilot Officer, it was supposed to be infra dig for me to play with them. This matter was easily overcome by my being made Officer In Charge of the Band, and I swanked about in front of them, trombone in hand, doing my Tommy Dorsey. The first time we played in the Officers' Mess, while everybody was out on the lawn enjoying a pre-prandial drink, I got the lads together on the dance floor to give them a bit of practice. 'First of all,' I said to them, 'let's get the National Anthem right. It sounds terrible.' Accordingly we went through it several times, and I was just about to launch them into yet another crack at it when the Orderly Officer came rushing up. 'What the hell's going on, Edwards,' he shouted. 'The old man's getting fed up with this.' It seems the microphone which relayed our music to the lawn had been switched on, and all the officers, plus their lady guests, plus the CO had stood to attention six times.

Target-towing, the most screechingly boring occupation that any pilot could do, continued daily, but was interspersed with occasional trips in a Harvard to various other aerodromes. And then one day the Lysander arrived. This was an odd-looking single-engined aircraft, with a high, bat-like wing, and a fixed undercarriage, which had originally been designed for Army Co-operation. Its greatest asset was its speed-range. You could get off the ground and land at extremely low speeds. There were all sorts of flaps and slots which increased the wing area. And yet, when everything was put away, as it were, you could work it up to about 200 mph. The great danger was that if you were going really slowly, and then opened the throttle too wide, it would climb uncontrollably. Once again, there could be no dual instruction on this one, so 'Tubby' Ellis and I pored over the manual, and then, in turn, loosed ourselves off into the air. It turned out to be far simpler than it looked, and far more reliable than the fading Battles, which were on their last legs. The 'Lissies' were being made brand new in Canada, but with the Battle you spent your whole time with one eye on the oil pressure, and the other on the Glycol coolant temperature. If one went down too far, or the other up too far, you simply abandoned target-towing and hurried back to the aerodrome.

It was at Kingston that I began to consider seriously the matter of growing a moustache. I had tried it first during a summer vacation whilst I was up at Cambridge. The following term, the first time I took a class at the Choir School at St John's some horrid little brute of a boy put up his hand. 'Please, sir,' he asked in the beguiling way that children have, 'what's that you've got under your nose?' They all tittered . . . How I love children! I blushed, and shaved it off that evening.

But now I thought I needed something to make me look old enough and stern enough and authoritative enough to carry the burden of my high rank. Well . . . and I am an expert, mind you . . . the only way to grow a moustache is to stop shaving your upper lip and see what happens. You can try to cozen the growth along by smearing a bit of vaseline on it now and again, but time is the great grower. I had another, more pressing incentive. I was dating the Squadron Leader Admin's daughter, and I desperately wanted to impress her with my maturity and worldliness. I even went to the length of buying an ancient Oldsmobile jalopy to take her out courting, but the first time I went to pick her up the damned thing refused to start. Nothing much came of this courtship—and very little of the moustache. I abandoned the one but persevered with the other, and I will tell you all about my several hirsute appendages as the story unfolds.

I had a thoroughly good time at Kingston, marred only by the towing, which was a mixture of monotony and lurking fear. But at least I was doing a job, and although nobody ever thanked me for it, there may be some ex-Royal Navy pilots around today who used my drogue to polish up their air gunnery.

Life in the Mess is always improved when there is a mixture of Services, and having these RN types around added to the fun. It was about this time that I started to venture on to the piano when sing-songs began after the beer had been flowing for a few hours. I had laboured at the piano for eight years at St Paul's Cathedral, and though I never achieved a very high standard, I could vamp for hours on end when the roistering was at its height. I never saw these songs written down, and very often didn't bother to learn the words, but they had no great musical quality, and conformed to simple musical patterns. On top of which, the singers themselves were not exactly musical geniuses, so that as long as I kept going everybody was happy.

Years later, at the Windmill Theatre I occasionally used to quote some of the cleaner lines to the audience, which was made up largely of ex-Servicemen. There was one line which always got a big laugh: 'Round and round went the dirty great wheel'. One day Vivian Van Damm, who was the manager, said to me, 'Why does that line get such a big laugh, Jimmy?'

'Come upstairs to the rehearsal room, VD,' I said (we all called him that—I don't think he actually knew what it meant), 'and I will sing you the whole song.' After I'd finished, he said, with an appalled smile, 'I wish I hadn't asked.'

When the chaps needed a breather, I would favour them with some bowdlerized versions of the only arias that *I* knew, which all came from oratorios I had sung at the Cathedral. Can you imagine 'Thus said the Lord, the Lord of hosts'—sung at a beery party in an officers' mess. 'Comfort ye' from the *Messiah*, was another of my hits.

And my trombone act was coming along nicely. It now took the form of a lecture on how to play the instrument, with all the technical, navigational, and meteorogical phrases I could muster thrown in. For example, before going on stage I would carefully fill the instrument up with water, so that when I first attempted to blow it there was a cascade onto the stage. 'Ah, liquid swirl,' I would say, and get a huge laugh. Don't ask me to explain the joke—it was something to do with magnetic compasses, which were filled with alcohol, which swirled about if you put the aircraft into too violent a manoeuvre. I wanted to give the lecture dressed as a Professor, and it was here, at Kingston, Ontario, that a kind local gave me his morning coat, striped trousers, and spats, which I had with me for years. One night we were performing in a village hall, where there was no water backstage. I panicked when my act was imminent, and, not wanting to lose the joke, filled the trombone with fizzy lemonade. Halfway through the solo, the slide jammed solid in the third position, and there was nothing I could do but leave the stage. The sugar in the lemonade had crystallized out. Good training for what was subsequently to be my profession, though I had no idea of it at the time.

By this time my brother Alan had won his wings also, and had been sent to a navigation training school at

Hamilton, also in Ontario. The town of Toronto was about halfway between us, and we had several wild weekends at the Royal York Hotel. We were anxious to serve on the same station together, and somebody put him up to a very ancient dodge, stemming from the First World War, whereby a serving officer can put in a claim for his younger brother to be posted to his unit. Some observant—or very old—officer at HQ got sight of Alan's formal application, and to our surprise it was granted.

Within two days of leaving Kingston, I was being shown the whys and wherefores of the Anson, at Hamilton. Whilst Alan was a navigation instructor, and spent a good deal of his time in the lecture room, I had been posted as a staff pilot. What a turning of the tables was this! Instead of scrambling about at the back, frantically searching for my pencil and dividers, as I had done at Port Albert, I would be up front in the pilot's seat, shouting orders and cursing the ineptitude of the pupils. The Anson was easy to fly—far easier than the Oxford—and I was soon off on my peregrinations around Ontario. Map-reading was easy out there in those days, with compact towns neatly joined by roads and railways. I don't suppose it's the same today, but back in 1942 it was a matter of a week or two before I knew the whole area like the back of my hand, even without reference to a map. There were also a lot of other Air Force aerodromes dotted about, which were easily recognizable by day, and flashed useful identification beacons at night. One had to fly the courses given one by the pupils, even if it was immediately clear that by so doing we would never reach our destination. Then, when the poor puzzled panicker came up and admitted he was lost, it was my job to show him where we were, so that he could start all over again. There were lots of little tricks one could play on them. My favourite effort was one dark night, when we were on the last leg of a three-hour, triangular trip, and should have been just about back at Mount Hope. My despairing navigator came forward, almost with tears in his eyes. 'I'm lost, sir,' he wailed.

'Well, then,' I said, pointing to an aerodrome beneath us which I knew very well was our own, 'we'll have to land down there, and you can go and ask where we are.'

I duly landed, and taxied in towards the hangars. He got out nervously and went and read a nearby notice-board. I shall never forget the look on his face as he came back to me. 'We're back, sir!!'

What a mean, rotten grinning devil I was.

Most trips lasted about three hours, and we often did two in a day, so we were kept pretty busy. And it was tiring work, quite different from the searing boredom of target-towing. You had to be on your correct course, and at the required altitude the whole time, and there was no George, or automatic pilot, in an Anson. The 'Annie' was a steady old machine, and could be flown with a very light touch—that is, provided everybody sat quite still. But the minute anybody on board moved so much as a foot or two fore or aft, the pilot could feel it on the control-column, and was forced to adjust the trim accordingly. If he failed to do so, in the twinkling of an eye he could gain or lose a few hundred feet, with the resultant decrease or increase in speed. But of course our persevering pupils had to move about the cabin quite a lot, especially if they wanted to go to the rear window and take a bearing on something or other. There was a simple drill for this. He just came up and tapped you on the shoulder, and pointed to the rear. Then our assiduous staff pilot (in the shape of me) would give the thumbs up, and be prepared for a radical change in the trim of the aircraft. But if the student failed to give this signal, and crept back all unannounced, with his sextant or whatever clutched in his trembling hand, the first thing the pilot knew about it was a wild change in the attitude of the Annie. I invented a cure for this lapse of manners. As soon as you saw, over your shoulder, our greenhorn navigator taking a bead on the object he wanted, you gave the control-column a sharp jerk fore and aft, which had the salutary effect of rapping the little brute's head on the roof.

Often we would do two trips at night, which meant a break in the middle, at about midnight, for eggs and bacon, which was the standard bonus for any night-flying. There was beer available after the second trip, and many's the time myself and a few hearty colleagues have been knocking it back as the bleary-eyed day fliers came in for breakfast.

Life in the Officers' Mess at Mount Hope was much enlivened by the presence of an elderly flying officer called Garvie. He was heavily built, sported quite a few campaign medals beneath his wings, and was reputed to have been sent to Canada as an instructor on Tiger Moths, but grounded for some wild feat much too near the ground and the control tower when he was rather drunk. He now worked in our control tower. He had a very loud voice, and always stood in front of the fireplace, with his tunic unbuttoned, and a pint of beer squarely in his right hand. If things weren't to his liking any evening, he would suddenly shout: 'Things are far too damned quiet in this mess.' Then he would lift his leg, rip off an immense fart, and yell: 'Balls, bollocks, and bang-me-arse. Chickweed and spinnygrass . . .'—and then continue to ramble on with a mad poem, the rest of which I have forgotten. Then it would be, 'Come on, young Edwards, let's have a party,' and I would be shoved in front of the piano. There were characters like Garvie scattered about all over the RAF. They'd usually done some service in one of the more remote areas like the Persian Gulf, or India, and had gone what was politely called 'doo-lally'. Like dear old Garvie, they usually disappeared one day, and all you could find out was that they had been 'posted'. This was a Service expression which simply meant 'sent to another station' and could always be recommended by a commanding officer if he wanted to get rid of someone. There were certain places which held a particular horror, either for their remoteness, or their frightful climate, or their lack of liquid refreshment facilities, or simply because nothing ever happened there. Back in England the greatest threat that could be uttered was, 'I could always have you posted to Wick.'

Mount Hope, Hamilton, Ontario, was definitely a 'good posting'. It was within weekend distance of Toronto, Niagara Falls was not all that far away, and you could also get into the USA very simply. We did a hell of a lot of flying, we churned out a hell of a lot of navigators, and we drank a hell of a lot of Canadian beer. The success of the station was mainly due to the benign yet firm rule of Group Captain Burnett, AFC, who had earned his gong for flying a single-engined Wellesley bomber to India before the war. A small, ginger-haired man, with piercing blue eyes, and a dapper uniform, he would occasionally appear in the most unexpected places, anywhere around the aerodrome, his swagger-stick tucked under his left arm. I saw him pop up round the corner of a hangar one day when flying had been cancelled, and then suddenly put on again owing to a change in the weather. Ansons were being pulled hurriedly out of hangars, and we were clambering aboard and starting up and getting airborne just as quick as we could. The Old Man appeared here and there from time to time, took a few salutes, and disappeared again. Later that evening, in a friendlier mood in the mess, I had the temerity to ask him why he did it. 'Edwards,' he said, with a twinkle, 'it's amazing the effect the old scrambled egg has on the chaps.'

I saw him, ages later, when my passage across Victoria Street was blocked by a royal procession. There he was, in his cocked-hat, gold braid, and sword . . . Commander-in-Chief, RAF.

Changes in weather were often a problem at Mount Hope. The runway was scarcely a mile from the shore of Lake Ontario, and if a fog developed over the water in the middle of the night, and began to creep towards the field, those of us who were out on exercises would get urgent radio messages: 'Return to base immediately.' I remember once getting the Annie down when there was only half the runway clear—I didn't want to have to divert somewhere else and spend the night in a strange mess.

We had one very irascible F/O, a Canadian, who was in charge of flying one night. He battled his way through a snow-storm to the met office to confirm his decision to cancel everything, and get into the bar. The met officer was poring over his charts, in a completely windowless office.

'Do you think we ought to cancel?' asked the F/O.

'No. It's perfectly okay,' says the met man, hardly glancing over his shoulder. Our F/O literally grabbed him by the collar, dragged him downstairs, and out into the snow. 'Then what the devil's this?' he roared. 'Snow,' said the met man, 'but it's not on my chart.'

There were plenty of non-flying activities for the brothers Edwards, soon to become known locally as 'AR' and 'JK'. For one thing, I became editor of the station magazine, the *Mount Hope Meteor*, which was published once a month, and was beautifully and glossily printed for next to nothing by a generous local printer, as his gesture of goodwill to the 'boys from the old country'.

Then there was, of course, the station concert party, which Alan and I took over together. We didn't exactly take it over—we formed it, by dint of spreading it around that there were auditions about to take place. I ran the cinema, too, and was often up in the projection room to broadcast messages to the audience between films. At one stage I began reading summaries from the world news as well, but my facetious comments soon brought the CO down on me. We found an amazing supply of talent. An airman in Accounts was a conjuror; a corporal fitter, who was very short, was a bit of a Cockney comedian; a mate of his, almost twice his height, teamed up with him, and we (brilliantly) called them 'The Long and the Short of it'. We had a wide choice of singers, and there was the inevitable flight sergeant steward in the Officers' Mess who liked to get up in drag. We became ambitious, and decided to do the best station show there had ever been, which we would present in the form of a revue, with the more talented among us doing our 'speciality' in between sketches. A high spot naturally would be the Trombone Act. One P/O Steele, another navigation instructor, revealed himself to be an excellent musician, so he was deputed to conduct the pit orchestra, in which I played when I wasn't on stage. We set a target date for the show, and started to work out some sort of format. The first stumbling-block, as with so many shows, was the title. There was no special theme to the whole thing, but it had to be called something.

Alan and I were sharing a reasonably-sized room, with a

double wardrobe between the beds, and a table and couple of chairs. 'Steely' was with us one evening when we started to discuss the title in earnest. I decided that the only thing to do was open a bottle of Scotch, wait for it to work its magic, and keep a paper and pencil handy. We jotted down every single idea that came up, however futile. 'One of them has got to be right,' I told them, as we quaffed away merrily. It was a great party, and we laughed uproariously as each scintillating thought went down in black and white. Next morning, in the cold light of post-breakfast recrimination, we pored over the list. 'Mount Hope Madcaps', 'Hamilton Hearties', one by one we crossed them out. But there was one we thought would do—'RAFter Raisers Mk One' and, once agreed, we stuck to it. I've used that method often enough, and it usually works. If there isn't an obvious title, hold a committee meeting, open a bottle, and write them all down.

My mind was brimming with ideas for songs and sketches, but, as time went by, not a lot of it was put on paper. I came back from breakfast one day to find the typewriter open on the table with a sheet of paper in it on which was typed simply, 'Scene one'. Over the table, on the wall, was pasted up a large sign, 'DO IT NOW!' How well AR knew JK.

Somehow it all came together. Alan wrote a brilliant little number called 'Mind, Body and Soul', which featured an education officer, a PT officer, and a padre. I did a sketch in three parts, in each of which I played a different submarine commander being interviewed on the radio— German, American and Royal Navy. In the last one I put on my most affected accent, and I always remember the last two lines:

Interviewer: 'And tell me, commander, did you actually sink the German battleship?'
Commander RN: 'Well, my second-in-command informs me that we did, and I've no good reason to doubt his good word.'

Then there were some 'Improbable scenes in the life of

97

AC Plonk'. In one of these I played the group captain in his office, and the huge joke was that I had some pilot's wings stuck over my moustache—and a huge pair of whiskers where the wings should have been.

I also hit on an idea for a church vestry committee meeting—mainly, I suppose, because I wanted to play the vicar. We were discussing the vestry cat, which was about to have kittens, when I was called urgently to the telephone. In my absence, the cat problem was solved, and the chairman moved on to the question of a certain lady of the village who was expecting an illegitimate child. Of course, when I returned to the meeting I thought they were still discussing the cat, so the scene was set for some typical misunderstandings. 'I always enjoyed it when she rolled on her back in the aisle . . . I used to scratch her tummy and she really purred . . .' and so on. Eventually the chairman said, 'But vicar, we are now discussing Miss Postlethwaite.'

'Oh,' I replied blandly, 'I mixed the cat up with the bag.'

The CO. who acted as our censor, wasn't very keen on this one, but I talked him into it. He was even less enthusiastic about a song I wrote for the diminutive Cockney, with his tall mate dressed as a hideous old woman. It was called 'Where There's Will There's a Way', and was full of the most appalling innuendos. I rewrote it twice to try and water it down, but he would have none of it.

The finale was my great work of art. The scene was the quayside at Halifax, with a cardboard cut-out of an ocean-going liner in the background. A group of airmen, about to sail back to England, stood facing the audience, with their kitbags in front of them. The song was 'Roll On That Boat', words and music by the Edwards brothers. It's odd how the phrase, 'roll on' gained such currency in the RAF. If you felt gloomy in the middle of the week, it was, 'Roll on Sunday!' At any time of the year it was 'Roll on Christmas!' And 'Roll on Pay Day' was a permanent sentiment. But for those of us who were overseas it was, 'Roll on that Boat!' Stationed in the luxury of Mount Hope, with easy flying conditions, no rationing, no blackout, plenty of booze, and even extra Overseas Pay, we must have been mad to want to go back to the blitz and all the other realities of war. But the thought was always in every airman's mind. So here's the song:

> Roll on that boat, 'cross the Atlantic's raging foam
> Back to where sweethearts are yearning for our
>   returning to home sweet home.
> Give us the blackout, and English beer, let's
>   get afloat.
> Though it's five Woodbines a day, and English rates
>   of pay . . .
> Roll on That Chugging Boat!

My mind boggles at the amount of time and energy I put into that show, and I was doing my full quota of flying as well. Not content with writing most of it, taking the rehearsals, playing in the band, and wangling all the cast off their duties so that they could join in, I also helped to paint the scenery. The only source of paint was the Dope Store, where they kept the stuff that was sprayed on the aeroplanes. And the only colours available were the green for the fuselages, and the red, white and blue for the roundels. The stink of it was appalling, but we persevered, and, between sneezing sessions, got it done somehow, but the paint was still wet on opening night.

It was worth every minute of it. The whole thing was an amazing success. I had given all the performers strict instructions that nobody was to take more than one curtain call. 'Keep it moving' must always be the motto in this sort of show. 'Don't give 'em time to wonder whether they're enjoying it or not.'

The only fly in the ointment was the conjuror—they're always the same. I stood in the wings mouthing threats, and, when he did come off, I grabbed hold of him until the next act was on. 'The Boat' was the wow of the evening. We had to sing it twice, and I think the CO was quite genuinely delighted . . . and even moved . . . when he came up on to the stage, and gave the standard CO's embarrassed thank-you speech.

The next week, by special request, we did a performance in the local village hall, and there the reception was not quite so rapturous. The totally Canadian audience missed most of the Service jokes, and the vestry sketch went over in utter silence. And when we came to 'The Boat', I think the question they asked themselves was why, after all the kindness and hospitality they had showered on us, we were so anxious to go home. You can't please everybody.

It was all such fun. I enjoyed the flying, I revelled in the concert party and the band. I wrote odd poems for the station magazine, I drank copiously, and Alan and I had invested in a rather ropey horse which we took turns to ride round the aerodrome, by special permission of the CO. We had to wait until flying had finished to do this, but it added a further dimension to what was a comparatively easy life.

I had begun to lean towards whisky at this stage. The shelf on our shared wardrobe was quite a sight, with Canadian rye whisky on Alan's side, and scotch on mine, with a long line of Canada Dry ginger ales in between. My drinking escapades had not so far got me into much trouble, but I had a narrow squeak one night when I was Orderly Officer. For this responsible job one wore an armband with a large 'OO' on it, and one was supposed to be in charge of all sections of the station, acting more or less as a stand-in for the CO. On this occasion I was carousing as usual with Alan and a few other officers, hoping subconsciously that no crisis would arise, and that I wouldn't be called upon to cope with anything unusual. In the middle of the drinking session, I was called to the telephone by the mess corporal.

'Orderly Officer here,' I said thickly, but with what I thought was a touch of authority. 'What is it?'

'It's the guardroom here,' said a voice. 'I'm sorry, sir, but we've got a drunk here needs dealing with.'

This was the last thing I wanted.

'Very well. I'll be along in a minute.'

I tottered to the cloakroom, and struggled into my greatcoat, overshoes, gloves and earmuffs . . . it was mid-winter.

When I got to the guardroom the corporal seemed

somewhat surprised to see me.

'What can I do for you, sir?' he asked.

'I believe you've got a drunk here,' I said, steadying myself against the door.

'Oh no, sir, there's no drunk here. Except . . .' there was a long pause as he eyed me sarcastically.

'Very well, corporal. Carry on.' I returned his salute to the best of my ability, and escaped, lurching back to the mess, to be met with great glee by everyone who was in on the joke.

'Been looking for a drunk, JK?'—and so on. My dear brother Alan was the most gleeful. It was he who had phoned, and I hadn't even recognized his voice.

It was hard to believe there was a war on. Many of the navigators who had qualified with our help were already in Bomber Command, and from time to time we heard of both decorations and casualties, which were duly mentioned in the *Meteor*. Thus we were able to feel that, at least in a roundabout way, we were helping the war effort. There was nothing we could do about it, anyway. Our lives lay in the mysterious hands of the moguls at Air Ministry.

RAFter-Raisers Mk I had been such a success, it was not long before Alan had me at the typewriter again, and I began to hack out songs and sketches for the next edition, which, naturally, would be called 'Mk II'. Things were well under way, and I had conducted the first tentative rehearsals, when the moguls stepped unexpectedly into the picture.

'Edwards, you're posted,' said the adjutant cheerfully one morning. 'Charlottetown, in Prince Edward Island. No. 31 General Reconnaissance School. So it's heigh-ho for Coastal Command.'

That was the way it always happened. No rhyme, no reason . . . no why or when . . . the magic word *posted* came along when you least expected it. You never found who had instigated the move, or whether it was just some goon in Kingsway shuffling lists of names about. I talked it over with Alan.

'We've got to get this next show on somehow.'

'Why not go and see the CO. He's bound to understand.

Probably postpone it till after the show.'

I asked permission to see the Old Man, and presented myself in his office accordingly. After slinging up my very best salute, I launched myself into my prepared speech.

'It's about this posting, sir. You see, we've just started rehearsals on the next show.'

He looked up from whatever he was writing. His clear, blue eyes locked onto me from beneath his auburn eyebrows.

'Well, Edwards. Don't you want to get back to the UK and get cracking against the Hun?'

What could I say?

'Yes, sir.'

There was a tortured pause. Should I try and persuade him? Should I start on the 'But we've got it all written, and they can't get on without me' gambit? What about 'Remember how much you enjoyed the last show, sir? This one is going to be even better.' I couldn't get a word out. He had gone back to his writing. He looked up again.

'Very well, Edwards,' and down went his head.

I slung up a somewhat tattered salute, and left.

The termination of such a long and successful stay had to be marked by a very special booze-up, and who better than the Edwards brothers to organize it? Things went with a great swing, toasts were drunk, trombones were played, and there was the usual session of dirty songs with me at the piano. In the blurred climax to the night, someone produced a razor, and next morning Edwards J.K. awoke with an almighty hangover, and only half a moustache! This half just had to be hurriedly removed before I made a somewhat sheepish appearance at breakfast. Soon I was on yet another Canadian train, heading remorselessly east towards Nova Scotia and England and determinedly starting on yet another upper growth.

I am proud to say that I was remembered at Mount Hope. Months later I received a copy of the *Meteor* of February 1943. I quote, with modest pride, from 'Station Notes':

Among those going to Prince Edward Island was P/O
J.K. Edwards, of the Edwards Bros. and Co. Unlimited . . .
a move, which, for ourselves we deeply regret. J.K.
had a spontaneous brand of humour that cheered up
many a homesick soul in moments of deep depression.
He was a rare humorist and no mean entertainer,
producer, librettist, trombonologist, horse-fancier,
toper . . . Oh, and Staff Pilot. Happy Hunting, Jimmy.

Nothing nicer has been written about me since!

That was forty years ago, as I write, and I realize now how
sharply my attitudes towards performing have changed.
Then, it was all fun, with the ebullience of youth to keep
me going. We did it all ourselves, voluntarily, to lighten the
darkness of our fellow airmen, and in the process to enjoy
ourselves, unrewarded, except by the thanks of the CO
and the applause of our mates. Little did I know that when I
eventually came into showbusiness it would involve hard
work, which very often became nothing but drudgery. In
1952, I recall, I went into a show at the Adelphi Theatre in
London, with Vera Lynn and Tony Hancock, which ran for
two years. And we did it twice nightly. During those two
years, Tony suffered three nervous breakdowns, and, but
for the grace of Scotch, I might have done the same. Vera
sailed along, seemingly unperturbed, always giving of her
best, and spending her time in the dressing-room with
knitting and tapestry-work. There are nights, in a show
such as that, when you would rather do anything than go
on the stage. Once I was attacked by influenza, and rang
George and Alfred Black to say I could not possibly
perform that night.
    'Just get down to the theatre, Jim, and do your best,' said
George.
    When I staggered into my dressing-room, there was a
bottle of Johnny Walker standing on my make-up table,
with a little note attached: 'You'll manage, Jim. Love and
Kisses, George and Alf.'
    They knew their Jim.

At the end of that run, during the magnificent party which this generous and kind management always threw, I asked Tony: 'What happens to you? Why all these nervous breakdowns?' (Each one of them had meant three weeks under sedation at the London Clinic.)

'Well, you see Jim,' he replied lugubriously, 'every night is like a first night to me.'

Poor old Tony. He, like me, had started by larking about in concert parties in the RAF. But eventually the burden of stardom got him down. Many years after this show, when we hadn't worked together for a long time, he came to dinner with me at my house in Sussex. When he arrived, as soon as he saw he was not the only guest, he sat morosely staring out of the window, hunched in his familiar misanthropic manner. I plied him with booze, and eventually he mellowed, and turned in towards us. Much later, when he had taken off his coat, and was in a happier mood, we took to discussing comedy, and showbusiness, as with him one inevitably did. One sentence from this chat remains with me.

'For me,' he said, 'the best drink of the day is the vodka in the bath before breakfast.'

One of the many problems in showbusiness is to know how to handle success. But an even knottier problem is to know how to handle a decline in your fortunes. Tony handled it by committing suicide. I went to a dreary pub in Tasmania not long after this melancholy deed, and as the landlord showed me into my bedroom, which had some sort of concrete frieze outside the windows so the minimum of light came through, he said to me with some pride: 'This is the room Tony Hancock had the week before he done himself in.'

I looked round the abysmally squalid accommodation.

'I can quite see why the idea came into his head,' I replied.

I was touring alone myself at the time, and had experienced many bitter moments. In Launceston, which is, if possible, even duller than Hobart, we were suddenly hit by Good Friday. I asked the landlord, my employer, what was going to happen.

'There's no show tonight, Jim. No worries.'

'What is there to do in Launceston today?' I ventured.

'Nothing, Jim. Legally, I'm not supposed to even open the bar.'

'If you don't,' I said quite simply, 'I shall kill you.'

At Charlottetown I was once again a pupil, sitting in the back of an Anson, fiddling about trying to work out courses to steer, and being taught the intricacies of Square Searches, Creeping Line Ahead, Radius of Action, and Parallel Track Search. I was able to take control myself a few times, but in the whole two months I was there I only logged up about twenty hours flying. The rest of the time was spent in the lecture room, and—need I say—the bar. And there was a snag here. Prince Edward Island was, technically, 'dry'—dreaded word—and one was only supposed to consume a limited amount of alcohol each day. But when the need is dire, thirst will find a way. There were just a few of those helpful mortals called teetotallers in the mess, and their vouchers could be bought at a price, by needful people such as myself. The civilians on the island, too, had their ways and means. If you could persuade a doctor that whisky was the only thing that would cure your cold, or save your life, he was empowered to issue you with a Prescription for Alcohol—known locally as a 'scrip'—and I made plentiful use of this loophole. And the CO was able, on special occasions, to increase the ration at the bar.

Also, as in all places where there is prohibition, bootleggers abounded in the town, and there was moonshine to be got at a price. Group Captain 'Woof-woof' Blake had a word of warning about this: 'For anyone returning to camp the worse for this liquor, the guards at the main gate have been equipped with a stomach-pump.' He was a lovable and eccentric character, and once you had been barked at by him a couple of times you realized how he had got his nickname. He was supposed, one morning, to have telephoned the adjutant, who had an office right next to his. When there was no reply, he apparently flung open the hatch connecting the two offices, shoved his head through, and yelled, 'Answer the bloody telephone' and then slammed it shut. He had the reputation of being the only pilot who had ever performed aerobatics in an Anson on one engine, a feat about which we were all very sceptical. Most of us thought it would be hare-brained to try it with both, but it was a legend which followed him around.

When the course was over I passed as Good Average as a reconnaissance pilot, and was ready to join Coastal Command. I didn't know it at the time, but I was saying farewell to the Anson, on which I had piled up well over 300 hours flying, and which I had grown to love as only a carefree pilot can love a simple aeroplane. Many years later, when, as a civilian, I landed my single-engined Cessna 172 at Gatwick, I found, just before I took off again, that one of the doors wouldn't stay firmly locked. I was standing on the tarmac, scratching my head and wondering whether I dared risk flying with a door that wouldn't lock, when the uniformed pilot of a British European Airways helicopter parked next to me, strolled over to see if he could help.

'Good lord,' he said, 'it's old Edwards—JK isn't it? Remember me at Mount Hope? What's your trouble?'

I showed him that the door would not lock.

'My dear fellow,' he said, 'didn't all those hours on Ansons teach you anything?'

He fished in his pocket, and brought out a ragged bit of string. 'I still stick to the old rule,' he said as he secured my door, 'never fly without a piece of string and a packet of chewing-gum.' In the Anson, chewing-gum was vital for blocking up cracks in the ageing perspex windows, Without it, especially in a Canadian winter, you were subjected to the most painfully icy draughts.

And it was farewell to Canada, too. But not immediately. The Commonwealth Air Training Scheme was now in full swing, and so many airmen, untrained and trained, were coming in and out, that a vast transit camp had been built at Moncton, not far from the port of Halifax, where they could wait for either train or boat. I was soon swallowed up in this huge complex of huts and drill halls, and eventually found my way to the Transient Officers' Mess. I had scarcely swigged down the first large whisky when I spotted a familiar face. It was David Porter.

I had not seen or heard of David Porter since he got me my wings at North Battleford, and, now that I had caught up with him in rank (we were both flying officers by now), we could drink together freely in the Officers' Mess. David told me that he had already been there for several weeks, as there seemed to be some shortage of troopships, and the rumour was that we were likely to be in for a prolonged stay. As a result of all this, the whole camp was full to bursting, and David revealed that he was already working on a satirical operetta set in the Officers' Mess. We found that there was a well-equipped stage in the recreation hall, and, as nobody else could be bothered, I got myself appointed Entertainments Officer. All we needed now was a composer. We didn't have to look far. In every Officers' Mess there was always a piano, and nearly always some heavy-handed bloke like myself strumming away at it so that the chaps could sing coarse songs. But one night we pricked up our ears. 'I say David,' I said, 'listen to that fellow on the piano. He can really play the damned thing.' David put some lyrics in front of him, and he immediately improvised a tune, with all the correct harmonies. F/O Kirtley was a real find, and in a very few days the score was complete, and we were looking round for performers. I picked a plum part for myself—an old, raddled flight lieutenant who had been there for ages, and despaired of ever getting moved on. My song, 'Please post me to another damned station', sung with great emotion and histrionics, was a big hit. But the real success was a heart-rending lament by an LAC who had come from England to learn to fly, and found himself, instead, sweeping up in the Officers' Mess.

My sketchy knowledge of RAF disciplinary procedure was put to the test one morning when we were rehearsing a number on the stage. Suddenly, all the lights went out, the cinema screen was dropped in and someone started running a film. I was overcome with rage.

'Turn that fucking thing off,' I shrieked. A voice came over the loudspeaker. 'I can show this film all day long if I want to.' It was the corporal in charge of the cinema. Blind with fury I rushed upstairs and started banging on the locked door of the projection room, shouting at the top of my voice. He refused to open the door, so I ran to a telephone and asked for the Guard Room. 'Corporal,' I yelled, 'I want you to come up here and arrest a man.'

The voice at the other end was cool. 'Now then, sir, what seems to be the matter?' I explained and repeated, 'I want you to come up here and put him under arrest.'

'All you have to do, sir,' said the corporal at the other end of the line, in that voice that means "I shouldn't have to tell you this, sir," 'All you have to do is simply inform the airman concerned that he is on a charge, and that he has to report to the Guard Room. You can come round here, sir, when you like, and tell us what the charge is.'

I hurtled back to the projection room, banged on the door again, and shrieked, 'You're on a fucking charge.'

Later that week, the case came up in front of the Squadron Leader Admin. Of course, by this time the airman had taken the opportunity to consult his fellow airmen, and when he was asked, 'Do you have any questions for the Flying Officer?' he was ready for me. He cleared his throat. 'Yessir,' he said, slowly and meaningfully. 'Did the officer at any time use obscene language?' This was a nasty one. 'Oh well,' I thought to myself, 'it's his word against mine.'

'Definitely not, sir,' I said firmly . . . and the unfortunate man got fourteen days. For the next four years I was never again tempted to put an airman on a charge.

During our two months of comparative idleness at Moncton, we were invited to do a show on the local radio station, which was situated in a tiny studio above a chemist's shop in that small town. They were called Radio CKCW, and naturally I took several opportunities to call it CK-WC by mistake. After the show, I asked the station manager what he thought of it. 'Too much goddam talking,' was his only comment. That was my first broadcast.

At last a boat arrived, and hundreds of us were crammed aboard HMT *Empress of Scotland*, which had been hastily renamed from *Empress of Japan* when the Japs came into the war.

The trans-Atlantic crossing took about seven, mercifully uneventful days. Once again there was no booze on board, so one had plenty of time to worry about torpedoes and fight against sea-sickness. I looked back on my two years in Canada, the initial setbacks and frustrations, and subsequent achievements, and decided that, on balance, it had been a good time. I had learned to fly. More important, I had learned to enjoy flying. I had learned to drink . . . and to enjoy that, too. And I suppose I had matured in a way that I didn't bother to analyze. Years later, when I was suffering my first professional showbusiness engagement at the Windmill Theatre in London, feeling frustrated after having had hardly any laughs, I would walk down to Piccadilly Circus underground on my way back to Barnes. In a window in Shaftesbury Avenue hung a lone neon sign, saying 'Emigrate to Canada—£10'. I was sorely tempted for eighteen long months—then along came 'Take It From Here'. After that, all was different. In fact, I didn't return to Canada until the early seventies, and by then I was sharing top-of-the-bill with Eric Sykes in 'Big Bad Mouse'.

COASTAL COMMAND

ON 24 MAY 1943 we disembarked, and made our way by train to Harrogate, where yet another holding unit had been established in some of the hotels. I wasn't there for more than a few days before I was told I had to go to Northern Ireland to learn to drop torpedoes. But first there was disembarkation leave, and I was able to get back to Barnes for a week or so, to quaff innumerable pints in the Market Gardener, and regale the locals with stories of my adventures in North America. But Barnes wasn't much fun, what with the blitz and the blackout and the shortage of booze. Still, I was able to see my mother, and get from her all the news of the other eight members of the family. But I didn't even see a lot of her, because she was by now a full-time air raid warden, and spent most nights in a surface shelter only a hundred yards from the pub. She didn't approve of my visiting her in the shelter, because the smell of beer offended her and her colleagues.

But one night they were glad of our proximity. I had been serving behind the bar that night, as Albert Clamp, the landlord, was shorthanded. I helped with the washing-up, had a farewell pint and tottered the half-mile or so home. I had only just got into the house when the sirens went signalling an imminent air raid, but I was too far gone to bother about our shelter at the bottom of the garden, and went upstairs to my attic bedroom. I stripped off my uniform and flopped into bed. My eyes were barely closed, when there was the most colossal bang outside. I rushed to the window. There were smoke and flames everywhere, and worst of all, it was the Market Gardener that seemed to be on fire. This was a grave setback to a drinking man, and I realized that I must dash to the rescue. I struggled drunkenly into my uniform, and tottered round to see what I could do. As I neared the scene, with fire-engines everywhere, and wardens running to and fro, I saw that the fire was on the other side of the road from the pub. What a relief. But when I actually got there, and saw what had happened, I groaned. The bomb had dropped so close that the whole of the front of the pub had been blown in. There was shattered glass and plaster everywhere. I picked my way through what was left of the door, and there was Albert, behind the bar, his warden's helmet on his head, a pint in his hand, surrounded by muck and rubble, with a silly grin on his face. 'It's all right, Jim,' he said thickly, 'the pumps are still working.' We set to, and cleaned the mess up as best we could. And then, for the rest of the night, we served the rescue workers with beer as and when they wanted it. After all, as Albert said, "ow can we close when the bleedin' doors won't shut?'

By seven in the morning I was so exhausted that I fell asleep leaning on the bar, with my head cupped in my hands. Albert gave me a nudge. 'You'd better go 'ome and get some sleep, my lad,' he said. 'We've got to open up again at 'alf past ten—and don't forget it's all on ole 'Itler.'

RAF Limavady, in Northern Ireland, was an Operational Training Unit (OTU), and here we were to learn to get into the action. At this stage in the war, Coastal Command strike forces, based in North Africa and Malta, were playing havoc with German convoys in the Mediterranean. One of the many techniques evolved was to drop torpedoes at night from Wellington bombers which had been specially modified for the job. On moonless nights, half the squadron would drop immensely powerful flares, and then the other half would run in for the attack with the enemy ships silhouetted against the bright artificial light. It was a very dangerous job, and RAF losses had been considerable. The first task was to learn to fly the Wellington, which I was looking forward to. But I was in for a disappointment. I found, to my disgust, that I had been put into a crew as a second pilot. As if this wasn't bad enough, the pilot and all the rest of the crew were flight sergeants . . . and I had a great deal more hours in my log-book than my skipper. I put up with this for a few trips, but they were such a sloppy outfit, and take-offs and landings were so hair-raising that I was emboldened to request an interview with the wing commander in charge of training. 'I'm sorry, Edwards,' he said, 'but you'll just have to get along with your crew as best you can. We can't run the Air Force just to please you.'

'But sir,' I began, not really knowing what I was going to say next. I was cut short by the phone ringing. The W/C answered it. He listened for a few moments and then said, 'Well, I've got someone here who might fill the bill. I'll send him over.'

'Well, Edwards, you're in luck. Somebody has just failed to go solo on the previous course. If you can get the hang of the Wellington tomorrow, and catch up with the required number of hours in one day, you can take over his crew.'

I went to bed early—and sober—that night.

Next day, all the flying experience gained in Canada stood me in good stead. The Wimpey (as the Wellington had been nicknamed) was bigger and heavier than anything I had handled up to now, and you had to be very strong in the wrist to hold the nose down once you had applied full flap. After two landings, my instructor turned to me in the cockpit. 'You know,' he said, 'you're a born Wimpey pilot.' For a moment I swelled with pride . . . and then I got the full implication of this 'compliment'. What he really meant was—'You fly like a lorry-driver.'

But I went solo, and flew the whole day long, did the hours they wanted, and inherited a crew that had been put together a week or so before. My bunch of flight sergeants, with some other unfortunate who had joined them as second pilot, flew into the sea one dark night a few weeks later. All six of them perished.

I met my navigator and three wireless operators next day in their classroom. Harry Green, who was to handle the maps and compasses, was a lino-layer from Wigan. Bill

In 1938, shortly before the War.

Summer 1941, before going to North Battle-ford soon after being commissioned.

Flight Lieutenant Hairs, my ab initio flying instructor, in 1941.

After the Wings Parade at North Battleford, Canada, in April 1942. I am on the left, Frank George is on the right, with two mates in the middle.

Frank George in 1941, before he smashed up his Tiger Moth.

Singing 'Roll On That Boat' in Canada. Brother Alan is on the left, watching nervously.

A little crash that I had in Kingston, Ontario, 1942.

July 1943. I am in the back row on the left next to Cartwright and MacNeil. Front row, left to right: Billy Randall, Harry Green and Bill Shaw.

My demob picture. I am growing the mous-
tache again – the same moustache put to
proper use at the Windmill.

At the Windmill Theatre after the War.

At a recent reunion with Randall on the left, and Sorensen on the right.

Shaw, who was to sit over the Morse key and climb into the upper turret in an emergency, came from Chester-le-Street, Tyneside. Bill Randall and Ernie Cartwright manned the front and rear turret. They were all sergeants, and we exchanged a few embarrassed pleasantries before we separated to go to our messes. I peered at a notice-board to see who was going to have the honour of being my second dickie.

'I wonder who this Pilot Officer MacNeil is?' I said aloud to myself as I turned away from the list, and bumped into a tall dark chap with 'Canada' on his shoulders. 'It's me, as a matter of fact,' he said, and we shook hands. 'Mac' was to fly beside me for eighteen months before he became a skipper in his own right. He survived the war, and went back to Canada. He has only just retired from the headmastership of a school in a small town in Ontario.

We had only been flying together for a week or so, when Bill Randall, with his ginger hair and freckled face, came up to me in the crew-room one day. Without a word, he handed me an old photograph of a chubby baby lying on its stomach, stark naked, on a velvet cushion. 'Recognize that, Skipper?' he asked, with a grin. I should say I did. 'Christ almighty, it's me,' I yelled. 'Where the hell did you get this?' 'One of my aunts was a nanny of yours in Woodlands Road. I live in Barnes, too—White Hart Lane.' 'Well, don't let everybody see it.' But of course, it had to be shown to the other four, amidst much merriment. The war was full of coincidences.

From now on, the six of us always flew together as a crew, and I began to feel the satisfaction of being the leader of a team. We soon grew to know and trust each other, and it was a matter of pride that we could work together almost instinctively. I enjoyed being referred to as 'Skipper' and felt that with all my flying experience, I could properly live up to the title.

We were soon doing long navigational exercises over the Atlantic and when Harry Green gave me a course to steer, I steered it with all the confidence that I had in navigators! We started off with daylight trips, and on these it was not difficult to tell whether you had made a successful landfall or not. After all, if we arrived a little bit too far south, the word EIRE was written along the coast in huge chalk letters. When we saw that, a sharp turn to port would save us from flying over neutral territory. I found these trips very satisfying. We never flew at more than 2,000 feet, and as we were over water most of the time there were no points of reference or landmarks to recognize, so it was very important to fly accurate courses all the time. There was plenty to do in the way of dropping smoke flares so that Harry could take sights on them and work out the wind direction and speed. And if we got too bored, we could take it in turns to get into the front turret and loose off a few hundred rounds from the four machine-guns mounted there. I only did this once, and found it far too draughty and noisy. One of the favourite exercises was to try and find the island of Rockall and take photographs of it. The catch was that Rockall has tremendously strong magnetic properties, so that, as soon as you got within a few miles of it, your compass began to play tricks, and you could soon find yourself going round in circles. I was one of the lucky ones. I kept the aircraft on a steady heading, and eventually the island loomed up. There wasn't a lot to photograph. Just a lot of seagulls sitting on piles of their own excrement. It was still standard practice in Coastal Command to carry a basketful of homing pigeons on every trip. The theory was that if you had to ditch, as soon as you were settled in your dinghy, you wrote your position on a piece of paper, placed it in a capsule, which was then attached to the bird's leg. The pigeon was then released, and, if all went well, the rescue operation could begin. I know there were numerous occasions when the system did work, and airmen's lives were saved as a result, but it never happened whilst I was at Limavady. So after each trip, when we had switched off the engines and climbed out of the Wimpey, we had the fun of releasing our feathered friends and letting them fly back to their loft. They always used to circle a couple of times first, as if to say, 'What's all the fuss about? We're only half a mile from home!'

In between navigational exercises, we did low-level bombing practice in a small bay just round the corner. This was supposed to be done from about 100 feet up, but of course, I was the keen one who went so low that we picked up tiny fragments of bomb-casing in the wings. We all enjoyed low flying especially when it was authorized, and in a Wimpey you had to work hard, diving down, zooming over the target, and then shoving open the throttles as you did a steep climbing turn away. All this compensated for the long hours of monotonous straight and level flying involved in the other exercises. Another excitement was 'fighter-affiliation'—at least, that's how you wrote it down in your log-book. A couple of Hurricanes from a nearby Fleet Air Arm station would rendezvous with us at about 6,000 feet and go through the motions of trying to shoot us down. Mercifully they were only armed with cameras, and our job was to throw the Wimpey about in violent evasive manoeuvres so that they couldn't get a good shot of us. If, for example, one of them came in from the port side, you were supposed to wait until he had definitely committed himself to the attack, and then turn sharply in towards him. In this way you mucked up his deflection, and with any luck he passed either over or under you without being able to take a pot. Or if he came in from behind, you went into a 'corkscrew' dive, which was pretty hard work in a Wellington. As usual, my enthusiasm overcame me the first time I tried all this out, and at one stage, to my shock and amazement, the Hurricane suddenly appeared upside-down under my starboard wing. Later, comparing notes with the Navy pilot, he told me that I had corkscrewed so violently that he had got caught in my slip-stream, and only just managed to avoid colliding with me.

Another favourite trip of mine was when we took off just at dusk and headed out across the coast and straight out over the Atlantic. This was about a six-hour flight— three hours out and three back. There was no actual destination at the other end. As night gradually fell, and darkness enveloped us, I would turn the cockpit lights down until, at around midnight, with one's eyes adjusted to the blackness, one could clearly make out the horizon, and the waves beneath us. The instrument panel was barely glimmering with dials, and woe betide any member

115

of my crew who came forward with a torch, which could stab at your eyes like a knife. And it was nearly always so smooth over the sea at night. Any clouds that had accumulated during the day soon faded away, and the old Wimpey settled into the sky and flew as steady as a rock.

And then Harry Green would be up at my elbow telling me to turn on to such and such a course in so many minutes, and we'd be on our way back. Limavady had its own beacon, flashing its own three-letter code, and on a very dark night you could see it from miles away—provided Harry had done his stuff. If, on the other hand, it didn't show up at the expected time, he would be up at my elbow again, peering into the murk, and muttering, 'Can yer see owt, Skipper?' in that tentative voice that navigators assume when they are not sure of their calculations. 'No, Harry, I can't see a bloody thing.' A long pause. And then, 'Perhaps yer best turn a bit to the left.' Suddenly there it would be, and our hearts lifted in unison. We all knew that in a few minutes it would be good Irish eggs and bacon, washed down with a pint of beer . . . or, better still, a Guinness or two.

All this flying was interspersed with lectures. There were occasions when we were expected to turn up to the classroom in the morning, even though we had been flying most of the night. All the members of our course took exception to this, and so one day, after discussing the matter among ourselves, we decided to boycott the lectures. Once again, as so often in my Air Force career, I was the one who was singled out as the ringleader, and summoned for a sticky interview with the wing commander. I managed to get our point across to him, and the schedule was changed, but I had the uneasy feeling from then on that I was considered to be the trouble-maker. Things weren't improved when, a few weeks later, I put my foot in it again. Some dozen or so of us were in the back of a three-ton lorry, on our way back from the airfield, when a small Hillman staff-car came up very close behind. Being in a jocular mood, I merrily gave it the two-finger Victory salute, in reverse—and it turned out to contain the station commander! Edwards was on the carpet again. It was only the fact that the course was nearly over and we were about to be posted to another station that saved my bacon.

At this stage I was moustache-less yet again. There must have been another party somewhere!

Now that we had mastered the art of seeking and finding the enemy, we had to have a try at sinking him, so we said farewell to Northern Ireland, and went off to Scotland to practise dropping torpedoes. The station was Turnberry, right beneath the famous golf-course, and our Officers' Mess was almost on the beach on the shore of the Firth of Clyde.

Once again we were flying the Wimpey and the whole course lasted less than a month. But we were in the air nearly every day, usually more than once. On 14 August 1943 I flew six sorties, two of them at night, clocking up nearly seven hours' airborne time, and doing six take-offs and landings. A couple of miles out to sea, between us and the island of Ailsa Craig, there lurked a destroyer, manned entirely by the Polish Navy, and their miserable task was to cruise up and down steadily whilst, one by one, we made mock attacks on them. I can't imagine anything more boring for them, but for us it was absorbing. In lieu of real torpedoes, each aircraft was fitted with a set of cameras, which were triggered off when you pressed the firing button. One camera photographed the ship in front of you, and the other took a picture of the aircraft's instrument panel at the same moment. From this information the whizzkids in the torpedo section were able to assess the success or failure of your attack.

Only at the very end of the course were we allowed to drop a real torpedo, and, naturally, it had a dummy warhead, and was adjusted to go underneath the ship (just in case you were that good), and then to resurface and give off smoke, so that it could be located and hauled aboard a launch for use another day. Tremendously accurate flying was called for. In theory, we were supposed to release the projectile at a speed of seventy knots, and from an exact height of 72 feet above the water. If you got it wrong, the torpedo would enter the water at the wrong angle and probably break up, thus costing the nation an unnecessary £2,000. The airspeed was not too difficult to control, but the precise height above the water was, for me at any rate, sheer guesswork. What it amounted to was that you flew towards the bows of the ship, looking at it through a sight on the windscreen, with the speed as nearly right as you could get it, and then, when you thought you were low, you levelled off. You then maintained that height and speed until you began to think, 'Strewth, that ship is close!'—and then you pressed the button. Out of exactly ninety simulated attacks recorded in my logbook, 44 were a 'hit' and 46 a 'miss'. In spite of that dismal record, I was assessed as 'above average as a torpedo pilot' and was considered ready to wreak death and destruction on the Jerries, wherever they might be sailing.

Mac and I were accommodated in a Nissen hut, with four other officers, a few hundred yards from the Mess. It was just our luck that on the night of the monthly party, we were down to go flying. We went to the crew-room, and glumly got everything ready and then sat about looking at our watches, waiting for the officer in charge to give us the go-ahead. Suddenly, at about nine o'clock, the Met Officer came in and said that the weather was going to deteriorate, and the whole thing was scrubbed. With a whoop of joy we rushed back to our quarters to get changed into best blue, and positively galloped to the Mess. Things were in full swing, but we were determined to catch up. After a few rounds I was certainly catching up, but Mac was overtaking in the fast lane. The din became uproar, the uproar surged into riot, I played the piano while everybody sang and by midnight we were all mightily flown with alcohol—not an unusual state of affairs—but it had been all too hasty. Mac began to slur his speech a little, and a group of us decided to pack it in.

'Come on, Mac,' I shouted above the cacophony, and we grabbed our caps from the cloakroom and made for the door, leaving the smoke and noise behind. Once out on the sandy beach road, the fresh air hit non-smoker Edwards like a tonic, and I gulped in great draughts to clear my head.

Mac did the same, but for some reason it had quite the opposite effect on our gallant Canuck. With a groan, he pitched forward, and hit the deck on his face. He passed out like a light. 'Well, chaps,' I shouted, 'there's nothing for it. We'll have to carry him back.' Easier said than done. Not only was Mac over six feet tall, and heavily-built, he was also about as easy to handle as a string puppet. Added to this, we were none of us utterly sober. But Edwards once again solved the problem. I trotted across to a nearby field, lifted the five-barred gate off its hinges, and shouted to the others to give me a hand. We put the gate beside the prostrate Mac, and rolled him on to it. Then, with a heave-ho, we had him up in the air and, with a fellow-officer at each corner like a pall-bearer, my mumbling second pilot was borne to his bed. Once we had pitched him on to it, we chucked the gate into a hedge, and hit the hay ourselves.

Next morning Mac awoke with a groan, and staggered to a mirror. Across his face where it had scraped the tarmac, was a great Groucho Marx mass of drying blood. He stared at it incredulously. 'Say fellows,' he said eventually, 'where was the fight?'

Many people have said to me, 'Ah, Turnberry, you lucky devil. I expect you managed to sneak in a round or two of golf while you were there eh!' But it was not so. At that stage in my sporting life I had not been introduced to that most obnoxious of games. I agreed with Mark Twain's attitude to golf—'A good walk spoiled.' When I eventually did take it up, at the insistence of my theatrical agent ('You'll get more work on the golf course than you will at auditions'), I managed to struggle to a handicap of 17, but every round was torture. You'd think a man of my bulk and substance could whack that tiny ball a mile, but I've never really got the hang of it. I have given the game up forever at least three times, but those damned clubs are still with me, and I occasionally go out when the weather's good and there's nobody else about. Afterwards when confronted with that inevitable question, 'How did you get on?' I reply, 'It's in the past.'

Once I was having a round with Tony Hancock at St Anne's. We were suffering a summer season in Blackpool, and, as I told Tony weeks before we went up there, 'You've got to have a pastime or you'll go mad.' By about the twelfth hole I was making a complete hash of it, and Tony was at least six up. How could this man be winning, with his poor physique, his caved-in rib-cage, his comical walk? I was in such a temper I could hardly bring myself to speak, but I drew myself up to my full height, and with all the dignity I could muster, addressed him thus: 'You are six holes up. You are one of my best friends, and we have not exchanged a word for the past half-hour. With your permission I shall pick up my ball, leave the course, and NEVER PLAY THIS BLOODY GAME AGAIN.' Tony took off his hat, and bowed courteously. 'Be my guest,' he said simply, and I stalked back to the clubhouse. Later that evening I was in my dressing-room at the Opera House when Nat Jackley, who was appearing at the Winter Gardens, put his head round the door: 'Hey, Jimmy, old boy, we're having a charity ball next month at the Imperial. Have you got anything you can spare for the auction?' I pointed to my golf-bag propped up in the corner. 'There they are,' I roared, 'take them.'

At Turnberry, just beside the Officers' Mess there was a squash court, as, indeed, there was on most RAF stations, and that was my recreation. I had started with fives at King's College School, Wimbledon, but that was a bit too hard on the hands, so up at Cambridge I graduated to squash, and continued to play it off and on until I got into polo. Then, in 1966, I was in *Big Bad Mouse* at the Shaftesbury Theatre in London. Eric Skyes had left the cast by this time, and Roy Castle had taken his place. We knew we would probably be there for a whole year, so I said to Roy, 'We need some exercise. Have you ever played squash?' 'No,' said Roy, 'but I'm willing to learn.' I dug out my gear, and Roy set himself up with the whole shebang, and off we went to the RAC club for his first game. After a brief lecture from me on the rudiments of the sport, we started off in earnest. We were just getting into the swing of it, and Roy was picking up the idea nicely, when we had the most almighty collision. 'You're supposed to go round me,' I gasped, as I picked myself up off the floor. Then I realized that the cartilage in my left knee had gone, so that was the end of my squash career. I never found out what Roy did with all his gear.

AFRICAN FIASCO

AFTER A BRIEF period of leave, spent mostly in the Market Gardener, our next task was to take a Wellington to North Africa, and, at long last, 'join in the fray'. I had been in the RAF for almost exactly three years, and was now to become part of its immense striking force. Let the Hun—or the Eyetie—beware! And so we duly reconvened as a crew at Talbenny, in Pembrokeshire, where there was a ferry training unit. We were still the same merry sextet, Mac sitting beside me, Harry lurking at the navigator's desk, Bill Shaw thumping the morse key and Billy Randall and Cartwright manning the guns. Down on the tarmac at Talbenny we were introduced to a brand-spanking-new Wellington Mk XIII—its number HZ962—which it was our duty to deliver to the RAF in a place called Setif, somewhere in the desert a few miles beyond Algiers. I was now almost overcome by the awesome task thrust so confidently onto my 23-year-old shoulders, and determined to get this aircraft safely and with all speed to its destination. It might well be the one machine that was needed to swing the tide in our favour. Somewhere in North Africa there was a squadron leader wringing his hands and crying out, 'If only they'd send me just one more Wimpey!' The rest of the chaps weren't quite so keen. The last thing they wanted was to turn their backs on English beer and their wives and girlfriends, and exchange it all for a tent in the desert. But I goaded them into a reluctant show of enthusiasm, and in only four days we had done all the tests on HZ962 and were ready to go. We took off and flew to Hurn, which is just outside Bournemouth, and which was to be our jumping-off place. But even now my keenness was thwarted by a sudden change in the weather, and we had to wait a couple of days for it to improve. I took the opportunity to visit Frank George's parents, who lived in Bournemouth, and gave them a first-hand account of our adventures in Canada. His father was particularly amused to hear how his name had been used during our stay in Ottawa, and told me that Frank was now a flying instructor at Calgary. Lucky him!

We were due to take off on this epic journey at about midnight, so that we could get across the Bay of Biscay in darkness. Not only was the sea in the Bay infested with U-boats, but the air above it was frequented by German long-range reconnaissance aircraft. We were under strict instructions not to attack a U-boat if we saw one, but as the only armaments we had on board were the three gun-turrets, a fat lot of use they would have been.

We were only supposed to fire at the Jerry aeroplanes if they attacked us first. The object of the whole exercise was to get these valuable reinforcements to the theatre of war where they could be put to some use. We were not going alone. At least another dozen Wellingtons were due to go, but we were meant to fly independently, and not in a gaggle. At about 8 p.m. on the third evening at Hurn, the operations officer said that, once again, the weather was not fit, but that there was just a chance it could improve in two or three hours. I made up my mind that we would go, so went to bed to catch up on some sleep; it would be at least an eight-hour flight. Mac agreed with me, but the rest of the crew decided that we would not be going, and went out on the beer. Just as they all came back from the pub, not exactly drunk but with several pints inside them, the word went round that flying was 'on'. I forced them into the truck, still in their best blue, and out we went to the aircraft. All our kit, including my trombone, had already been slung into the bomb bay, so all we had to do was climb aboard and get going. I was in a high state of excitement . . . mixed with considerable trepidation . . . as we trundled down the runway. At last the Wimpey (heavily weighed down with extra fuel) was airborne, and it was, as I wrote in my log-book in capital letters, 'NORTH AFRICA HO!' We climbed up to about 2,000 feet, and flew westwards over shadowy, blacked-out England, on the first leg to Land's End.

I had planned to navigate by means of 'pundits'. A pundit was a bright red light on the ground, which at regular intervals flashed two letters of the Morse code, and they were scattered all over England. To make it impossible for the Germans to take advantage of this simple aid, every week the two letters on each beacon were changed, and the new code was available to navigators. It wasn't long before I realized that Harry had not collected this week's new list, so that all the readings were wrong. However, we pressed on, more or less following the coast, as I had worked it out in my brilliant mind that when we finally run out of land, that was bound to be Land's End. I had put Bill Randall in the front turret, in the hope that it might clear his head, and it was he who drew my attention to the foamy sea dashing itself on the rocks, just ahead. We had finally run out of England, and there was nothing to help us between here and Africa except Harry's Dead Reckoning Navigation.

As we set course more or less due south, Bill's voice came over the intercom. 'Hey, Skipper, there's something in front of us, just a bit to port. Seems to be at about the same height as us.' I leaned forward and strained my eyes to see what it was. Then I saw it—the shadowy shape of another aircraft, just visible against the minimal horizon. Everybody could see it now, and the intercom was buzzing with voices. 'I can see it now, Skipper. Christ! It's moving across in front of us. It's a Jerry. No, it isn't. It's a Sunderland.' Whatever it was, it continued its eerie progress, passing in front of us at a slight angle, while I held grimly onto my course. I reasoned to myself that if we made any sort of manoeuvre that drew attention to us it would be certain to attack, whether it was one of ours or one of theirs. Now there was total silence on the intercom, as we all held our breath to see what would happen. Looking back, I can only think that it was, indeed, a Coastal Command Sunderland setting course on a long-range patrol, and that its crew was having exactly the same thoughts and doubts as we were.

Slowly it merged into the darkness. Theoretically our next sight would be Gibraltar.

I had planned to cruise at a very economical airspeed, so that there would be no danger of our running out of fuel, but this was not a very brilliant ploy, because it meant that, when dawn eventually came, we were still over the Bay, with all its dangers. I think at the back of my mind I had a sneaking hope that we might actually sight a U-boat, and, with great dash and verve, disregarding all orders, I would gallantly strafe it into submission with my twelve machine-guns. It was a nice thought, but it didn't turn out quite like that. The only result of my economical use of fuel was that we took a whole hour longer to get to Africa than the rest of the party. We bowled along at about a thousand feet above the waves, eating sandwiches and drinking tea, with Harry's visits to the cockpit increasing in frequency, and the frown of worry on his brow getting deeper all the time. After he had said, 'Can you see owt?' a few times, he eventually volunteered his standard piece of advice . . . 'I should turn left a bit, Skipper.' I obliged, and slowly a coastline emerged out of the hazy visibility. 'Well, that's OK,' I thought. 'That's got to be Spain. Hug the coast and Gibraltar is bound to appear some time or other.' We spotted a few ancient fishing-boats, and I went down low to look at them. With the coast just under the port wing we were having a merry old time, and I was genuinely enjoying myself. So much so that a moderately heavy squall of rain did not deter me in the least. I got the windscreen wipers going, and hugged the coast even closer. For a moment I glanced at the compass—Christ! we were flying due east! East? The realization hit me like a sandbag. We were flying straight up the mouth of the Tagus. A few more miles and we would be over Lisbon . . . another neutral country. I banged open the throttles and threw the Wimpey into a steep turn to starboard, and in no time we were safely out to sea again.

Another international incident safely avoided. We got a good pinpoint on the Portuguese coast, and set course for Rabat Sale. When we finally landed there, the whole trip had taken exactly nine hours. This was the longest flight I ever did, and the change from the rolling countryside of the west of England to the Moroccan desert was dramatic indeed. We slept well that night—too tired for drinking—and we were off again next day, keen to get to Algiers and see what was in store for us. This was friendly territory, so the whole crew was as relaxed as if on a school outing. For most of the journey I flew low as we all marvelled at the novel sights beneath us—undulating desert, with here and there the vivid green of an oasis; occasional flocks of seemingly wild camels, but with a few nomadic natives in charge; and other more orderly strings of working camels, wending their way with bobbing backs all loaded up with merchandise. Every few miles there was something to see. 'Look over there, Skipper,' would come over the intercom, as somebody spotted something fresh to see—and I would swing the aircraft over in a steep banking turn to investigate. And the natives—Bedouins I suppose—marvelled at us, too, as this great black bird, engines steadily purring (the Perseus engine didn't roar) swooped over their heads. It was all over too soon.

After four hours of this free excursion over Africa, I climbed up to a respectable 2,000 feet so that we could orientate ourselves, and make a proper approach to Setif. But what a shock lay ahead. As we joined the circuit and were given permission to land, we looked down and saw—not, as we had expected, a couple of squadrons spread out round the perimeter, but row upon row upon row of Wellingtons, exactly the same as ours, standing wing-tip to wing-tip in their hundreds, all over the aerodrome.

A scruffy airman in tatty khaki shorts, and with no socks and no shirt, waved us in to our parking space with a bored look. He gave us the signal to switch off the engines and slouched away. We climbed out into the hot sun and clambered aboard a dusty three-ton lorry that had been sent to pick us up. I handed over the aircraft documents to a flight sergeant in a scruffy tent. 'Thanks,' he said. 'I don't know where to put the bleeding things.' My keenness was now totally dissipated. 'What do we do now?' I asked miserably. 'The lorry will take you up to your Messes, and then you'll probably go by train to Algiers. There's a holding unit there.' Oh God, another holding unit.

In the lorry we bounced along a dusky track at the side of the airfield, noticing the many different types of aircraft that were lined up everywhere. I even saw some Spitfires, and thought for a moment we might have come to the wrong aerodrome. I was standing up, hanging on to the canvas roof of the lorry and looking back. Suddenly, in the swirling sand behind us, I noticed a small bunch of pilots walking along in the same direction as ourselves. Amongst them was a short, untidy flying officer, with a filthy cap— and a pronounced limp. I looked again. It was IVJ! Of all the incredible coincidences, here was the chap with whom I had joined up, and whom I hadn't seen since I went to Canada. The limp was the result of a crash he had been in when he was training. One leg was now an inch shorter than the other. I cupped my hands and shouted: 'Ioan!' He looked up and waved, and then broke into a shambling trot. Our driver hadn't heard me shout, and pressed on.

But at the Officers' Mess a few minutes later we met, and as it was about six in the evening, the celebrations began immediately. On his recommendation I drank the local muscatel ('It can't do you any harm') and we exchanged notes about our separate careers. He had been on a squadron in the desert, and was now officially 'on rest' but from time to time he had to do delivery flights, taking Spitfires from one place to another. I told him that I had hoped to join a torpedo-dropping unit but, as he explained, there was no chance of that. The British had already landed in Italy, and the war in the Mediterranean was virtually over. All the Wellingtons I had seen parked around the aerodrome would never be needed, unless things went very badly. I was destined for the camp on the beach at Fort de L'Eau, just outside Algiers, where I would have to wait, with my crew, until someone decided what they were going to do with us. In fact, we were supposed to catch a train that very night, but IVJ soon scotched that. 'I'll talk someone in to flying you over there tomorrow.' This was my first experience of the haphazard way things were carried on in the desert. My crew disconsolately hauled themselves into a lorry, and set off for the railway. 'I'll see

127

you all tomorrow,' I said merrily, as I went back to my muscatel.

The RAF had taken over a big, old Algerian house for a Mess—all white walls and marble floors, and IVJ and I sat on the verandah tippling wine and exchanging reminiscences, while the stars twinkled above us, and the moon eventually came up, and the desert air was full of the sound of groups of drunken airmen staggering back to their tents. The muscatel was a damned sight stronger than IVJ had led me to believe, and it soon had charge of my tongue and finally my head. I lurched upstairs and rolled into one of those foldable canvas travelling beds which were standard issue to officers, and which I was going to see a lot of in the next few months.

Next morning, nursing my first but by no means my last North African hangover, I crammed myself into the back of an Anson which was full of South African aircrew on their way to Algiers for the weekend. After struggling over the mountains, we landed at Maison Blanche, and I managed to hitch a ride to the camp at Fort de L'Eau. Mac had collared a bed for me in one of the hundreds of bell-tents that were pitched underneath the pine trees on the beach which overlooked the Bay of Algiers. It was the perfect setting for a holiday camp, with sloping sand, and just enough surf to make the swimming interesting. But there was nothing else there to give that holiday feeling. The food was terrible, the booze limited, and the beds uncomfortable. But, above all, there was absolutely nothing to do. Each morning we formed up in what could loosely be called a parade, and waited to hear if there was any news of a move for any of us. There was a patchy attempt at a roll-call, but it was quite easy to get someone to shout 'Here' for you if you wanted to lie in bed, and, more often than not, the so-called parade just fizzled out as group by group we strolled away and got into our bathers. Morale sank rapidly. When the bar opened at night we quickly demolished the small stock of reputable booze that was available, and then switched to the only thing that was left. This was the local eau de vie, the age of which could be gauged by the fact that it came in English beer-bottles.

128

It soon became clear that we were destined to vegetate at Fort de L'Eau for an indefinite period, and I got so fed up with the daily round of parades and pointless booze-ups, that I went one day to the Algiers airport, which was called Maison Blanche, and hitched a ride in a Wimpey that was going to Setif. But when I got there, I found that IVJ had been moved to rest camp near Tunis, so I hitched another ride, this time in a Bisley, back to Algiers, and rejoined my bored crew on the beach. Mac had found no difficulty in answering for me at the roll-call, in spite of his Canadian accent, so after a further four days of this meaningless existence, I went back to Maison Blanche and toured the tarmac, looking for anybody who was Tunis-bound. I tried an American Air Force Liberator, and the pilot, who had just ferried it all the way from the USA was delighted to have me aboard. Yet another type of aircraft to put in my log-book.

This was the largest plane I had ever been in, and I had a fascinating trip exploring its vastness and getting in and out of its numerous gun-turrets. Once we had touched down at Tunis, I scrounged around until I found an RAF jeep that was going towards Hammam Lif, and there, naked on the beach, I found IVJ. 'Christ,' he said, 'what the hell are you doing here?' 'Oh, just visiting, there's absolutely nothing to do at Fort de L'Eau.' 'Well, you might as well say a few days and get some sun. Nobody knows anybody here, anyway.'

And so I had a glorious time on a beach which I believe is today one of the most fashionable in Tunisia. Back in 1943 about a dozen of us had a whole mile of glorious golden sand to ourselves. The camp was supposed to be exclusively for pilots who were resting from flying operations, but I was asked no questions, and just joined in with the rest. We swam, we lounged around on the beach (I was careful always to wear a shirt and trousers, whilst IVJ was sunbathing in the nude, as I did not want to get burnt), and we threw hand-grenades into the water to stun a few fish for the Mess. Altogether it was an idyllic existence, and the only sign of the war was the fact that the hand-grenades were German, and had been left behind by

Rommel's retreating army.

One day we were visited by a pilot who outdid even us in his scruffiness. We learned that his squadron was stationed not far away between us and Tunis, and so, to break the monotony, we went along in his jeep to pay them a visit. They were flying the Bisley, a short-nosed version of the Blenheim, which had been in use since before the war. Their job was Army Co-operation, and they were one of the last of the truly mobile squadrons. Everything, including the Ops-room, was on a trailer, and even the Officers' Mess was in a heavily-camouflaged marquee. Here, over a few jolly beers, the wing commander explained their situation. 'We've done absolutely nothing here since Rommel got kicked out. I think we are the original Lost Squadron, but I expect they'll find something for us to do eventually. We're terribly short of aircrew, but I suppose they'll send us some along some day.' I was incredulous. 'But sir,' I said, 'that's absolutely potty. There's literally hundreds of us back in Algiers doing absolutely sweet Fanny Adams. We're all dying to find something to do.'

'Different Command, old boy,' he replied. 'Coastal wouldn't let you go.'

'Could I come and see you in the morning, sir?' I persisted.

'If you want to. But I'm sure there's nothing I can do.'

Next day I found him at his portable desk in his portable office, and explained to him about all the flying I had done, and told him how keen I was to get cracking. He jotted down my details, and promised to 'put in' for me, and those of my crew who would be of use in a Bisley. 'I'll do what I can,' he said cheerily, 'but don't bank on it.'

After a few more days on the beach, I began to feel uneasy about my continued absence-without-leave, so down I went to the Tunis airport of El Ouina and hitched another ride. This time it was a South African crew in a Boston who obliged. I was really becoming an airborne hobo. Nothing had happened back at Fort de L'Eau. Mac and the others were still there, bored stiff, and nobody had commented on my disappearance. I endured the mock parades, the swimming, and the fiery eau de vie for a few more days, and then found a convenient Wellington on its way to Tunis, and hopped aboard that. IVJ's spell of relaxation was nearly at an end. 'I've got to start this ferrying business again,' he said, 'I tell you what. Next time there's some Spitfires to be fetched out of Algiers, you can fly one with me.'

'But that's ridiculous,' I said. 'I'm a Wimpey pilot.'

'But you've flown a Battle. It's the same sort of thing, only smaller and faster.' I thought he was crazy, but, just in case the opportunity should arise, I got him to write down all the details of the Spit—where everything was, and what speeds you did everything at, and kept it with me to study from time to time.

I paid one more visit to the desert squadron of which I hoped I would be a member some day, and, as one of their Bisleys was making a trip to Blida, I hopped aboard. Then it was a quick hitch in a jeep, and once again I joined the doleful band at Fort de L'Eau. On all these crazy trips, I had learned to carry my own parachute and harness. Most pilots wouldn't let you bum a ride without, and we had all been issued with them back in the UK and they were part of our personal kit. Ours were the type in which the harness and the chute were separate, so that you could walk about the aircraft without too much difficulty. Your parachute pack was stowed somewhere near your seat, and, in an emergency, you hooked it onto your chest, and pulled the ripcord with your right hand. When IVJ turned up a few days later and said there were a couple of Spitfires to be ferried from Algiers to Setif, I gamely and perhaps foolishly accepted the challenge. 'Just follow me into the flight hut, sign for the aircraft, and off we go.' It seemed an awful nerve, but it is an indication of the general slackness which prevailed that I was able to get away with it. An airman showed me the machine which was to be mine, and, as I climbed onto the wing and prepared to get into the cockpit, he asked me if I had a parachute. Then it dawned on me. All single-engined aircraft had a bucket-type seat, and the pilot was supposed to have the appropriate harness where the chute was already attached to his bottom. He should have smelled a rat, but he said nothing as I crammed my chute into the seat, and then climbed in and sat on top of it.

I got out my bit of paper with the basic details and balanced it on my knee. Then I fumbled around with the controls, and somehow got the engine started. The mighty Merlin roared, and I suddenly realized that it was at least a year since I had flown a single-engined machine. I taxied out, swerving from side to side as you had to in a Spit to see where you were going, and got to the side of the runway. IVJ was talking to me on the radio, and was soon on the runway, and swiftly airborne. It was easy for him! He'd been flying the damned things for months. Reading haltingly through my list, I ran the engine up, tested the magnetoes, then laboriously went through my cockpit drill. By the time I was ready to go, the temperature of the Glycol which cooled the engine was well over the limit, but I couldn't be bothered about that. What the hell! With IVJ's voice in my earphones urging me to pull my finger out, I teetered out onto the runway and eased the throttle open. Fortunately I remembered the Battles, and was not completely amazed when the nose disappeared in front of me. After a few more seconds of terrifying weaving along the tarmac, I eased it off the ground, and gropingly found the undercarriage retraction lever. I was airborne—in a Spitfire! IVJ's cheers rattled in my ears, and I swung into a climbing turn to join him above the airfield. Already I was glorying in the feel of this wondrous little aeroplane, with its fantastically quick response to the controls, and my spirits soared with every hundred feet I climbed. I reached IVJ's side in just moments, and as I throttled back to keep formation with him, his voice came through again: 'Isn't it it splendid? Now, hang on and follow me.' I had been so busy catching him up that I had not had time to see exactly where we had got to, but as I followed him in a steep dive I realized that we were heading straight for the beach at Fort de L'Eau! 'Wait till they see this,' IVJ chortled, and I could do nothing but hang on to him grimly as we swooped down to sea level and zoomed in over the unsuspecting bathers beneath. Some of them who had seen us coming waved a greeting, and I was busy looking over the side of the cockpit and trying to find a hand with which to acknowledge their greeting, when we hit the turbulence coming up from the palm-trees. The Spitfire rocked violently, and my instinctive reaction was to pull the stick back and slam open the throttle. 'Whoops!' said IVJ in my ears. 'Let's do it again.' Up and round we went, over the sea, and then down we swept again for an even lower 'beat-up'. This time the chaps were all on their feet and ready for us, arms and towels waving.

We climbed away and I just had the strength to shout over the radio, 'That'll do, Ioan!' for I'm sure he would have gone round again if I had said nothing. We set course for Setif, and at 6,000 feet I was glad to level off and relax. Not so my crazy friend. Chattering away jovially on the r/t he proceeded to show me all the aerobatics that I had not done since my days on the Harvard at Trenton. Then it was: 'Come on, James. Try a roll. It's easy!' Not bloody likely. The whole escapade was madness, anyway. If the slightest thing had gone wrong, and I had crashed or even damaged the aircraft, a court martial would have been an absolute certainty.

But we had got away with it—so far! Now I had a landing to cope with. We joined the circuit at Setif, and I watched IVJ as he demonstrated a typical Spitfire approach, with a gliding left-hand turn which finished just over the start of the runway, for in the landing attitude you had practically no forward vision whatsoever. As he taxied out of the way, the stage was set for my debut. Miraculously I pulled off a perfect three-pointer, undercarriage and tail-wheel touching the ground simultaneously. As I turned off the runway, I slammed the throttle shut with a sigh of relief, and the engine cut out and came to a complete stop. I climbed out on to the wing, too weak to even bother to restart it. Let them tow it in, I thought. I've had enough. IVJ's smile was huge. 'Well done, James! A perfect three-pointer. We'll make a fighter-pilot of you yet.' 'No thanks,' I groaned, staggering along under the weight of my parachute and harness. 'Let's get to the Mess and have a socking great drink. And NO muscatel this time!'

I returned to Algiers by my now habitual method of hitching a ride—in an Anson once again—and I had only just settled down to the hideously dull routine of the holding unit, when IVJ turned up again. 'Want another trip in a Spit?' he said. I shuddered. 'No thanks, I don't think I dare risk it.' 'Oh come on, James. Be a sport. Besides, it may be your last chance. I've been posted to a squadron in Italy. I have to report next week.'

'Very well,' I said, 'But, Ioan—no shoot-ups, eh?'

This time I had a Spitfire Vc, which had an even larger engine than the first one, and also sported a five-bladed propeller. But I was an old hand now, and the whole trip went off quite smoothly. I even forced myself to try a roll, but funked it halfway round.

So then, it was back into the war for my friend, and back on my backside for me.

'Why, hi there, Skipper, you're quite a stranger,' said Mac, as I rolled up once again at Fort de L'Eau. I had to admit that I had been neglecting my crew. It was always a little difficult to keep a crew together when they weren't doing anything constructive, and it was doubly difficult when they weren't all in the same Mess. And it certainly didn't help morale when the skipper kept bogging off on hare-brained excursions. So I organized a bit of 'togetherness' in the town of Algiers. There were some damned good French restaurants there, and we were able to enjoy such delicacies as frogs' legs, and even roast thrush. The local wine wasn't all bad either, but these bored and frustrated airmen wanted something more piquant to tickle their appetites—and I'm not talking about food.

Someone found out where there was an 'exhibition' going on. Well, it wasn't very difficult—every little Arab in the street was touting for something. One of the most scrofulous of them accosted me one day: 'Hey, meester—I show you man and woman—woman and woman—woman and donkey—' I laughed at him mockingly, 'What about man and donkey, eh, you dirty little beast?'

'Anything can be arranged.'

I was persuaded against my will to join the gang at one of these pornographic displays. We mounted some sleazy stairs and went into a filthy room, in the middle of which was a low table, covered with a threadbare, flea-ridden blanket. I groaned inwardly. The room was packed with a motley collection of Servicemen, some of them—mostly the sailors—sitting within a few inches of this horrid little podium, on which unmentionable things were about to take place. There was much laughter, and a strong smell of liquor and the thick smoke-haze added to the bizarre effect. The lights were turned out, leaving just one blue bulb glimering on the ceiling. A throaty cheer of anticipation went up as the participants appeared and shuffled their way through the crowd. Oh God! It was going to be 'woman and woman'. My stomach began to turn. I groped my way to the door, thinking I would wait outside until it was all over. Damn. The door was locked. What could I do? I was trapped, and it was all my own fault. Nothing would induce me to watch the obscenities being perpetrated in front of this grotesque gang of malodorous males. I leaned my head against the door and counted the minutes, and, after what seemed like hours, the door opened. I was first out. I was a prude then, and, by some standards, I still am.

I may not have been very self-indulgent about sex at this time, but I have to admit that the same cannot be said about alcohol. As has so often happened in my lifetime, idleness led to boozing, and boozing led to hangovers, and hangovers led to even more boozing. It is a vicious spiral in which millions have been caught up at one time or another. The awful thing was that I actually enjoyed drinking. I enjoyed the taste of it, and I enjoyed even more the painless manner in which it swept away my personal inhibitions. The shy, retiring, introspective, unconfident Jim soon became the roaring, red-faced buffoon who pounded the piano or blasted on the trombone. I was always among the last to leave the Mess at night, and very often the first to swig down a livener next morning. My only excuse is that there was absolutely nothing else to do—unless you were into chess or card-games. The swimming was fine, but you can't swim all day. And chaps did try to get up scratch games of football, but that was not a lot of fun in the dust of the parade-ground. We ate a lot of local dates which could be bought very cheaply in the markets and bazaars, but this pleasure was cut short for me when I noticed, too late, that I had been absentmindedly consuming maggots as I munched dreamily through a packet. Someone said, 'Don't worry, Edwards, that's the first fresh meat you've had for weeks!'

I suppose the severity of my hangovers was lessened by my not smoking. Ever since I had tried the weed at the age of ten as a choirboy at St Paul's, I had been a confirmed non-smoker. It was a boy called Windross who had tempted me. He was staying with my family in our house in Barnes, and he somehow talked me into smoking a Woodbine in the rhododendron bushes in Richmond Park. I must have inhaled the poison pretty deeply, for in a few moments I was lying on the ground retching like a grass-eating dog. I was so violently ill that I thought I was going to die, and this experience made such a lasting impression on me that I have never, to this day, smoked another cigarette. I have only once or twice fancied myself as a pipe-smoker, thinking that it would give me some sort of intellectual image, but I did not inhale. I soon gave it up anyway because the juice got into my system and gave me stomach ache, and I got thoroughly fed up with my pockets being full of remnants of tabacco. On top of that, the stink used to linger in my moustache, and there is nothing worse than waking up in the morning and breathing stale Three Nuns. These days I will sometimes accept a good Havana cigar after a splendid meal—but half-way through it I usually go on a slight 'trip' and talk more nonsense than usual. How I survived the entire war without smoking cigarettes is a tribute to the delicacy of my stomach rather than the staunchness of my self-denial. What would I have done if booze had made me ill? The mind boggles.

Cigarettes were cheap enough for Servicemen in any case, but when we were in Africa there was a free weekly ration of the stuff. Although I had no intention of using it, I always accepted my allocation; it gave me a certain bargaining power over addicts who might like to trade it for some booze. There was a strict anti-smoking rule in all aircraft, and though some skippers turned a blind eye to an occasional puff, I found it easy to enforce the rule rigidly. I was not always popular with my crew, but in an aeroplane like the Wimpey there were fuel lines everywhere, and if you caught fire once, you wouldn't live to do it a second time.

I could just about stand the Officers' Mess parties, because, although nearly everybody except me had a cigarette going most of the time, one could always slake one's parched throat from time to time with a beer, or pop out into the desert for a leak and a lungful of fresh air. But what was almost insupportable was a long ride in a three-ton lorry, with canvas cover tied down, and sixty-odd aircrew all dragging at their fags in the dark. These days, when travelling, I always seek out a non-smoking compartment, and if anybody has the temerity to ask me, 'Do you mind if I smoke, old boy?' I reply, 'Not if you don't mind me coughing.'

The tedium at Fort de L'Eau was eased one day when I was actually called out of the morning parade and told to report to a Group Captain at Headquarters in Algiers. I shaved and did what I could to smarten myself up, and slung up a snappy salute.

'Edwards?'

'Yessir.'

'Edwards, I can't quite understand this, but the wing commander of a squadron in the desert near Tunis has asked for you to be posted to him. How did this come about?'

I hesitated. 'Well, sir, there are ways—if you know what I mean, sir.'

He smiled. 'Yes, Edwards, I do know what you mean. Perhaps I'd better not ask any more. I'll see what I can do about it.'

Whoopee! At last I was going to be on the move. All that hitch-hiking to and fro had at last paid off. I was so excited, the pints flowed thick and fast that night, and I was in a fever of anticipation for the next few days. My crew picked up my enthusiasm. After all, I was bound to take some of them. A Bisley had to have a navigator and at least one wireless-op. Possibly a second pilot too. But the days went by, and I heard no more. As my spirits sank, so my intake of alcohol soared, and, increasing quantities of the local fire-water were slung down the Edwards gullet. Then, one morning when my hangover was particularly crippling, I asked Mac to represent me at parade. He came back bubbling. 'Hey, Skipper, guess what? We're going to India . . . Ceylon, actually.'

I sat up in my untidy, unmade bed. 'We what, Mac?'

'It's true. Thirty Wimpey crews are posted to Ceylon. We're ferrying the aircraft out from Setif next week. Anti-sub patrols in the Indian Ocean, and all that.'

Well, at least, it was action. We celebrated this new development with an even merrier party than usual that night, but somehow I could not get my enthusiasm up. And next day I felt even more lethargic than before. My mood blackened, as I vainly tried to raise my spirits each night, and by the time we assembled to take the train to our point of departure, I had no spark in me whatsoever. At Setif station, the three-ton trucks were lined up for us, but I had scarcely the strength to climb aboard. And, at the familiar Mess at RAF Setif even carrying my parachute was an effort. Mac, who was so looking forward to the trip, voiced the opinion of the whole crew, 'There's something the matter with you, Skip. Why don't you see the MO?' 'Oh, I'll be all right. But I'll go, just in case.' The doctor took one look at me, lifted one of my eyelids, and said one word: 'Jaundice.'

And that's how I never got to see Ceylon.

Mac and the others were bundled on to a train to Algiers, and I was bundled into a hospital right in the middle of the town of Setif. It wasn't a real hospital. The upstairs floor of a school for Arab children had been equipped with twenty or so beds, and a few miscellaneous pieces of medical equipment had been installed. This was an isolation ward, and the only other occupant was a malaria case. There is no treatment for jaundice. You simply lie in bed feeling miserable and waiting to feel better. More or less the same goes for malaria, except that you sweat a lot, I believe. My fellow-patient had got over that stage and was sitting up feeling fairly cheerful. I was lying down feeling awful.

There was practically nothing to eat but that didn't matter, as I had no appetite for food. Once a day an Army doctor in a white coat came into the ward, casually swinging a stethoscope, and said, with grating cheerfulness, 'And how are you today?' He was always gone before I could reply. After several days of this I was ready for him. Almost before he had finished his fatuous question, I blurted out: 'Bloody awful! How d'you expect me to feel?' He stopped in his tracks, laughed, and came and sat on my bed. 'Sorry, old boy,' he said, 'only I'm just as bored as you are. All I've seen for nearly two years is jaundice and malaria. In fact, if and when I ever get home, I'm going to have to read everything else up all over again.' After that, we had a little chat every day.

The other patient, an Army captain, introduced me to that great game 'Battleships'. We had no equipment at all except a piece of paper and a pencil each, but we got hours of fun out of it, and Macintosh always won.

Every day we played Battleships; every day the Army doctor paid his duty visit, and every morning the voices of the Arab children in the classroom below came drifting up through the floorboards, as they chanted their nouns and verbs and numerals in French. Until at last came the day when I was pronounced fit enough to leave. My eyes, which fortunately were the only part of me which had turned yellow, were clearing up nicely, and I was almost looking forward to food once again. With strict instructions to drink no alcohol for at least six months, I was packed off to a convalescent camp which had been set up in a cluster of villas overlooking the Bay of Tunis. Here I found myself amongst a gang of largely Canadian aircrew, all recovering from some malady or other, and all bent on disregarding all the doctors' orders. Very soon we were playing cards and swigging beer, and feeling a hell of a lot better for it.

Here, too, I found myself sufficiently recovered to

restart my moustache . . . for the umpteenth time. This one seemed to be different. At last it began to flourish in the way that I had always hoped it would, and I guarded it carefully during boozing sessions.

Macintosh and I never met again. Life in the Services, especially as there was a war on, was studded with little incidents like this, when one was thrown together for a short time with other chaps, got to know them very well, and then never encountered them again. I wonder what happened to him, and to the doctor. The one may be a tycoon, and the other a royal physician, for all I know.

These days I often meet chaps who remember me, but whose names I have completely forgotten. Well, it's easier for them. I was the noisy one with the loud voice and the trombone. At Perth airport in Australia a greying, slightly bald man came up to me and said: 'I bet you don't remember me, Jim. I was your second pilot way back in 1943.' 'Second pilot?' I said. 'All right then, sit profile and I'll try and get you.' He swivelled round and sat as he would have done when flying with me. I racked my brains. Then: 'I've got you. Flight Sergeant English . . . Right?' 'Well,' he said with a laugh, 'the name's actually Britten. Not bad after thirty-five years, Jim.'

The Canadians were crazy about poker, and taught me the madness of 'Dealer's Choice', in which whoever had the cards could more or less invent his own game. The French currency that we used in these games was pretty worthless, but it gave you a good feeling to plonk some money down and say: 'Your thousand and up a thousand.'

My convalescence over, I was sent back to Fort de L'Eau, supposedly fit for flying duties. But there wasn't much of that going on. The crew were all still there, very cheesed off, but, I found, quite pleased that my illness had prevented them from going to India.

Now came a black period. I had missed my posting to the Bisley squadron, who had by now moved on from the desert and were in Italy. IVJ was there also and so was David Porter. David was fully operational, doing night-bombing on Mosquitoes. Somewhere about this time I heard, through that mysterious thing we called 'the grapevine', that he had been shot down and killed, but there was no way one could verify this sort of rumour.

We had nothing to do but sweat it out until word of a posting came through. For the whole of November and December we sat disconsolately in our tents, killing time in the only way that I knew. Sometimes a period of inaction when it is not a well-earned rest but simply enforced idleness can be a real test of character. I'm afraid I failed the test this time. As it became clearer and clearer that there was no hope of spending Christmas at home, my morale sagged to its lowest ebb. But it didn't show from the outside. To my crew and friends I was still Jolly Jim, jovial to the last, and I was always last to leave the Mess at night. But then, when I threw myself on to that canvas bed, and stared straight upwards, sometimes the tent would start to spin, and I would hang on to the sides and shout at the top of my voice to halt the rotation. This must have been a charming experience for my tent-mates, but they got used to it. 'Edwards has got 'em again,' they would shrug, and just hope that I didn't get 'em every night. Finally, we got word of our next move. We were being returned to the UK, surplus to requirements in the British North African Force, and the troopship would leave on Boxing Day.

So there was time for one final fling. By the time that the three-tonners were ready for us around dawn, I was so roaring drunk that I refused point-blank to go. Mac and the crew hauled me out of bed, shook me out of my stupor, and dragged me to the quayside. Once aboard the SS *Otranto*, I had ten days in which to dry out, so that when we arrived at Greenock I was more or less my old self.

As we motley collection of scruffs hung over the rail and stared at the grey, forbidding Scottish landscape a hundred yards away, a voice came over a loudspeaker on the quay. 'You are back in the UK now. Things are a bit different from North Africa, you will find. You will be properly dressed at all times, and officers will be saluted at all times. The war is not over yet, and we expect maximum effort from every airman' . . . or words to that effect. We raised a feeble jeer, and one or two of the braver ones even managed a raspberry. But there were a great many red-capped Air Force Police at the bottom of the gangway when we trooped ashore, and we realized we would have to pull our socks up.

But first, disembarkation leave in Barnes . . . mostly in the Market Gardener. I had one minor triumph there at the first lunch-time session. 'Give me a large gin-and-tonic,' I said in my grandest voice to Albert, 'and, landlord, I'd like a slice of lemon in it.'

'Don't talk daft,' said Albert from behind his thick spectacles. 'We haven't seen one of them since rationing started.'

'Oh, very well then,' I said, 'I suppose I'll have to supply my own,' and promptly pulled a huge fresh lemon out of my pocket. I had thrown half a dozen into my kitbag in Algiers, hoping for such a moment as this.

Believe it or not, my mother—or 'Mrs E' as she was known to most people—was still soldiering on as a full-time air raid warden. But, on top of her long hours of duty, she managed to keep a bed available for any of her nine children who might be on leave. We were all in one or other of the Services, and, when we were overseas, she kept us up-to-date with family affairs through her long and informative letters, which she usually wrote if things were quiet on night-duty. There was always room for a few others as well, so I sometimes took members of my crew to enjoy a few boozy nights in London. Most of the pubs just carried on as normal, in spite of the shortage of supplies, and when there was an air raid the simple philosophy was that if you made enough noise you couldn't hear the bombs coming down, anyway. There was one classic night when Mrs E was on night-duty, and I had failed to warn her that I would be staying the night, and bringing Billy Randall and Harry Green with me. I got them installed in the attic, hours after closing time, placed an empty chamber-pot in the middle of the room, showed them the light switch, and bade them goodnight. At six in the morning, Mrs E came in, and as she opened the front door, there was Billy coming down the stairs wearing only a shirt and carefully carrying the brimming jerry, obviously looking for the loo. 'Good morning, Mr Randall,' she said, without turning a hair. 'How nice to see you.' Bill gave her a fatuous smile. All he could think of saying was: 'Skipper's got me teeth.' 'Oh, I am glad,' said my mother, and marched past him into the kitchen. Bill had a habit, if he was very drunk, of giving me his full set of false teeth for safe-keeping, because they used to come loose, and he had already lost one set. I would wrap them in a hankie, and keep them in my pocket until he next wanted to eat.

Another time, I was coming home alone from the West End and decided on a bus pub-crawl. Nearly all the stops out to Barnes were outside a pub, and as each stage was only a penny, I had only to spend about a shilling to get all the way to the Railway Hotel on Barnes Common. I had a pint or thereabouts at each stop, so that, when I set off after closing time to make the short walk along the Upper Richmond Road to the Market Gardener for my nightcap, I was weaving a little. On the corner of Vine Road there was, and still is, a bench inscribed 'For wounded soldiers'. I sat down on this for a breather, and passed out. Soon afterwards a bunch of local chaps must have come by, and said 'Gawd blimey! It's Jim. We'd better take him 'ome.' I was too far gone to know anything about it but Mrs E told me next day that she had been sitting quietly reading when there was a thunderous knock on the front door. When she opened it, she was confronted by the sight of her son, Flying Officer James Edwards, being carried shoulder-high by six none-too-sober friends. 'We fahnd 'im on the common, Mrs Edwards,' they explained. 'Where do you want him?' She indicated the drawing-room, so they carried me in there, and pitched me unceremoniously on to the sofa. And that's where I woke up in the morning.

17 Woodlands Road, Barnes, certainly saw some strange happenings in the war years, but it also saw the birth of all but one of the nine Edwards children. It was from there, too, that we had all toddled across the common to Miss Wright's kindergarten in Ranelagh, and it was from there that I had walked across to Barnes Station to take the train when I went to St Paul's Cathedral as a choirboy. Later on,

I had cycled every day to King's College School, Wimbledon, a fair old ride, and torture in a headwind. No. 17 was my home when I was on vacation from Cambridge, and my base when on leave from the RAF. And, much later on, I sallied forth from there for my audition at the Windmill Theatre.

TRANSPORT COMMAND

MY LEAVE AFTER arriving back from North Africa was cut short one hungover morning by a telegram from the Air Ministry . . . 'Report to RAF Station, Doncaster . . .' I lay in bed wracking my aching brains for anything I knew about the place. Yes, it did ring a bell. I got out my log-book. I had flown there once from Limavady in a Wimpey to take some senior officer home on leave. A grass aerodrome, I seemed to remember, right next to the racecourse. And in the corner, a collection of ancient twin-engined, biplane bombers, which, I had been told, were converted into transport aircraft. There was some story about them doing a cabbage-run to the Orkneys once a week. I then recalled that the aircraft had been known as the Handley-Page Harrow, and had been unofficially renamed the 'Sparrow' now that it had been relegated to the unglamorous task of delivering vegetables to outlaying RAF stations. So they needed a replacement crew? Oh well, at least it was a job, and better than sitting on your backside trying to get cirrhosis of the liver. I sent telegrams to the rest of the crew suggesting we all turned up at the appointed time . . . might as well make a good first impression. They might need us urgently.

At Euston station it dawned on me that I had completely misread the situation once again. The platform was crowded with familiar faces . . . mostly from Fort de L'Eau, and the air was alive with gossip and speculation. The odd thing was that Bill Shaw and Ernie Cartwright had not shown up. Bill Randall told me that they had not received telegrams. Clearly the moguls were cutting down the size of the crew. It's hard to believe, but we were once again all completely in the dark as to our destiny. On the long journey northwards I shut up the chatter with my usual laconic: 'Gentlemen, speculation is useless. All will be revealed when the Air Ministry sees fit.'

At Doncaster, in an overcrowded crew-room, a tall, fair-haired wing commander finally put us in the picture.

'My name is Wing Commander Booth. I am in command of No. 271 squadron, of which you are all now members. The Sparrow flight will continue to operate from here, but we shall be equipped with a new American Transport plane, which the RAF is calling the "Dakota". As soon as they arrive, we shall learn to fly them, and the whole effort will then move to an aerodrome which is being built in the south-west. There are too many of you to be accommodated in this Mess, so most of you will be given a billet not too far away. I suggest you go there now, unpack, and get back here in time for the squadron party, which begins at seven.' A cheer went up at this last piece of news, and I staggered off with my kit to get acquainted with my new landlady, Mrs Moon. She was very north-country and very kind . . . and also had two very pretty daughters. 'Come upstairs,' she said. 'I've moved out of our best room so that you can have a large bed.' Such luxury, after that ghastly tent in Algiers. I told her about the party so she gave me a door key, and said, 'I'll leave a light on in the hall, and see you in the morning.'

I walked cautiously back to the Mess, memorizing the route, and pitched into the beer with a will. There were so many old faces, so much to talk about. Our morale had soared sky-high. We were members of a squadron at last. Transport Command had only just been formed, and we were in on the ground floor. I don't think any of us knew what we were going to be called upon to do, but it didn't matter. Booth and his flight commanders very sensibly saw that a good get-together at this stage would pay dividends later, and the bar stayed open until only a few stalwarts like myself were left. Then I set course for my billet, head spinning with a mixture of beer and a natural elation.

146

I found Mrs Moon's house with the precision of an experienced transport pilot, and crept quietly up to my room. My deep sleep was interrupted in the early morning by a compelling desire to empty my bladder, so I stumbled out of bed and tried to find the light switch. What drunk has not been in this dilemma? I groped along the walls, in a room pitch-dark because of the blackout, and eventually found a fireplace. There was nothing for it. This would have to do. With a groan of relief I unburdened myself, and slumped back into bed.

I was up early, and had gone off to the Mess for breakfast before my landlady or her daughters were about. Our first lecture was at nine, and I wasn't going to miss it for anything. After a very full day, I went back to the billet at tea-time. Mrs Moon was at the door, arms folded, cold fury on her face. 'Come into my front room, Mr Edwards,' she said menacingly.

Cap in hand, I followed her. She pointed silently upwards to a great, yellow stain on the ornate ceiling, stretching from the wall half-way across the room.

'What's that?' she asked. I muttered something fatuous about 'Must have knocked over a chamber-pot', but it was no use. I never lived it down, how ever many times I took her and her girls out for a drink. Thousands of years later I bumped into one of the daughters when I was working in a cabaret somewhere up north. By this time she herself was doing very nicely singing in night-clubs, and, thank goodness, she laughed the incident away.

Soon after this, the first Dakota arrived, flown across the Atlantic by Ferry Command, and picked up from Prestwick by W/C Booth. He quickly familiarized the flight commanders with the machine, and, as more and more of them came in, we all made our acquaintance with this gentle lady of the air. Much has been written about the dear old 'Dak', both by and for enthusiasts, so I will content myself with a paragraph or two for those who know nothing about it.

It was a twin-engined, low-winged, monoplane, designed in 1931 as an entirely new concept in passenger aircraft, and known as the DC1. Two years later it went into service with slight modifications, as the DC3, and had been flying in the USA ever since. It came to us with all the internal refinements removed—no sound-proofing, no posh seats, no bar (more's the pity!). Along each side of the fuselage there was a line of bucket seats, designed especially for paratroops to sit in on their way to their target, and extremely uncomfortable for anyone without a parachute strapped to his bottom. There was a large cargo-door at the rear, and with any luck a jeep could be coaxed up a ramp and into the fuselage. The mollycoddled air-traveller of today would be astounded by the two propellers, driven by Pratt and Whitney piston engines, amazed by the absence of a nose-wheel, and confused by the fact that, when you entered, you walked up quite a slope towards the nose. At the top of the slope was a metal door which led into the crew compartment, and here we just had room for two pilots, a navigator and a wireless operator. There wasn't a machine-gun anywhere. The great luxury for myself and Mac was the dual control. Each pilot had a control column and his own panel of flying instruments, and the engine controls were placed between us. On the Wimpey there had been only one stick, so that, if I wanted Mac to take over, he had to slide into my seat as I slid out, while the not-very-good automatic pilot did the flying.

At first, the airfield at Doncaster didn't seem to us a very good choice for learning to fly a new type, being small and bumby, and all grass. But we soon realized that these were just the conditions on which the Dak thrived, especially when carrying no load. Nor is that part of England exactly ideal for practising new navigational techniques. Many a time at the end of a cross-country flight I came back to find that the aerodrome had completely disappeared under a cloud of thick black factory smoke. On these occasions, one diverted to Church Fenton, which had runways plus landing aids, there to wait for a change in the wind. Very soon I was as relaxed in the Dak as I had been in the Wimpey, if not more so. Everyone who has bought a new type of motor car has experienced the sort of familiarization process that we had to go through on new aeroplanes.

You know how maddening it is to try to indicate a turn, and find that you have started the windscreen-wiper and then some idiot runs across in front of you and you can't find the hooter. Frustrating in a car, but possibly fatal in the air. There was a maker's handbook, as with a car, and when you'd studied that you sat in the cockpit, learned where everything was, both by sight and by touch. And there were little rituals that you learned by heart. Before take-off . . . H-T-M-P-F-F-S. Hydraulics, trim, mixture, pitch, fuel, flaps, switches . . . to which you added carburettor heat, gills-on-trail, and lastly, as you lined up in the runway, tail-wheel locked.

Landings were quite different too. For the first time I had to learn to 'motor on' to the runway, coming over the threshold with plenty of power still on, and not cutting the throttles back until the wheels touched the tarmac. There was no question of attempting a 'three-pointer'. Then, when the tail-wheel touched, deceleration was very rapid, with the great wide wings acting as an airbrake. They used to say that only a fool could make a bad landing in a Dak, but in the two years that I flew them, I must confess that I qualified for the cap and bells once or twice, mainly through absentmindedness. They were coming across the Atlantic in a steady stream now, the journey being made possible by the fitting of large plastic fuel-tanks in the fuselage. These were removed before we took delivery— but we were to need them ourselves before the war was over.

It was decided that as one of our jobs was going to be glider-tugging, it would be an improving experience for all pilots actually to go up in one of these fearsome contraptions, so that we could appreciate for ourselves the difficulties involved at the other end of the tow-rope. Accordingly, a few of us were despatched to RAF Brize Norton, where the training of army personnel to fly the Horsa glider was in progress. We were only there for two or three days, and I was only airborne four times, but it put years on me. They were using the Whitley bomber as a tug, and this ancient dilapidated machine, which had once been the mainstay of Bomber Command's striking force, was scarcely up to the task. I did two trips sitting beside the pilot in one of these, and each time it seemed as if we would never get off the ground. But this knuckle-whitening experience was nothing compared to the two trips I was forced into making in a glider. The Horsa was constructed on rudimentary lines of three-ply wood and piano wire, and was designed to be crash-landed on enemy territory, and was therefore regarded as entirely expendable. The pilots of the Glider Pilot Regiment were all volunteers, some sergeants and some officers, and they had been given a very swift and sketchy course of basic training on Tiger Moths. The fellow whom I sat beside did the whole thing as if he were loading up a machine-gun, and finally, when he was ready for take-off, he was sitting, ramrod-backed, with the stick shoved forward by rigid arms as far as it would go. To double the terror, the very first trip was at night. I can just recall a pitch-darkness, relieved only by the stabbing flames of the Whitley's exhausts in front of us. We were airborne first, and stayed above his tail until we had climbed in a gradual turn to 2,000 feet. And then our pilot pulled a lever, and we were alone, and I knew that the only way we could go was down. The Horsa had immense manually-operated flaps, so we had some sort of control over our rate of descent, and we managed to juggle our way to the threshold at a reasonable height. Then, with a last wrist-cracking application of flap, we sank down and hit the deck with an almighty crunch. After that, silence . . . except for the sound of my heart beating.

I never sat in a Horsa again, but on the many subsequent occasions that I towed them, I had a lively understanding of what those Army boys were coping with.

Back at Doncaster once again, 271 Squadron was up to strength, both in aircraft and personnel; but what was this I noticed in the Mess?—a 'Brown Job'. A short, wiry, swarthy individual in the uniform of a Major in the South African Air Force was introduced to me. He was Major Pier S. Joubert, who had been seconded to the RAF and, owing to his age, had been farmed out to Transport Command. I soon found out that he had been a commercial pilot for donkey's years in South Africa, but had joined the Services in his own country as soon as the war started, and had immediately applied for a posting to Europe. All he wanted to do was to see some action, but, as he was well over fifty at this time, he had to be content with us and a Dakota. He had been put in charge of 'C' Flight, of which I was a member, and I subsequently got to know him well. His voice had that distinctive gutteral quality that belongs only to the Afrikaner, and his impish sense of humour made him well able to cope with the ribbing he got from us. But, although we ribbed him mercilessly about his uniform, and his voice, and his total lack of knowledge of things administrative, we all loved him, and admired him for joining in a war which he could so easily have avoided. He was a good drinker, and devilish keen on the WAAFs, and we soon established that easy rapport that is founded on respect, but allows familiarity in the right places, at the right time. To us aircrew he soon became known as 'Jouby', but in his office every morning he got a salute and a 'sir' without any prompting.

At last came the day when, after a farewell binge in the Officers' Mess, we said farewell to Doncaster and left it for the Harrow Flight to continue their mercy runs with greens for the Scottish Islands. We headed south to look for the tiny Cotswold village of Down Ampney, where our own aerodrome was supposed to be ready for us. It was not difficult to find, with Cricklade and its distinctive church tower a mere two miles away, and the beautiful old town of Cirencester less than ten. The operational part of the aerodrome—the three runways, set as a triangle, and the hangars and control tower—were all laid out neatly on the flattest piece of land in the neighbourhood. But the rest of it—the living quarters, the Messes, the Headquarters buildings—seemed to have been jumbled up with the village in a most haphazard manner. The Officers' Mess, for example, had been plonked into the orchard just behind the largest farmhouse, and there seemed to be Nissen huts scattered higgledy-piggledy everywhere. But we soon settled down, and the villagers got used to our frenetic comings and goings at all times of the day and night. I found myself sharing a hut with seven other officers in the middle of a field just two minutes' walk from the Mess, which was very convenient after a late-night drinking session. These seven unfortunates included Phil Hollom, a keen ornithologist who was later to become an international expert in this field, Simon Rowan, a redheaded Irishman who was the wing commander's navigator, and Tim Beddow, another pilot on 271 Squadron, who shared my interest in the countryside, and shooting in particular. We hadn't been at DA more than a couple of days before Tim and I decided to pay a courtesy call on the local squire, a Major Dennis, to ask his permission to have a crack at the game which abounded on the airfield. 'My dear fellows,' said the Major, 'since the Air Ministry took over the land the shooting has belonged to them.' Then he added ruefully, 'I'm afraid I can't stop you.' When I had the cheek to enquire if he had a horse I could ride, he looked me carefully up and down, and replied, 'Nothing up to your weight, I fear.'

Somehow I had got hold of an ancient twelve-bore shotgun, and Tim had a .22 rifle, so we had plenty of fun potting at hares and rabbits on the runways when there were no aircraft about. But there was plenty of flying to do. I went off with Jouby to Hampstead Norris, where we learned the art of glider-tugging. There were two tricky moments in a take-off with a Horsa behind you. Firstly, you had to take up the slack on the rope by gently letting the aircraft roll forward until the glider pilot, who could talk to you through a wire in the rope, told you when the rope was taut. If you opened the throttles too suddenly, you could either break the rope, or you could yank it out of its two attachments to the glider's wings. Then, when you had at last applied full power, and had got the Dak's tail up, and were accelerating, albeit painfully slowly, down the runway, the glider would get into the air before you, and manoeuvre up to about twenty feet in order to get out of your slipstream. So, for a few moments, he was up, and you weren't! And if he was hamfisted enough to get too high, he would lift your tail, so that your nose dipped, and you had a hell of a job to get up at all. It's not difficult to imagine the language that went flashing along that rope at times like this. Once you had climbed to a reasonably safe altitude you could all relax, but there was no question of putting in 'George', the automatic pilot, while the Horsa was wallowing behind you.

If you ran into bad weather, and there was a danger that your glider pilot would lose sight of you in cloud, he could opt to go into the 'low-tow' position. This involved his pushing his nose down and bucketing through your slipstream until he was a few feet beneath you, and he then relied on some crazy string device that ran from the hawser to an instrument in his windscreen. This was meant to help him fly 'blind' behind you, and was known colloquially as the 'angle of dangle'. I never knew a glider pilot who had any faith in one of these contraptions. When you reached your destination, and your Army mate behind you reckoned he was in the right position to make a landing on the airfield, he only had to pull a lever, and the tow-rope fell away from his wings. We then made a slow run over a prepared field, and dropped the hawser into it so that it could be used again. In an emergency, or in bad weather, it was a matter of some delicacy as to who disengaged himself from the rope. If the glider unhitched, the Dak pilot would take the rope home with him; if the tug unhooked the glider, its pilot would hang on to the hawser until he was down. In each case, the theory was that, if a court martial resulted, whoever was in possession of the hawser was exonerated.

Next, dropping paratroopers. Here the problems were quite different. You had to bring your Dakota over the dropping zone (known as the 'DZ') at the right height, usually about 500 feet, and at exactly the right speed (somewhere around 70 knots), but also in the right 'attitude' which was supposed to be slightly tail up, so that as the men went out of the door, they didn't hit the tail-unit. All this meant a good deal of fine juggling with the throttle and the flaps. When you judged that the drop was imminent you pressed a warning button on the instrument panel, which brought on a green light immediately above the door. Then when you thought that with the aid of the prevailing wind the stick of paratroopers would arrive smack on the target, you pressed the 'jump' button, which rang a loud bell in the fuselage—and out they all went. Sometimes there were ten of them, sometimes twenty, but you could count them going as each jump caused a slight judder of the control column. When we had practised this a few times at Down Ampney, we were ready for the real thing, so I took a Dak with my crew along to Netheravon on the Salisbury Plain, and we spent a few days there graciously allowing Army types to leap out of our aeroplane. Naturally I was a little nervous on the first trip. After all, quite a few things could go wrong. This was not the 'free fall' that we know about today. These men could not pull their ripcord as and when they felt like it; it was attached to a 'static line'—a strong wire in the roof of the aircraft, and as they jumped, so the parachute was automatically opened. If you were going too fast, the whole thing could be torn apart. And if you were too high or too low, they could all land in a river or on top of a town—although on Salisbury Plain that was not much of a hazard.

I watched nervously as my twenty stalwarts climbed up the steps, with all their battle gear; sten guns and heaven knows what, and then assuming my most nonchalant expression, I got in and walked up between the two rows of them to my cabin. As I opened the door, one of them asked, 'Do you do a lot of this?' I forced a smile, 'Oh—any amount, old boy,' I said, and hurriedly disappeared. I suppose if I had told them the truth they would all have rushed out again. But all went well, and they all landed unscathed. Some time later, however, when we were doing a large mass drop in formations of three, I saw how easily things could go wrong. I was on the left of my 'V' and my stick of twenty had all just gone, when I glanced over to see how my opposite number on the right was getting on. To my horror, I saw that one paratrooper had somehow got his foot caught in the door, and was dangling helplessly out in the slipstream. He seemed to hang there for hours, and then at last, inch by inch, he was hauled in. As luck would have it, a couple of groundcrew were taking a totally unauthorized joy ride in that particular aircraft, so there were enough men to drag him back in. To their surprise, he turned out to be a padre—dog-collar and all. He went up the cabin. 'Don't worry, sir,' said the pilot, 'I'll get you back to base as soon as I can.' 'No thanks,' said the padre, 'could you possibly go round again so that I can jump with the chaps?' My squadron mate was taken aback, but did as he was asked. A week later, he received a charming letter thanking him for his trouble.

On the same day, another Dak from a different squadron had a similar problem which did not have such a happy ending. This time a chute got caught up in the tail-wheel, and the unfortunate soldier was trailing behind unable to disentangle himself. The pilot wracked his brains for a way out of this predicament, whilst fellow-airmen flew alongside telling him what was happening. Eventually, in consultation with the radio ground control, he flew out over the Solent, and went down as low and as slow as he dared. Airsea Rescue launches followed him as his crew hacked at the harness with an escape hatchet. The paratrooper, with whom, of course, no one had been able to communicate, fell into the water, but the impact was too much for him. When the launch picked him up he was dead. The incredible thing was that accidents like this, which could not have been foreseen, never once put men off from volunteering to be in this gallant brigade.

This was March 1944 and there were three more months to go for the great event for which we were being trained. I suppose I must have had a rough idea of what it was all about. There was a lot of talk of opening the Second Front now, and it wasn't difficult to deduce that all these gliders and paratroops would be used for some sort of invasion. But nobody knew when or where. Besides, I had plenty to occupy myself when I wasn't actually flying. Soon after my arrival at DA I had sought out the Recreation Hall and found it well equipped, both as a cinema and a theatre. I met F/O Johnny Day from the Admin who was the station entertainment officer. A Cockney who had had some contact with showbusiness before he joined the Air Force, he gladly welcomed my co-operation and assistance, and I was soon helping him put on variety shows. I revived one or two old favourites from Mount Hope, and started writing new sketches which were more appropriate to our present conditions. Johnny already had a nucleus of talented performers. Syd Sharr, a corporal in the MT section, was an East End comic who could do a stand-up act of fruity gags of any duration; Dave Chambers, another corporal, was a comedian of a slightly lighter touch, and I cast him as a humble airman in my immortal series 'Improbable Scenes in the Life of AC Plonk'. The first of these was set in the CO's office . . . (and guess who played the group captain).

Another airman, a strange, quiet Scot with the broadest of accents, was a brilliant violinist in the Grappelli style, and he was the backbone of a splendid little jazz band. My trombone act was soon given its first Down Ampney airing, and there were many more to come. Tim Beddow and I continued our shooting excursions, committing many breaches of etiquette which I had better draw a veil over, and, wonder of wonders, I bought myself another car.

It was an Austin Seven, which, if it were around today, would be described as 'vintage', but which cost me exactly £50. I practised driving it round the aerodrome perimeter-track. There was only just room for me behind the wheel, and changing gear was a work of art. The clutch pedal was only about an inch off the floorboard, and to change down you had to perform that now obsolete manoeuvre known as 'double declutching'. I took three pals for a spin as soon as I'd got the hang of it. As they squeezed into the tiny body I announced: 'By the way chaps, no pub crawls in this.'

'Oh,' said one, 'we could just pop to the Bull at Fairford for a trial run.'

'Just this once,' I replied, and off we went. In those days, beer was in such short supply that many pubs would be shut for several nights a week. We persuaded some of the landlords to run up a flag if they were open, and this saved a lot of mileage and a lot of clambering in and out of the tiny car. Petrol was severely rationed, too, and my allowance of coupons was pitiful. That's where Syd Sharr came in handy. When things were quiet, I would sometimes slip into the MT Section when he was in charge, and he would quickly pop a gallon or two in from the service pumps. This was not only illegal, it was courting disaster, because Services petrol had a deep red dye in it which eventually showed all round the carburettor. One dark night Syd threw a couple of jerrycans of the stuff in the back seat, and I drove hurriedly up the lane. This would be enough to keep me going for weeks! But where was I going to hide it? I turned into the gateway of a field, and lugged the jerrycans a few yards along the hedge and dumped them in the ditch. Carefully memorizing the spot, I drove hurriedly away. 'I'll leave them there until I really need it,' I thought.

Not more than a week later the need for this illicit juice arose. A visit to Cirencester had been planned, and I simply could not cadge a coupon off anyone. Tim was melancholy. 'We'll have to scrub it,' he moaned. 'Oh no,' I said smugly. 'I have the matter in hand.' We waited until things were pretty quiet after tea-time, and sneaked down in the Austin to the farm where the stuff was hidden. I took the car right into the field, and after a few minutes of frantic searching found the jerrycans. In a few moments we had filled the tank and I quickly dumped the can back in the ditch. 'That'll do for next time,' I said happily as we hopped into the car. Once out in the lane, Tim slammed the gate shut and we were away. But we didn't get far. Just round the corner the engine choked and spluttered, and finally conked out altogether. Tim leaped out and pumped away at the starting handle. Nothing happened. We opened the bonnet and I gazed at it hopelessly, knowing nothing about engines. All I could see was the tell-tale dye all round the carburettor. A court martial offence! A small gang of airmen came by on their way to their huts, and I trembled as they approached and saluted. 'Anything wrong, sir?' 'No chaps,' I lied. 'Everything's all right.'

As they disappeared, Tim jumped into the driver's seat,

while I took a panicking turn at the starting handle. And then a vehicle approached. 'This is it!' I could see myself stripped of my rank and peeling potatoes for the rest of the war. The MT van stopped, and out stepped a corporal. It was Syd Sharr! 'What's up, sir?' 'Thank God, it's you Syd. I've filled it up with that bloody petrol and it's conked out.' Syd glanced professionally at the engine, bent down and sniffed carefully. 'That's all right, sir. Just a little water in the petrol.' He swiftly opened up the carburettor. drained off some fluid, filled it again, tasted it, and put the whole thing together again. 'She'll go all right now, sir' and off he went, as with one turn of the handle my engine fired. Another year older!

And saved from the cookhouse!

Down Ampney held two squadrons, ourselves and No. 48, and just the other side of Cricklade, Blake Hill Farm held two more. Nearer to Oxford was RAF Broadwell, which accommodated a further two, and these six squadrons, all equipped with Dakotas, made up 46 Group. Each squadron was divided into 'A', 'B' and 'C' Flights, all with six Daks each, so the entire group comprised just over a hundred machines, and there were plenty of Horsa gliders to go round. This meant that we now housed a good number of members of the Glider Pilot Regiment, and so at last Jouby was not the only 'Brown Job' in the mess. These chaps had a wonderful leavening effect on what might have become a very stodgy RAF loaf, and they also provided a colourful addition to our Mess nights, when each of them turned up in his own regimental Mess kit, complete with tight trousers and spurs. Major Jackson, who was in charge of them, was an ebullient eccentric who drove about in a vintage Bentley with huge headlights, and gave forthright and down-to-earth briefings. One of his classic remarks was: 'If you do have to make a crash-landing, make it as near our gliders as you can, and then march back with us. But—don't forget—bring your own water-bottle'.

The pace of our training was gradually stepped up, and soon we were doing mass take-offs with gliders loaded with real troops and real jeeps and guns, and also teaming up with the rest of the group in large-scale practice paratroop drops. Tugging a heavy Horsa off the ground on a dark night was an eerie experience. The main snag was that none of us could clearly see the rope, so you had to more or less guess when it was taut. To overcome this, one of our wing commanders devised a very simple apparatus, just like traffic lights, which was placed to the left of the runway, and controlled by an officer on the ground. As you swung your aircraft on to the tarmac, you then stopped on a steady red. When the amber started to flash, you eased the throttles over and moved gently forward. Then, when a steady green showed, you knew the rope was taut, and 'gunned the motors', as the Yanks would say. The hairy bit came when you were airborne, for at this moment all the runway and aerodrome lights were switched off, and you felt in limbo until you had staggered up to a couple of thousand feet.

Late in April we knew that the invasion could not be far off, for we were briefed to do a 'nickel raid'. This was a code name for dropping pamphlets over France, warning them of their imminent liberation, and advising them what to do when our forces arrived. Up to now, these raids had only been carried out by operational aircraft, like the older types of bomber, which could defend themselves if attacked. But some brain in the higher echelons of command now decided that things were so quiet over France at night, that we could usefully and safely perform this function. At this stage our bomber offensive was mainly directed to targets in Germany, so most of the Luftwaffe was engaged over their own country. Even so, it gave us an eerie feeling to realize that we were going straight over the Channel to wander about trying to find the right place to distribute our reading matter. All our Daks had by now been equipped with the latest navigational aid, a thing called a 'Gee'. I had only the sketchiest knowledge of its workings, but gathered that strong signals were sent out from various transmitting stations in England and they made a sort of pattern which was then superimposed on our maps. With the aid of a receiver the navigator could get two separate signals and where their lines crossed on the map was our precise position.

Harry Green reckoned that he had mastered this by now, so, on the appointed night, we set off for our target, which was in Tours in the Touraine district of France. By now Mac Macneil had left my crew, and was a skipper in his own right, and in his place I had been given Flight Lieutenant 'Daddy' Wallis, who earned his nickname by being older than all of us, and by wearing a long-service medal. He was amiable enough, and had spent so long instructing on Oxfords that he found the Dak a bit of a handful, and I had not had much time to let him try his hand. I had also my own personal Dakota which rejoiced in the serial number KG444, and which I had nicknamed 'The Pie-eyed Piper of Barnes'. This had been painted in large yellow lettering on the nose. This was a wheeze that Wing Commander Booth had borrowed from the Americans, and it certainly gave one much more interest and pride in the job. Tim Beddow had called his 'Boozer's Gloom' and everyone else had concocted something jolly. This nickel raid was only my first trip in Treble Four, and I did many more before it came to a sticky end. Mind you, I did my best to get rid of it on this sortie. We set off with our cargo of bundles of bumph for the French and climbed, on a pitch-dark night, to some 8,000 feet over the Channel. We saw nothing of the French coast, but I assumed that Harry had things under control. However, after an hour he came forward with the dismal news that 'the Gee was jammed', and he couldn't get any signals from it.

'Never mind,' I said in my most press-on mood, 'Carry on with normal navigation, and we'll drop the stuff on ETA.' Harry looked crestfallen at this, and two sergeant pilots who had been sent along for the ride, and to help chuck out the literature, both begged me to turn back. But I would have none of it. 'I shall do as I say,' I said sternly, 'and if you mention it again, I shall report you when we get back.' A terrible silence settled over the cockpit as we chugged on over France, seeing absolutely nothing. Harry was just staring at his maps so I maintained the course he had given me with great, and I thought, admirable, resolution, until at last he said miserably, 'I reckon we're about there now.'

The paperwork was duly thrown out of the open door as I made a slow left-hand turn, and when it was all gone, in the absence of any help from my own dejected navigator, I set course due north. I calculated that wherever we were in France, as long as we hung on to a northerly course, we must eventually see some part of England. How the time dragged. Daddy Wallis was asleep, Harry was gazing hopelessly at his 'Gee' set, Bill Randall was maintaining a discreet silence, and the sullen antagonism of the two sergeants could be felt all through the cabin. By this time I knew I had been a damned fool in pressing on for so long, and one could tell by the painfully slow way in which the occasional light on the ground grew nearer, that our groundspeed was desperately low. Now there was literally nothing to do but hang on to that course. We had been in the air about five hours, and not a word had been spoken for the last two, when the bright lights of an aerodrome appeared straight in front of us. Inch by inch, it grew nearer, and moment by moment the crew began to come alive.

'I know what . . . it's Hurn,' said one. 'No, it isn't, it's St Mawgan,' said another. 'It's bloody Lynham . . . It's Brize Norton . . .'—they were all guessing now. 'Wherever it is, I'm not landing until we've called them up,' was my firm answer. We could see the whole place lit up now, and there were three searchlights set around the perimeter, whose beams met together over the runways at about 2,000 feet. This was standard practice in the UK for aircraft who had perhaps had their radio knocked out and who were completely lost.

The runway lights were on, too, and the whole thing looked very inviting. But I was uneasy. If it was an English aerodrome—and after all that time flying due north it could even be somewhere in the Midlands—why wasn't there a light anywhere flashing a code signal? I continued to circle, calling out: 'Darky, Darky' on the emergency frequency. But there was no reply. 'OK chaps,' I said, 'we've got a fair amount of petrol. I'm going north a bit further until I'm positive we're over England.' There was a groan from the entire crew, but I swung on to 360° and maintained my altitude. By now the same thought was in everybody's mind. When dawn comes, if we are still over France, we'll be a sitting duck for any fighter who cares to take off. The night was still as black as your hat, but when we had been airborne for fully six hours, the horizon began to lighten, and we could at last make things out beneath us. And there it was . . . the coast of England! But where? Suddenly there was an airfield, and as I rapidly lost height, we could all clearly see the large white letters by the control tower . . . TR. 'Tarrant Rushton!' we all chorused, and, with a turn to port, dear old Down Ampney was soon in sight. It was daylight now, so without bothering to call them up on the RT, I dived down and swept past the tower almost at ground level. As we pulled away, up came a green Very Light, and in a matter of minutes we were on the ground. Six and a half hours, it says in my log-book. Where the hell had we been? All the others had been back ages ago.

At the post-mortem next day, although the CO was grateful that I managed to bring my valuable aircraft back, I was severely criticized for not turning back when the Gee went u/s. A week later when the group navigation officer had had time to mull the whole thing over, it was proved that I had distributed the news of the impending invasion to some unsuspecting peasants close to the Pyrenees. But I had been right not to land at that inviting aerodrome, because it was near Cherbourg and the Germans' ruse of lighting up the whole place so beautifully had already netted them several lost but intact British aircraft, whose crews were now in the bag. For Daddy Wallis, it was just a nice night's rest. Without our knowing it, the wind had swung round 180° and swept us much further south than we should have gone. Naturally when we turned and set out for home, we were flying straight into a headwind.

Of course I was the target for some derision after this episode, and the RAF monthly magazine awarded me the Finger of the Month, and the whole trip was set out in some detail as a warning to others. I was, however, able to derive a little satisfaction from the story that was later leaked. Ralph Fellows, who was navigating for Jouby at this time, told me privately that as they were approaching to land back at DA he had discovered that the intrepid Boer had done the entire journey with his white tail-light switched on.

Although we had risked life and limb in this exploit to warn the French—the wrong ones, as it happened—of the invasion, there was still more than a month to go before the event actually took place. During this time our training was intensified, and we were in the air nearly every day, either with gliders, troops, or dummy supplies. This last activity required yet another technique. The floor of the Dakota was equipped with two parallel sets of metal rollers, and the panniers containing the supplies were placed on them, with their static lines attached to an overhead wire. The routine then was more or less the same as for paratroopers, except that these great laundry-baskets had to be pushed down the rollers towards the door. For this purpose we carried four privates from the Royal Army Service Corps, many of whom had never been off the ground before. So our frequent practice drops were as much for their benefit as for ours. Our dropping-zone was only a few miles from Down Ampney. On one occasion a major from the RASC said he would like to come up with me to see what went on. I put him in the seat beside me, determined to give him the shock of his life. Having climbed up and dropped the panniers, I said: 'Watch this!' Cutting the throttles, and dropping the wheels and flaps, I had Treble Four down on the runway before the panniers hit the deck. 'Phew!' said the major, as he unstrapped and left his seat. 'You fairly scared the pants off me then.' Of course I was delighted. I had just logged up my 1,000th hour, and was full of confidence.

Daddy Wallis had now been put full-time on to flying our small clutch of Oxfords, which were used for radar and Gee training, and also, incidentally, for flitting about England taking senior officers about their lawful—and often unlawful—occasions. His place was taken by Flight Lieutenant Hunter, an Observer who had earned a DFC on operations in Bomber Command. He was a cheery, blond-haired chap, with a great taste for beer, and we went on many booze-ups together in my Austin Seven. 'Tiger', as he was quite logically nicknamed, had unfortunately never had his hands on the controls of an aircraft—at least only in straight and level flight—so I resolved to teach him to take off and land the thing. With great bravery, I put myself in the right-hand seat, and monitored his somewhat shaky dash into the air. I noticed a slight juddering as we neared the end of the runway, so grabbed the stick myself (I would never have made an instructor!) and got it into the air. But all seemed to be well, so I let him take over again, and we executed a copybook circuit. On the down-wind leg, I let the undercart down, and was idly gazing out of my window when I noticed that the landing-wheel just beneath me was gently waving about in the slipstream. So that's what the juddering was! We had blown a tyre on take-off. 'Take her up to 2,000 feet,' I said to Tiger. 'I'm not letting you make your first landing with a bloody flat tyre! And I'm not going to try a landing from the right-hand seat, either.'

I put George in, and we hastily swopped places, and then I told the control tower what had happened. 'You'd better land on the grass,' they said. 'We'll have the fire-engine and blood-wagon standing by.'

We had all been taught what to do in a situation like this. I landed as slowly as I possibly could on my left wheel, and kept the right wing up as long as there was enough airspeed to do so. Then, when the flat tyre touched the grass we did a bit of a ground-loop and came to rest facing the wrong way—just like an Oxford on one of its off days!

After that, poor old Tiger never got an opportunity to do a landing, for we were far too busy getting ready for the Great Event.

11

IN ACTION AT LAST

WE ALL FELT that D-Day was looming, and our suspicions were confirmed when the station intelligence officer issued an edict that all aircrew moustaches were to be shaved off. His reasoning was somewhat convoluted. We were all to carry passport-size photographs of ourselves which, if we were unlucky enough to be shot down, could be pasted into false identity cards to be supplied by the French underground movement. He thought that RAF-type handlebar moustaches looked far too British, so, before the photos were taken, off they had to come. And what a hirsute harvest it was. We appointed one of the senior WAAF officers as Official Shearer, and with great merriment and not a little beer she performed the solemn ceremony. So another Edwards facial effulgence fell by the wayside.

The invasion was supposed to take place on 5 June 1944, and about a week before that we were given a detailed briefing on the various jobs we had to do. I was one of a group of Daks which were to go over the night before and drop gliders on various special targets like bridges and gun-emplacements, so that these could be captured before the main onslaught took place. We did our best to memorize the lie of the land from maps and reconnaissance photographs, and the day before the 'off' all the Dakotas and Horsas were duly marshalled on the runway.

There were going to be so many machines in the air over the beachhead that, to simplify identification, all Allied aircraft were to be painted with wide black and white stripes on the wings and the tail end of the fuselage. This was such a well-kept secret that we didn't know about it ourselves until the day before D-Day, and it had to be done so speedily that our groundcrew couldn't possibly cope with the task in the short time available. Accordingly, all the aircrew had to rally round, and out we went to the dispersal points armed with large whitewash brushes, and lent a hand with sloshing the stuff on to the wings. I was wearing my second-best peaked cap, which was already splitting open at the front of the peak, and the addition of liberal amounts of white paint added to the rakish appearance. The CO eyed my get-up with a disapproving look, but said nothing. This was hardly the time for bullshit.

However, as everybody knows, the whole operation was postponed for twenty-four hours because of the weather in the English Channel. This placed a great strain on all of us, but to save our mooching about with our morale sagging, we were all piled into a fleet of coaches and taken to Netheravon, where we filed into a very secret Ops room where we were allowed to gaze at a large-scale model of the actual piece of coastline we would encounter when we finally went over. Every house and farm building was there, as were all the Jerry emplacements.

Both squadrons were gathered into the Operations Room to be addressed by the C-in-C of Transport Command. He was an elderly man with a mass of ribbons on his rather ill-fitting battle-dress. 'Your task,' he said impressively, in a quite passable impression of Winston Churchill, 'is to support all the services in their various endeavours. You will nourish the Army. You will nourish the Navy. And you will nourish the Air Force.'

I muttered to Tiger, who stood beside me—'There you are. We're nothing but a bunch of bleeding nourishers.'

Our stay was far too short, and soon we were back in the coach, desperately trying to remember what we had seen. Conversation was not very brisk, and back at the Mess drinking was sporadic and merriment short-lived. Every spare bit of grass on the aerodrome was occupied by the tents of the troops who were going with us, and their nerves were pretty taut as well. Some of the remarks tossed to us 'boys in blue' as we went to the comparative luxury of our Nissen huts, were definitely bordering on the unfriendly! We were all strictly confined to camp, because we held the dread secret of our actual target in our heads, so there was no question of a sortie in the Austin. I sat on my bed, and, in an uncharacteristically sombre mood, wrote a letter to my mother which has fortunately been lost to the nation. This must have been the longest 24 hours in the lives of all of us, and it was a tremendous relief when the next day the whole thing was 'on' again.

There was a further complication when we did at last go down to the airfield to take off. During the delay, the wind had changed completely, and was now blowing in the opposite direction from the day before. And there was no time to take all the Daks and gliders to the other end of the runway. This meant a down-wind take-off with a heavily loaded glider in tow, but fortunately it was not a very strong wind, so as Wingco Booth said, 'We'll just have to make the best of it.'

I was the third to go and we just made it and then for an eerie hour we droned across the Channel in the darkness. As we came to the French coast, I forced myself and my glider pilot to believe that we had made the correct landfall, but I was not really convinced. And then, in a few minutes, it all came unstuck. We had been warned that 'Bomber Command will be dealing thoroughly with gun-sites near your targets,' but we hadn't bargained for the massive clouds of smoke and dust they would leave behind. Suddenly the ground was completely obscured. I struggled on for a few minutes, with the conversation between myself and my Army friend behind me getting more strained, and finally I said to him, 'I can't see a bloody thing. I'm turning back to get a pinpoint.' It was a foolish decision. No sooner had I made a rambling, lurching turn back towards the coast then we ran head-on into the formations of Daks bringing in the paratroopers who were to follow us up. In the chaos I somehow managed to avoid a collision, and turned yet again back towards our target. Suddenly, as we crept about at a ridiculously low altitude, there were gun-flashes beneath us, and I heard one or two muffled explosions. 'Missed us,' I thought, and waffled on. By now we all knew that I had made a complete hash of it, and on top of that there was simply not the petrol available for another search for our bridge, so with a shout of 'I'll have to let you go, goodbye, and good luck,' I persuaded him to disconnect. I rammed the throttles open, dropped the rope, and climbed away.

In a few moments we were in unexpected cloud, and I put George in and set our prearranged course. Being empty, we gained altitude rapidly. 'I believe we got hit back there,' said Tiger nervously, 'Nonsense,' I replied. 'We'd know all about it if we had.' My panel told me that we were OK but when we finally came out of the cloud into the moonlight above, we were at a very strange attitude, with the left wing down. I straightened her up, and turned on to the course which would take us round Dieppe and back over the Channel. It was only when we were nearly back at DA that I realized that something was wrong. The wheels and the flaps refused to come down, which could only mean that we had lost all our hydraulic fluid.

That explained our crazy emergence from the cloud back over France, for that same fluid activated the automatic pilot. As Tiger frantically operated the emergency hand-pump to get the undercart down, I flashed my headlights on and off as a signal that I was in trouble. Soon I got an answering flash of green from the sound-controller and came straight in without flap to make a landing on the grass beside the runway. I knew that I would have no brakes, either, so as soon as we touched down I switched the engines right off, and prayed. I kept old Treble Four pretty straight with rudder for a while, but finally it was all in the lap of the gods. She swung round in a wild ground-loop, but the wheels stood up to it, and eventually we came to a stop. I can't remember who was first out, but none of us took very long! As we gathered in the gloom under the wings, dim headlights came bumping towards us, and a small van pulled up. Out leaped Flight Lieutenant Swann, one of our medical officers. 'Christ, it's you Jim. Everybody all right?' 'Yes, thanks, Doc. There's nobody hurt,' I shouted, as another Dak roared on to the runway beside us. Then he was off in his van in no time—we were of no further interest to him if nobody was hurt—but soon there were others all around us, and with their torches we inspected the aircraft to try and see exactly what had happened. 'Hey, look at this,' shouted someone, 'you've been hit here.' He was standing underneath the port engine, pointing upwards. Sure enough, there was a small jagged hole in the exhaust pipe. But that wouldn't explain the complete loss of hydraulic power. I grabbed a torch, and flashed it on to the wheel. 'Aha!' There was a tiny slit in the oil pipeline leading to the brakes. So it had been an explosive shell, and all the fluid had drained out of that minute hole in that eighteen inches of pipe not covered by the engine cowling.

Several more holes were discovered in the underside of the port wing, and next day Jouby was seen inspecting them with unusual interest. It seemed incredible, but he was actually jealous of them, and expressed disappointment that no Jerry had had a go at him in the pre-invasion darkness.

Treble Four being now unfit to fly, I had to use a spare aircraft on this day to take another Horsa over in daylight.

This was the real thing, at long last: 6 June 1944—D-Day, which we had been working up to for so long. And, although I was part of it, I felt more like a spectator than anything else. Crossing the coast near Worthing at about 2,000 feet, in the most glorious weather, we had a grandstand view of the whole impressive show. In front and behind, there streamed a steady flow of transport aeroplanes of all shapes and sizes. Above, and all around, massed formations of fighters, forming a huge umbrella which no enemy aircraft had the nerve to try to penetrate. And beneath us, as we approached the French coast, the assembled might of the British and Allied Fleets. I simply followed the man ahead and marvelled at the spectacle that I was so privileged to see. The Navy for once recognized us as friendly and forbore from pooping off at us as we trundled up to the coast and along the mouth of the River Orne. Our dropping-zone was already half-filled with gliders as we delivered Captain Mills and his men to their destination with all the panache of a postman delivering his mail. We dropped the rope, and, losing height rapidly, turned for home as low as we could get. Halfway across the Channel we spotted a Dak floating in the water with its tail up in the air, and circled it twice to make sure that it was not one from Down Ampney and that the crew were OK. Sitting in their dingy, with two Air Sea Rescue launches already bearing down upon them, they gave us a merry two-finger salute, so we headed for home.

As far as 271 Squadron was concerned, the invasion had been a piece of cake. Back at base old Jouby was jubilantly displaying three or four holes in his starboard wing with a smile on his monkey-like face that stretched from ear to ear. Ralph Fellows told me afterwards that the old maniac had deliberately held on to his course after dropping his glider, in the determined hope of attracting enemy fire. And when they did hit him, he had ordered Ralph into the astrodome to inspect the damage.

'You've got several holes in the starboard wing,' Ralph had reported over the intercom.

'Are they bigger than Jim's?' was all that Jouby could say, and chortled when Ralph had described them to him. He was the happiest man in the Mess that night.

Having played our part in mounting the biggest ever land invasion in history one would have thought that we would now be plunged into a mad whirl of hectic 'nourishing'. But it was not so. Everything was going so well that there was no need for supply-dropping, but the army had not yet pushed far enough forward to be able to carve out landing-strips for us. Major Jackson and his band of glider pilots had walked back to the beaches and, in company with one Dakota crew, had been ferried home in an empty landing-craft. They were itching to be ordered into the air for further adventures, but they too now kicked their heels in the Mess for a matter of four weeks. Soon we were occupied once again with seemingly endless 'exercises', interspersed with pointless and frustrating hours in the 'Link Trainer'. There were also a great many 'Charley trips', as we called them, when, under the guise of a 'navigation exercise', you bogged off somewhere to collect some beer or take somebody on leave.

On one occasion I had to go to St Athan in Cornwall, and whilst in the Mess at lunchtime, I noticed they had a good stock of Guinness behind the bar, which was one drink we were singularly short of back at DA. With the welfare of my fellow-officers in mind, I bought a couple of crates with my own money, and chucked it in the back. Halfway home, some wag in the crew said, 'I wonder what Guinness tastes like at six thousand feet?' There was only one way to find out.

'Very frothy, but very tasty!' was my verdict, and after a couple more I got back into the seat, dropped down to tree-top level, and arrived over the control tower in a tremendous low-level beat-up. Not content with that, I went round and did it again. Fortunately the officer on duty was a mate, and nothing more was said about it. But I never drank in the air again. I didn't know then, that at that sort of altitude alcohol goes into the bloodstream much more quickly than normally, but these days I am grateful for the knowledge, and very rarely arrive sober on the many trips I make around the world.

I suppose I have flown to Australia over twenty-five times, and, like most ex-pilots, I positively loathe it every time, so I make the best of it by drinking liberally all the way. I usually take a silver tankard with me, and, as I board the aircraft, I hand it to the chief steward and ask him to charge it with champagne—and keep it charged. High in the air over the Pacific one day, I wrote this telling little memo to myself: 'RULES FOR FLYING: 1) Always try and get on a 747; 2) Always travel first class; 3) Never refuse a drink; 4) Never look through the curtain at the poor bastards in the back.'

I have spent many a happy hour in the upstairs bar of a Jumbo, playing chess, or Scrabble, or, on one occasion, the trombone. Eric Sykes and I were on the way from Chicago to Hawaii, and he obliged with an accompaniment on a couple of ice-buckets used as bongo drums. Unfortunately, a steward had to ask us to stop, as we were 'interrupting the film downstairs.'

These days most airlines have filled this splendid bar with so-called 'executive' seats, so that first class passengers are robbed of the undeniable pleasure of being able to stretch their legs as they clamber up and down the spiral staircase. But, I note, not one airline has reduced the price of first class seats by a commensurate amount. I suppose this could be described as false pretences, and it is high time someone did something about it.

On a flight from Singapore, I was toting my miniature chess set round the cabin, trying to get an opponent, when a small Malaysian boy with large horn-rimmed spectacles took up the challenge. After twenty minutes this twelve-year-old little brute had me nicely checkmated, and his six-year-old brother, who had been watching the game, offered to take me on. After another twenty minutes, punctuated by infuriating remarks like, 'It's a pity you did that,' and 'Are you sure you meant that move?' he too had my king in a corner. As the two little swine sat giggling, I went back to their parents and said, 'Haven't you got one three years old?' The air hostess was very consoling. 'Perhaps it is the champagne,' she said with a smile.

I make a practice of carrying a hunting horn in my pocket whenever I go on a long journey by air. This may seem eccentric, but it has its uses. At Abu Dhabi once there was a tremendous crowd of white-robed Arabs impeding my way. One blast of the horn, and they scattered to let me through. More than a year later at the same airport the taxi-drivers at the gate recognized me and called on me to give them another tootle! On the same trip, at Bahrain the Customs Officer was suspicious of one of my pieces of baggage which actually contained a euphonium. 'Open it,' he said sternly. I did so, and he frowned at what he saw. 'What's this?' he demanded. 'A musical instrument,' I replied in my most subservient manner. 'You play!' he commanded. I was delighted to oblige, and was just warming up to the 'Serenade' by Drigo, when a heavily-armed soldier approached, waving his arms and shouting 'No, no, no, no,no.' The metal roof of the Customs Shed was amplifying the sound splendidly, but I took the instrument from my lips, and said jovially, 'Make up your minds, chaps. You want it, and he doesn't.' I packed the euphonium hurriedly and left them busily arguing the point.

I once conducted a mock hunt in a DC9 of Ansett Airlines of Australia somewhere between Adelaide and Melbourne. I was well flown with wine, and there was only one other passenger, and she sat reading a book throughout the whole mad episode. I 'Found' the fox in the loo, and whooped and holloaed and tootled at it all the way up the aisle, until it finally went to ground in the cabin, right underneath the pilot's seat.

There were no such jollifications on board Treble Four in that long, boring month after the invasion. I seemed to be flying somewhere nearly every day but at the end of four weeks had only logged up some twenty-odd hours. The rest of the time I was busy doing shows and touring the countryside in my Austin Seven in search of open pubs.

Also, at this time, in a mood of sheer defiance, I stopped shaving my upper lip—and lo and behold, at last something fairly respectable began to take shape. For a long time the ground crew, and in particular my rigger, AC2 Meanwell, had referred to me as 'Hank'. Now, at last, I began to feel that I could live up to the nickname.

Then, at last, the chaps in Normandy managed to lay out a strip suitable for Dakotas, and in we went. In my first trip we were ferrying an entire fighter wing to its new base at Sommevoire, and my own load consisted of sixteen groundcrew, with all their kit. I made my first landing on one of the new metal-strip runways. It had a lot of give in it as you touched down, and made an ominous clanking sound, but it was perfectly safe and later on literally hundreds of such strips were put down. On the return I carried a load of stretcher cases, and this was to be the pattern for the whole of July and August—freight on the way out and wounded on the way back. To look after these men we carried a couple of RAF nursing sisters, and they did a wonderful job. Walking up the fuselage on the way to my seat, I would marvel at the conglomeration of apparatus they had to tend the three layers of stretchers. Some had legs in plaster, hoisted above them; some had bottles of blood-plasma hanging over their heads, and all were festooned with labels which would tell the next doctor how far the treatment had gone. Once, as I revved the engines to taxi out for take-off, the nurse came forward and said, 'Captain, I want a smooth take-off and landing. I have one man here with a broken back . . .' How I sweated over that trip! Often we carried a number of walking wounded as well. Some were cheerful, with maybe just an arm in a sling. But many had bandages about the head and body, and these had that glazed and stunned look that I grew to recognize as a sign of shock. On 22 August I was the first to land at Carpiquet, the aerodrome at Caen which had seen so much bitter fighting before we captured it. I had to make a low pass over the strip to scare away some cattle before we could come in, and it was incredible to see the potholes in the runway which the army had been obliged to fill in before the strip could be used.

On the 27 August, after Paris had been recaptured, we flew relief food in to a base at Orleans, from whence it was rushed to the starving city in a huge convoy of American army trucks. I noted the load in my log-book '5,000 lbs of biscuits'—and the next day it was the same amount, but this time, herrings in tomato sauce. Cynics in my crew said it was all NAAFI reject food, but whatever it was, I hope the Parisians appreciated it. This operation was master-minded by the Americans, and it was a revelation to see their organization at close quarters. There was only one runway available at Orleans, so an American major was roaring up and down in a jeep, shouting through a loud-hailer, 'Come on there. Get moving! Get your ass going', and other Yankee extravagances. When one of his Dakotas, or C47s as they called them, burst a tyre, he had it bull-dozed on to the grass just so that things could be kept going. I had scarcely stopped my engines before the load was gone and I was instructed to 'Get the hell outa here!' On the way back from one of these trips, I passed over the

Falaise gap, which had just been the scene of the slaughter of a great number of Germans. Being empty, I took Treble Four down low, dropped a bit of flap, and had a slow look at the sight. It was my first real glimpse of the devastation of a battlefield, and afterwards I rather wished I hadn't seen the twisted wreckage of tanks, the slumped bodies, and even, to my disgust, the mutilated carcases of horses and the ammunition trucks they had been pulling. But far worse than the sight was the stench of it all.

I shut the window, opened the throttles, and climbed away. Nobody said much until we got back to DA.

The Allied advance was so swift at this stage that we made frequent trips to newly-constructed airstrips carrying loads of petrol. The potential danger of this cargo, distributed along the fuselage in two or three long rows of jerry-cans, never really dawned on me, but one shudders to think what would have happened if rough weather had broken them loose from the canvas rope that held them to the floor. To me it was just another load, which one signed for almost without looking at the manifest. My confidence in the Dakota was such that I had become very casual about details such as the distribution of load, and the slide-rule provided in each aircraft for the calculation of such things remained firmly wrapped up in its container. Besides, we had a Freight Section whose job it was to sort these things out, and—from sheer idleness—I had complete confidence in them.

The Dak was wonderfully adaptable. When the freight door was opened wide, it was amazing what could be squeezed in, from jeeps to motorcycles and ammunition, and now that the advance was going so deep into enemy territory, we began taking thousands of brand-new battledress uniforms for prisoners-of-war who were being released. And always the canvas harness was there for slinging stretchers on the return journey. One day we were briefed for another major airborne assault, ahead of the front, but that evening I went down with severe tonsilitis, and waited miserably in the sick-bay to hear the others taking off. But nothing happened, and soon Jouby was beside my bed to tell me that the whole thing had been cancelled because General Patton had reached the dropping zone before the gliders had even taken off. As soon as I was well again, it was back to the almost daily re-supply trips. Brussels was our main destination these days, and I spent many a boozy night in the cafés there.

The whole thing was building up to a tremendous climax, when suddenly we were all grounded for a whole day and we saw the ominous signs of those long-range fuel tanks being dragged out and refitted in the fuselage. What had the moguls thought up now? It wasn't long before we knew. As we filed into the briefing room there on the wall was the usual large map of Europe and on it a thick line of red ribbon stretching from Down Ampney right across the North Sea, and deep into Holland. At the very end of the line, written in large blue letters, was the word 'ARNHEM'.

Treble Four's days were numbered.

The story of Arnhem has been told many times, in words and on film, and is now widely known. Some ten years ago I somewhat foolishly allowed myself to be included in TV documentary on the subject, compiled by Anglia Television. I went to Norwich specially to make my contribution. We had a splendid, rather alcoholic lunch in a hotel, then went to the studio, where I was interviewed at some length before the cameras, without script or audience. Weeks later when the show was broadcast, the editors had been at their devilish work and had interwoven and intercut several interviews with other people—more eminent then myself. The result was a hodge-podge of disconnected chat, ending with the most unfortunate juxtaposition of opinions. General Urquart was seen standing on his lawn in front of his country residence saying, in his best military accent: 'As far as I am concerned, all my men would willingly have gorn again.' Immediately afterwards, I was seen lolling in an uncomfortable studio chair, uttering, 'As far as I was concerned, the whole thing was a cock-up'.

And from the viewpoint of one of the hundreds of tug-pilots involved, so it was. It all began with the best intentions. More men were going to be dropped than ever before, and were going further into enemy territory than ever before. The first glimpse of that map in the briefing room brought whistles of incredulity from many of us. Clearly, the moguls had gone mad. It seemed to many of us that the generals were determined to use this massive airborne force simply because it was there, and all their previous plans had been thwarted. It was all made to sound so simple at the briefing.

'You will take off and fly in pairs to Aldeburgh on the Suffolk coast, where all the other aircraft involved will join you in a steady stream as you set course for the Dutch coast. It has all been worked out with split-second timing so that a continuous flow of gliders will arrive at exactly the right time over the dropping-zone the other side of the river at Arnhem.' All well and good. But it didn't happen like that. For one thing, the 'other aircraft' involved were not all Dakotas. By this time, the lumbering, stolid Stirling bomber had been relegated to this humble task of dragging three-ply and piano wire through the sky, and so had the Albemarle, a medium-sized bomber that had done very little to commend itself up to now. The snag was that they all flew at different airspeeds, so that even with the most immaculate precision flying, the 'steady stream' was just a briefing officer's pipe-dream. In the event, it was more like a dog's dinner.

At the outset I was in trouble. Halfway down the runway one of Treble Four's engines decided to play up, developing a thing called 'boost surge' which meant that the power fluctuated like mad, and was gathering speed far too slowly. My glider, which had about six soldiers and 5,000 lb of ammunition stuffed into it, got airborne okay but by the time we had reached the end of the tarmac we were still going pitifully slowly. 'We'll never get up,' shouted Tiger nervously. 'Pull the bloody wheels up and we will,' I roared back, and up they came. We sagged into the air and inched our way up, passing the tower of Cricklade church lower than the red light on top of it. Somehow or other I managed to coax the combination up to our allotted altitude, and gradually the faulty engine righted itself, and we joined the stream on the way to the east coast. Aldeburgh was easy to pick out on such a fine day, and we settled down for the crossing of the North Sea.

A few miles out we saw a Dak floating helplessly in the sea beneath us, with its glider not far away. The chump of a pilot had chosen that place to switch over to his overload tanks, and got himself an airlock in the pipeline. Both engines stopped, and down he went, but we could see launches speeding on their rescue mission. We made the Dutch coast, and tightened our backsides in preparation for the long daylight flight over enemy territory. Fighter Command were doing their stuff, but most of them were so high up you could scarcely see them.

We drew comfort from our brand-new flaksuits. I had draped mine over my uniform as instructed, but Tiger had decided to sit on his. 'That's the part of my anatomy I want to protect,' he said. 'If I get that damaged, I might as well be dead anyway.' There was a very occasional puff of smoke in the air to show us that the Jerries were extending a welcome, but below us the Typhoons were taking care of their gun emplacements as soon as they opened fire. Then, with a whoosh, all hell broke loose. Not German fighters; not ack-ack. The Stirlings came up from behind with their superior speed and flew through the lot of us. We rocked and swayed in their slipstreams, but there was nothing we could do except hang on to the stick and swear. Then it was the Albemarles' turn, and soon the sky was a huge jumble of aeroplanes and gliders—but I didn't see one collision.

We were getting nearer the target now, and there was an increase in the ack-ack. In front of us, a tow-rope was severed by the flying shrapnel, and down went a glider all on its own, while the Dakota turned and headed for home, the shredded length of hawser still dangling from his tail. 'If he's got any sense,' I thought, 'he'll take that back to England with him.'

We plodded on. The Stirlings were well out of sight now. They were dropping the chaps who would set up small radar transmitters for us to home on to. Hertogenbosch passed under us, then Eindhoven—and eventually Arnhem. As we crossed the river, the ground was already littered with crashed gliders, and the air full of many more on their way down. I bade farewell to my pilot Captain Joe Mills, with whom I had supped many a pint, got rid of the rope and climbed away at full throttle. Some two hours later I was back at Down Ampney, comparing notes and swapping yarns with the others. I don't think we lost anybody that day. I had been in the air exactly six hours.

The next day we did it again. This time my take-off was without incident, but on the climb up to our cruising level I stupidly did a rather tighter turn than usual, and suddenly I was being yanked uncomfortably about the sky by my glider, which this time contained a jeep and two trailers, with a few soldiers as well. 'What the hell's going on back there?' I shouted down the intercom. I soon found out when Bill Randall got into the astrodome.

'One of the front bits of rope has got the wrong side of the glider's nosewheel.'

'Can you cope?' I asked the two staff sergeants.

'We've got the controls almost upside down, but we can manage.'

I knew full well that we couldn't fly for four hours like that, but they wouldn't hear of me taking them back.

'We'll carry on like this,' they insisted.

Then I had an idea. 'I'm going to ease the throttles slightly,' I told them, 'and then, when the ropes have fallen away from the nosewheel I'll take up the slack.'

Bill proceeded to give me a running commentary and after a few minutes of agonizingly careful flying, the rope tautened without breaking, and we rejoined the stream.

Again I was impressed by the almost fanatical keenness of these airborne troops. They intended to get into the action at any price. This trip was almost easier than the first, and we all marvelled at the lack of opposition as we passed over Arnhem and dropped our gliders on to the now overcrowded target field. Back at Down Ampney I logged up another six hours of flying. The date was 18 September 1944.

Next day while we waited to hear the result of the action, I put in three more hours in the Pie-eyed Piper taking a further 5,000 lb load of petrol to Belgium. 'Tiger' had been taken ill with a tummy bug, so in his place I was given Flight Sergeant Clarke, one of a large bunch of new pilots who had recently arrived in case replacements were needed. He had been trained in Rhodesia, and after returning to England had just spent a whole year in a hotel in Harrogate waiting for a posting. I found him sitting on the grass with his mates, and laughingly threw him a small pamphlet which we all had to carry, entitled 'Useful phrases in the event of being shot down behind enemy lines.'

'Read this, Nobby,' I said, 'You never know!'

Three days later he was using it.

I wasn't able to land at Brussels to unload my petrol, because of the weather, but I got into Lille all right, and was back at base before dark. Next day came the news that the forces at Arnhem had met with unexpectedly violent opposition, and had been hemmed into a very small area by a German Panzer division. Fresh supplies of ammunition were urgently needed, and plans had been made for a mass drop of panniers. There wasn't time to fit Treble Four with the necessary metal rollers, so I took KT 500 on the trip. This entailed another five and a half hours in the air, and, although the outward journey went off without incident, it was clear as soon as we approached the dropping-zone that things were not going well. The whole landing area was now ringed with German guns, which seemed to be firing continuously at our chaps down there, but the moment we arrived, they were elevated in our direction with scarcely a pause. We were down to about 600 feet, easy targets for the Jerry 88 mm howitzers—but here again luck was on our side, because the Huns chose to fire at the Stirlings which were mixed up with us, because they were twice our size and made much easier shooting.

In the few minutes that I was over the target I saw several Stirlings brought down, and they hit the ground with a frightening shower of flames and sparks and smoke. I lost no time in climbing away after we had made our contribution, and, although several Daks had been hit, when we got back to DA and eagerly assembled on the tarmac to talk it over, we found that nobody in our squadron was missing. Jouby's eyes were sparkling. At last he had seen some action! 'We've got to put in another effort tomorrow, Jim,' he said. 'I need one more, but I can't ask you to go. You've been flying four days on the trot as it is.' 'If Treble Four is ready, you can count me in,' I replied. I didn't feel in the least bit tired, and was quite ready to volunteer. There were no heroics about it. We would all have gone anywhere to please the old man.

So, on 21 September 1944, another maximum effort was mounted to try and relieve the beleaguered 1st Airborne Division. As before, the long haul from base to Holland was trouble-free. I was so relaxed that I went back into the fuselage to write on a label on one of the panniers a jocular message 'Delivered courtesy of Jimair'—or words to that effect. Then there was the grim run-in through even heavier ack-ack than before. I was just about to ring the bell for our RASC friends to start rolling out the panniers, when, just a little over to our left, I saw a lone green Very light come up from the garden of a large house in the town. I swung Treble Four over, and we dropped right over some tennis courts alongside the house, which, we now know, housed the Brigade HQ. We also know that although the supplies were right on target the chaps were not able to break cover to get at them because of the concentrated fire. I pulled up and away, and, to the consternation of my crew, did a fairly leisurely circuit at 6,000 feet as I looked down to watch what was going on. Then, climbing up to about 8,000, I set off for home on this my fourth trip to Arnhem. There was no sign of fighter cover, but I was quite confident that the lads were up there somewhere, so I engaged George, and called for coffee and sandwiches. We had passed Eindhoven and Nijmegen, and I was feeling pretty pleased with myself. But suddenly the scene changed. Gazing out through my window, I saw a fighter plane approaching rapidly, and at our level—and—I couldn't believe it—little sparkles of light on its wings, which could only mean it was firing at us. As it flashed by, I could see plainly the black cross painted on its side. 'Fighters!' I yelled at the top of my voice. Frantically disengaging George, I grabbed the control column and ordered Bill up into the astrodome. At last our training in

Northern Ireland was going to pay off.

First thoughts in an emergency are often strange. Mine were, 'This won't do. We've got a show to put on tonight!' I had written some more sketches, and was going to incorporate them into a variety show. But there was no time to dwell on that aspect. My job now was to try and get away from this bloody German. My training in aircraft recognition had already told me it was a Fokke-Wolfe 190, and was therefore armed with some eight machine-guns. He had climbed away by now, but soon came in again from the port side in a copybook diving attack. I responded, as taught, by turning in towards him as sharply as I could, and he didn't touch us. He tried again from the starboard, and again I eluded him. Bill was calmly describing his moves to me over the intercom. And now I noticed broken cloud a few thousand feet below us. 'I'll make for that,' I thought, and stuffed the nose down. Here, in my panic, I made a mistake in not closing the throttles. Had I done so, we would have dropped like a stone. Instead, our speed built up, and the aircraft struggled to go up again. I pushed with all my strength, and at last we made the cloud. But he was on us again all too soon, this time from dead astern. 'He's right behind you,' shouted Bill. 'It doesn't matter which way you turn!'

The cloud was too broken to give me complete cover, and every time I came to a patch of clear air, the F-W was on me again. He hit us again and again, until, as Bill put it, 'The wings were full of holes.' I twisted and turned, throwing Treble Four into tighter and tighter turns, cork-screwing this way and that, until all the flying instruments were spinning crazily and I had lost all track of time and all sense of our whereabouts. It was amazing that the plane was still flying, we had been hit so often. And there was nobody coming to my rescue. After what seemed an age—but which was probably only a matter of twelve minutes or so—and when I had reached the stage of not really knowing what to try next, the decision was taken out of my hands.

With a high-pitched scream, both propellers went into 'fully fine', which means, in effect, that the hydraulic fluid had been lost, and the blades ceased to have any traction. As a result, the engines 'ran away' and the rev-counter needles went right round the clock. At the same time, the starboard engine burst into flames, and I knew we had had it. There was nothing more to do than yell 'Bale out!'—and Nobby Clarke and Harry Sorensen grabbed their parachutes and ran to the back. I turned to get mine, and saw a little huddle of men in the rear of the cabin. It was three of the army privates. 'Why the hell don't you get out?' I roared. One of them looked up weakly, and said hoarsely: 'We can't.' I saw then that they had been wounded. Bill said later they had been hit by explosive bullets and were in a terrible state. So there was nothing for it but to try for a crash landing. I yanked open the escape hatch in the roof above my head, and stuck my head out to avoid the flames which were now enveloping the cockpit. The wheel of the steering-column was now completely upside down; with one hand on that and with the other held in front of my face for protection, I managed to keep her fairly level as we plunged down towards the ground. I instinctively pulled out of the dive at tree-top height and held the nose up as best I could while the speed dropped off. Then, with a rending and crashing, we plunged into the forest. I had not had any chance to choose a landing spot, but, as luck would have it, we pitched into an area of saplings, so that the impact slowed us down instead of tearing us apart. Finally, as I clung desperately to the sides of the escape hatch, the nose dug into the ground and the tail came up in the air. We hung poised for a split second, with the fuselage almost vertical, and then, with a sickening crash, the tail came down again, and with the impact I was shot out of the hatch like a cork from a bottle. Down I came again on to the roof, spun round a couple of times, and then fell to the ground beside the now blazing aircraft. Picking myself up, with the strength that comes to a man in desperation, I ran through the trees to try and take cover. Bill and one of the army privates had somehow managed to hang on and then jump from the rear door, and as I ran I sensed rather than saw them following me. But even now, having brought us to our knees, the German hadn't finished with us.

Wheeling overhead, he saw our predicament, and turned away to come in for a final strafing run. As we heard his guns approaching, we all three literally tried to claw our way into the ground, for with our bright yellow Mae Wests we were easy targets. But the inept Kraut was gypped of his prey, for halfway through his run, he ran out of ammunition, and passed harmlessly overhead with a roar from his engine. Then . . . silence, except for the crackle of flames, and the occasional explosion of Very cartridges and petrol tanks, as Treble Four became the funeral pyre of the three luckless wounded men still inside.

Moaning and cursing, I stumbled to a safe distance from the fire, and three of us threw ourselves into a ditch among the trees. Then, remembering our training once again, we ripped off our Mae Wests and, scrabbling with our hands at the soil, hid them as best we could. Then we lay there, panting and trembling, and waited to see what would happen to us next. I had absolutely no idea where we were, except that it must be Holland. I didn't really care much, for my hands were now shaking with shock, and the left side of my face was taut and stinging where I had been thrown through the flames. I had instinctively put my arm up to shield myself, and my battledress was badly singed. Bill had sprained his ankle, but was otherwise unhurt, but our army friend, although he had escaped physical injury, was in such state of shock that he could not say a word. Poor fellow. He had been thrown all over the cabin during my hectic evasive manoeuvres, and had spent some time with his head pinned to the roof while we were in our final dive, and it was quite probably his first operational flight.

As we lay trembling in the ditch, with the last explosive convulsions of Treble Four dying down in the background, we exchanged a few whispered sentences. 'What do we do now?' said Bill. 'Well,' I said, 'I've no idea whether we're in enemy territory or not. As far as I'm concerned, I've had it. If anyone comes along, I'm giving myself up.' Bill nodded in agreement, and we lay there in silence for some time. Then we heard voices approaching, and instinctively we crouched lower in the ditch. There seemed to be quite a few people, and they stopped just a few feet from us, chattering and arguing in a language that I did not recognize. I peered at them between the branches. They seemed to be civilians, but in my state of shock I couldn't work out the situation. I lurched to my feet, and staggered out into the clearing, my hands raised above my head shouting, 'Kamerad! Kamerad!' at the top of my voice. I must have been a strange apparition—with my filthy uniform, my blackened face, and my shaking hands above my head. It's a wonder they didn't burst out laughing. As they jabbered away, I fumbled for my 'Useful phrases' pamphlet and desperately tried to find the appropriate page. With Bill and the other chap standing behind me, I tried to find out what nationality they were. 'Bosch?' I shouted. 'Bosch?' One of the women nodded. 'Yah, yah, Bosch' she said, nodding her head towards the oldest man in the group. Then they all joined in, pointing to the old man. 'Oh God,' I thought, if he's a German, I'll have to shoot him.' I groped for my .45 revolver, and got it halfway out of its holster. A few of the women ran towards me, shaking their heads, and shouting, 'No, no, no,' and with a gabble of mixed languages and smiles I somehow gathered that they were trying to tell me that he was their Boss—not a German at all. He was, in fact, the foreman in that part of the forest, and I also pieced together that the place was full of German troops, and it was imperative that we hid in the ditch until dark, when they would bring us food. I pointed to my now extremely painful face and they indicated that they would also bring a doctor. We fell back into the ditch, and suddenly they had all gone, and a heavy silence fell upon the whole place. For what seemed hours we heard nothing, and said nothing. Once we heard the unmistakable sound of a Spitfire approaching, and he eventually flew low right over our heads. 'A bit late now,' we thought bitterly, but we were too tired and confused to think of trying to attract his attention, and gradually the sound of his Merlin faded into the distance.

As dusk approached we again heard voices. It was the foreman and the village doctor, who seemed very out of place in the middle of a forest dressed in striped trousers, with a black jacket and a butterfly collar, with his little black bag in his hand. They had brought us some food, but as it was only bread and some very fatty bacon, I was unable to eat it in my condition. While Bill and our pannier-pushing friend picked at that, the doctor examined my face, which by now was extremely tender to the touch. He said nothing but clicked his tongue and shook his head as he smeared on some vaseline. Then he pulled out a bandage and tied it tightly round the left side of my head, so that I could only see out of my right eye. Neither of them spoke much English, but by their demeanour and constant glances over their shoulders we gathered that the Germans were not far away. As soon as my bandage was tightly secured, and the food basket was empty, they got out of the ditch, and, indicating to us by sign language that we were to stay put until they came to fetch us, they made their departure. Once again, a hush fell over the forest. Conversation between the three of us was not very brisk.

I was exhausted, shocked, and badly burned. The army bloke maintained a stunned silence. Bill was his usual cockney self, essaying a cheerful remark from time to time. My mind, what was left of it, was still going over and over the past hours, wondering what had gone wrong, and, worst of all, where I had gone wrong. There are so many 'if onlys' after something like this. If only I had closed the throttles when we dived for the cloud. If only we'd had some warning before the attack. If only I hadn't had George in, with a cup of tea in my hand. I couldn't stop thinking about it. And I couldn't go to sleep. Darkness came eventually and the foreman came back with another friend, and they led us, stumbling, along the ride to a log-cabin some miles away. Inside we found a strange collection of Dutchmen of all ages sitting round a table heavily loaded with drinks of all kinds. The leading light seemed to be the local religious leader, dressed in a monk's habit, and he had a smattering of schoolbook English.

I gathered that we were to spend most of the night there, and then, before dawn, would be taken somehow or other to the nearest 'Tommies'.

I told him about the three men who had been killed in the crash, and he replied solemnly: 'Do not worry. I will grave your friends.' He asked him to hand over to him my revolver, and when I pointed to his clothing with surprise, everybody laughed as he drew up the skirt of his habit and revealed a murderous collection of pistols, knives, and even hand-grenades. I gave him my .45 with pleasure and he added it to his stock amidst general laughter and approval from his comrades. After an hour or so of their excited jabbering, I grew tired, and made them understand that I needed some sleep. My face was giving me hell by now, and I could feel it swelling up under the bandage. Some doughty Dutchman saw my distress, and went to fetch a piece of cracked mirror. They all roared with laughter when I winced at what I saw. My lips had swollen from beneath the bandage, and I looked like a charred Satchmo. But the biggest shock, which of course the Dutch wouldn't be able to comprehend, was that my beloved moustache was gone, burned to the roots by the flames during the crash-landing. There wasn't really time to grieve over this loss; at least I was still alive, albeit face-naked. Bill and I crept up into the loft, and got a little fitful sleep before we were wakened again, this time to be piled into a two-wheeled farm-cart drawn by a jet-black cart horse.

It was a weird journey, the old cart rattling and bumping over the tufty grass in the wide fire-breaks of the forest. As our eyes became accustomed to the blackness, we peered into the gloomy trees, desperately hoping not to see any German troops. Suddenly in the darkness ahead, we saw a figure, and fear gripped my throat. But the old foreman drove the horse on until we were abreast of a shadowy Dutchman leaning on the saddle of his bicycle. We stopped for a moment, and he leaned forward to whisper the word 'Safe!'—and on we went. This happened several more times, until we realized that there was a whole team of foresters scouting ahead to see that all was clear. Then there happened one of those things that you laugh about afterwards, but which at the time had my hair standing on end. Bill suddenly evinced a desire to empty his bladder. There was nothing for it but to stop the waggon, let down the wooden flap at the back, and watch him drop out into the darkness to perform this urgent task. In the silence of this vital operation, all I could hear was the clink of the horse's bridle and the grunts of Bill's relief. And, as far as we knew, the forest was stiff with Germans. At last he finished the job and clambered back into the cart. The emergency was over. To this day Bill swears that it was I who had the leak, but there is no rancour in the argument.

At last we reached our destination, which turned out to be a slightly more substantial house right on the edge of the forest, with a reasonable road leading away into the countryside. Outside the front door stood an ancient saloon car, and we gathered that this was to be our escape vehicle. Our foreman friend who had been the first to help us said his farewells, turned the cart round, and was soon lost in the gloom of the forest. (Some fifteen years later I was to shake hands with him again when that jolly Irish genie Eamonn Andrews pulled him out of the hat during my ordeal in that macabre TV show 'This is Your Life.' His command of the English language had not improved, even then. He drew himself up, took a deep breath, marched forward with outstretched hand, and blurted out, 'Goot-bye!' 'Surely you mean "Hallo"?' I said jovially, hating it as much as he did.)

The crowd sitting round the table in this next house was larger and more animated than the last. Everyone was wearing a large yellow rosette, and all were brandishing firearms of some sort. The 'Tommies' were very near, they assured us, and they clearly thought that for them liberation was close at hand. As the schnapps circulated, their spirits rose, but I, for once, was in no condition to accept a drink. By this time I was nearing the end of my tether. My face was swelling every hour, the tightness of the bandage exacerbating the pain, and my brain was reeling with shock and fatigue. At last, dawn came, and it was deemed light enough to make the last dash to safety. We poured out of the house, and the three of us were crammed into the old car with as many Dutch patriots as could fit in. The rest clung on wherever they could, on the bonnet, the rear bumper and the two running boards, waving yellow scarves, and gesticulating with their pistols.

In this fashion, we careered along country lanes, turning this way and that, until once again I had lost all sense of direction. As we passed groups of other Dutch people by the roadside or in the fields, shouts of greeting were exchanged and great cheers went up. Clearly we were regarded as a triumphant prize. Suddenly, amidst the clamour and the dust and the wildness of it all, I saw straight ahead, smack in the middle of crossroads, standing erect and immaculate in his red peaked cap, gleaming white belt and even whiter gloves, the figure of a military policeman calmly directing the traffic. We had made it! As my heart surged with relief, we drew alongside him and our friends showered him with questions. He peered into the car, saw the dirty, singed RAF uniforms and my head swathed in bandages, and immediately gestured towards a hut not far away, with a large Red Cross flag beside it. As I entered this makeshift first-aid post our mad rescuers turned the car round, and made off back towards their village, still shouting and waving. Poor devils. I learned afterwards that, owing to the general slowness of the Army's advance, they had to go to ground again, and it was weeks before they were truly liberated.

DOWN BUT NOT OUT

IN THE FIRST-AID post, my bandage was quickly whipped off
to relieve the pressure on the swelling, and replaced with
proper dressings and a bag of lint with holes cut in for my
eyes and nose. I was given an injection of penicillin, and a
sedative, and large labels proclaiming this treatment were
tied to my battledress. On the other side of the hut sat a
surly blond young Luftwaffe pilot, and I wondered in a
confused way whether he might be the little sod who had
shot me down, but there was no way of finding out. Bill's
ankle was strapped up, and the three of us went outside to
a waiting ambulance, which was to take us south as quickly
as possible. Apparently my burn was more serious than I
had thought, and proper treatment was needed urgently.
On the grass beside the hut we saw a line of bloodstained
parachute harnesses; the eight occupants of a Dakota, we
were told, had been machine-gunned to death as they hung
in the air after baling out from their stricken aircraft.

The ambulance, driven by a private in the RAMC, set off
southward down the main road from Nijmegen to
Hertogenbosch. It was not a very wide road, and it soon
became clear that it was the only thing that the British
army held in that part of Holland. On either side, troops lay
on their stomachs manning machine-guns and up the
centre came a stream of tanks and personnel carriers.
Orders had been given that traffic went only one way—
forward—and more than once the helmeted commander of
a tank shouted to our driver to 'Get out of the bloody way.'
But each time he yelled back: 'Badly burned cases, sir,' and
we were allowed to pass. This was the nearest I ever got to

190

seeing the Army in action, and seemed to be nothing but noise and confusion to me. We passed over a bridge and into a small town, and, inexplicably, our driver took a right-hand turn. In next to no time the noise and confusion had gone, and we were travelling along a fairly quiet country lane, when the truth dawned on me. 'You bloody fool,' I screamed, 'you're driving straight towards the Germans!' 'I think you're right,' he called back, and swung the ambulance round and hared back into the town.

As we progressed slowly southwards, the sense of urgency subsided, and we pulled into Hertogenbosch in good order. There I was bundled into a bed in a huge marquee crammed with wounded, and after a further sedative injection, collapsed into a deep sleep.

When I awoke, my head still covered in a Ku-Klux-Klan style hood of lint and my battledress festooned with labels like a school trunk at the end of term, I said feebly to a doctor who leaned over me, 'I must get back to my squadron.' 'You are staying here, my boy,' was all he replied, and there I did indeed stay for several days.

Eventually the doctor considered me fit enough for further travel, and I was sent in another ambulance all the way to Brussels, where I found myself in a proper hospital, in a special ward for burns cases, which had only just been opened. In fact, I was their first customer, and sat up in my bed in lonely state for the first day. Then I was joined by another flight lieutenant, who listened patiently to my constant complaints and my frequent requests to be sent 'back to my bloody squadron.' Nearly three years later, when I was at the Windmill Theatre in Piccadilly, I was carousing in a nearby club between shows one day, when an RAF Flight Lieutenant came in and sat at the bar beside me. After a few minutes, he turned and said: 'You are Flight Lieutenant Edwards, aren't you?'

'How the hell do you know that?' I replied.

'My name is Hogan,' he said. 'I was in that burns ward with you in Brussels. I never actually saw your face, because of your lint bandage, but I'd know that bloody binding voice anywhere.' He was still serving in the RAF, and used to come up to town frequently to see the show and swap a few pints with me. That was the first inkling I had that my voice was in any way distinctive, but after eleven years of the BBC Radio show, 'Take It From Here' I grew accustomed to total strangers coming up to me and saying the same sort of thing. More recently, having grown a beard for the part of Mr Bumble in the musical *Oliver!*, people would say to me, 'I wasn't sure it was really you at first, but it was the voice that did it!'

Somehow or other I had now lost touch with both my fellow-survivors. The army private had been claimed by his own service, and Billy Randall, I supposed, was in a non-commissioned officers' ward somewhere. But I was too deranged to make it all out. Every day I repeated my request to get back to 271, but I was always fobbed off with 'You're not well enough to travel.' Then, one day, the doctor added: 'Besides, the casualty aircraft are fully loaded, and you must take your turn.' 'But you don't understand,' I yelled at him. 'That's the line that I'm in! Just get me down to Brussels airport and I'll hitch a ride back!'

Reluctantly he agreed, and a few hours later down on the tarmac at Brussels Ivere, I spotted a Dak from 48 Squadron, and the pilot gladly let me sit up in the cabin with him as we chugged back to DA. When I walked into Jouby's office and slung him up a somewhat sheepish salute, the old boy's eyes glistened as he grabbed my hand. I had been 'Missing, believed killed,' for a total of eight days. Jouby had himself telephoned my mother to say he was positive that he had seen Treble Four crash, and that there was no hope of my survival. Back at the Market Gardener they had had a two-minute silence for me. And in my Nissen hut, Tim Beddow, who had been appointed my executor, was about to hold an auction of all my kit.

I was interrogated pretty thoroughly by the Intelligence Officer as soon as I was well enough to stand it. He questioned me closely about what had happened to my revolver. For a moment I thought I was going to have to sign another blasted form and pay for the blooming thing, but he decided it was now being put to good use. The three RASC men, I was told, had been posted as 'Missing', so I was able to tell him emphatically that there was absolutely no hope for them, and that their unit must definitely post them as 'Killed in Action': I only mention that because it had the most astonishing and touching sequel. Some time in the 1970s, I was touring with a show in New Zealand, and one evening had an unexpected visit from a young woman who had emigrated from the UK. She told me, very simply, that she was the sister of one of these unfortunate men. The whole family had gone through a harrowing two weeks, not knowing for certain what had happened to the poor chap. Then they heard what I had said in my report. 'Thank you, Mr Edwards,' she said, 'for putting us out of our misery.' She then thrust a silver cigarette-box into my hands, turned, and left the theatre without even giving me her name.

My stay at Down Ampney was short-lived. The MO soon decided that my burns were beyond the scope of our small hospital, so I was sent to a larger establishment near Swindon. Here again the doctor clicked their tongues and shook their heads, and it was decided on a further move, this time to a place that had a special ward exclusively for burns. When I heard that I was to be sent in an ambulance in the company of one other burned flight lieutenant, to RAF Ely, I quickly got out my map and saw that with very little detour we could go through Barnes on the way. 'It doesn't matter to me,' said the corporal who was to drive. And my fellow burnee, whose hands had been the target for the flames, was equally co-operative. So off we set. It was a Sunday, and I timed the whole thing perfectly, making a spectacular entrance into Albert's saloon bar just when the lunch-time session was at its zenith. As I walkd through the door, Albert was in the act of drawing a pint. He looked up, saw me through his thick pebble glasses, said—'Gorblimey, it's Jim!' and pulled on the pump with such ferocity and glee that bitter poured all over the floor. My Ku-Klux-Klan hood was no handicap when it came to downing a pint, and of course all the drugs that I had been taking enhanced my euphoria, with the result that it was two very drunken officers who reeled into the hospital at Ely. The Matron was furious. 'They told me to expect two serious burns cases,' she stormed, 'and I have cleared a special ward for you. And then you arrive in this condition.

Well, really!' We giggled feebly, and fell into bed.

The next few days were tough. The medics had just come up with an entirely new treatment for skin burns. The idea, quite simply, was to wash the wound with a saline solution, and at the same time scrape away the scabs with a pair of surgical tweezers. This had to be done every day, and in this way new skin would grow, and with any luck there would be no scar. On the first day, as I sat in the bath, a corporal medical orderly carefully removed my bandages, and inspected the wreck of the left side of my face. 'I'm afraid, sir,' he said softly, 'I'm afraid I shall have to shave you first. You see, sir, you've got quite a stubble there now, and it will only encourage germs.' I moaned in disbelief. 'I'll be as careful as I can, sir. And I'll change the blade as often as you like.'

I don't remember how many blades he used, but there was a lot of swearing by me before he had finished. Next, he very gently covered the whole area with something called Tullegras, which in effect was fine lace curtain material cut into small squares and steeped in vaseline. Then another bandage was wound round my head, and on went another lint mask.

The unusual feature about this ward was that it catered for All Ranks. It mattered not whether you were an officer, a sergeant, or the lowliest of the low—as long as you'd been through the flames, you were welcome. My routine was simple. Every morning I sat in my saline bath and suffered the torture of the tweezers. Then, with a new dressing to ease the smarting pain, the rest of the day was mine. To begin with I stayed in the smaller room with my new friend with the burned hands, but very soon my spirits picked up, and I would don a blue dressing-gown and wander into the main ward to chat with the other cases. Some enlightened MO had decided that all burns cases should enjoy an ample diet. After all, there was nothing much wrong with our bodily functions, and I suppose we needed our morale building up after suffering from so much shock. We tucked into three good meals a day, and—this was the gilt on the lily—we were allowed a bottle of beer each per day. Needless to say, I soon found one or two chicken-hearts who didn't want to drink their ration—and once again, my allocation of cigarettes came in handy when the bartering began. It was now just a question of patiently waiting for the new skin to grow on my face.

Those of us who could get about easily were given little odd jobs to do, and our spare time was spent sitting round a table in the middle of the ward, chatting and playing cards or chess. They were a fascinating bunch.

At the bottom of the ladder were two airmen who had been hoisting a large flare into the belly of a Lancaster when it slipped and fell on to the tarmac. Their burns were not too serious, but the flash had temporarily blinded them. Their main worry was that it had been mostly their fault, and they kept asking me: 'Do you think we'll get court-martialled?' I did my best to allay their fears, but, with my sketchy knowledge of things disciplinary, I wasn't much help.

There was a corporal whose job was to tend the huge engine of an air-sea-rescue launch. While they were sitting below decks one day out in the North Sea, some sort of leak had developed in the exhaust system, and the escaping fumes had knocked him unconscious. He slumped over the red-hot engine casing, and it was only the smell of burning flesh finding its way up on deck that had saved his life. His whole right forearm was in a shocking mess—but he smiled bravely and never complained.

I recall also a good-looking young sergeant pilot who had various minor burns, but whose jaw had been fractured when his Hurricane fighter crashed. His jaw bones had been screwed together, so that the break could heal, so he had to talk with clenched teeth, as it were. When he got angry or impatient and tried to shout he literally foamed at the mouth, and some of the unkinder inmates would deliberately get him going so that they could enjoy his frenzies of frustration. It was quite impossible to tell what sort of an accent he had, and I had great fun privately trying to assess his real voice. Eventually his jaws were unscrewed, and gradually, day by day, he regained the use of them. To my intense surprise there emerged the cultured tones of a university man.

Our most senior inmate was a squadron leader who had

received his wound in a very ungallant manner. He wore pilot's wings, and had a few gongs under them as well, but one night, at a Mess party to celebrate something or other, late at night he had clumsily reloaded his cigarette lighter to overflowing, and foolishly struck the flint before the stuff had time to evaporate. Naturally the whole thing burst into flames, and, in his drunken state, he had just stood there, laughing, with flames shooting from his hand, without feeling any pain. When his second-degree burn had finally healed, it was adjudged a self-inflicted wound, and he was presented with a bill for his food and drink. He was the only one among us who didn't join in the general laughter.

One night my room-mate and I were woken by the nurses and unceremoniously bundled into the larger ward. The reason was soon clear. A young pilot, whose plane had crashed that night not far away as he came back from a raid, was wheeled in on a bed surrounded by nursing staff with all sorts of medical apparatus. He had received such terrible burns that there was little chance of his surviving, but all night long we heard the sisters fighting to save his life. Then, towards dawn, we heard his rate of breathing start to rise in a ghastly crescendo, and then suddenly stop. Sadly, they trundled him out through our ward, and we knew that, in the familiar Service slang expression 'he'd had it'. You had to try to be philosophical about these things, but there was a gloom over the games table next day.

One morning the Matron came bustling in with a special air of urgency. There was to be an inspection by a senior medico, and she wanted everything to be 'just so'. In fact, she prepared the whole thing with all the precision of a command performance. Standing in the middle of the ward, she gave her orders. 'Now, that man will be having his bandages changed. And you over there, will be having your blood-pressure checked. And, nurse, you will be taking this man's temperature. And you, Mr Edwards, will be having your saline bath.' I dutifully went and sat in it, and the corporal stood with his tweezers poised for action, but our VIP visitor failed to arrive on time. As the air of urgency gradually evaporated, I got the corporal to fetch me a book, and sat reading whilst he occasionally topped me up with hot water. Then suddenly, in she darted, snatched the book away, and ushered in the great plastic surgeon, Wing Commander MacIndoe, who, we learned, made frequent tours of all the RAF burns units, looking for serious cases to work on. He bent over me, put his hand on my forehead, and with his thumb gently opened wide my left eye. Then he straightened himself up, and said with a smile. 'Well, my boy. They didn't even get your eyelashes.' Then he was gone. Our paths didn't cross again until years after the war, when he had been knighted for his wonderful work, and I was invited down to East Grinstead to entertain the Guinea Pigs. It was incredible to feel the warmth of affection that this band of disfigured aircrew had for the man who had operated on them all, and whom they laughingly referred to as 'the Butcher'. I have been there several times since, and being with these men always makes me feel how lucky I was to get away as lightly as I did.

It was naturally a relief to know that I was not in need of plastic surgery, but I still had to go through my daily torture in the saline bath, with the corporal picking away with his tweezers. My left ear seemed to have caught the worst of it, and I began to worry when I woke up one night with the most awful pain up there. I sent for the night nurse, and she introduced me to a new pain-killer called Vegenin. In ten minutes the hurting stopped as if by magic, and I was soon asleep again. But it didn't seem to be long before it was back again with twice the ferocity. I asked for more Vegenin, and it was duly crushed up in a pestle and mortar and mixed with water for me to swallow. Next morning, when my dressing was removed, I told the nurse, 'This will have to be operated on.' 'Stuff and nonsense,' she said, in that way that nurses have, and for two days this running battle went on. I even got my watch out and timed the sequence of events. Exactly ten minutes after the Vegenin, the pain went. Three hours later, it came back. 'You're just becoming a Vegenin baby,' the nurse said sarcastically. Then, on the third day, the senior surgeon came round for an inspection. I asked for the bandage to be removed, and he took a long and searching look at the ear.

'Yes,' he said. 'Nurse, I shall have to operate on this.' I grinned in triumph, and behind his back gave her the two-finger sign. Then I looked at my watch. 'More Vegenin please,' I said, and she stomped away to prepare it.

The top part of the ear had become infected with streptococcus, and the operation to remove it, performed by Wing Commander Morley, did not take very long. Whilst coming round from the anaesthetic, I dreamed that I was trying to fight my way out of a huge paper bag, and when I finally woke, two nurses were desperately trying to hold me down on my bed. Apparently I had given them a terrible struggle.

This was the first time I had ever been subjected to 'the knife' and the recovery was not much fun. The surgeon had left a piece of narrow rubber tubing embedded in the ear so that the poison could drain away, and this remained there for several days, until it felt as though it was actually growing into the ear. 'How the hell are you going to get that out?' I asked Nurse Riley. 'It'll mean yet another operation.' 'What nonsense you do talk, Flying Officer,' she said crushingly, as she bent over the ear. I didn't notice the large pair of tweezers in her hand. Then: 'What's that aircraft going by, Flying Officer?' she asked. I glanced out of the window to astonish her with my knowledge of aeronautics, and let out a piercing oath as the most horrendous burning pain shot through my ear. She stood up and waved the rubber tubing gaily in front of me. 'There we are. That didn't take long, did it?'

Today she lives not more than five miles from me in Sussex. She says she still remembers me as the most difficult patient she ever had, and I can quite believe her.

The actual wound healed up steadily, but it remained very tender for a long time, and, of course, a chunk of ear was missing. At first, I was extremely self-conscious about this, imagining myself as some sort of freak, but over the years I got used to it, and after leaving the Air Force I was able to grow my hair a little longer and camouflage the whole thing, so that nobody ever notices it these days. More important, my hearing was not affected.

One day, in the middle of one of our innumerable games of cards, a nurse came in with a telegram. 'It's for you, Mr

Edwards.' Who the . . . ? What the . . . ! I opened it, dreading bad news. Then I stood up and shouted: 'Hey fellows! They've given me the DFC!' There was a chorus of congratulation, but my jubilation was tempered when I heard a much-battered veteran from Bomber Command telling the chap in the next bed: 'Old Edwards has got a chop-gong.'

On my return to Down Ampney, dear old Jouby was in a bit of a predicament. I had been categorized as totally unfit for flying, so strictly speaking he should have had me posted somewhere for other duties, but he seemed loath to part with me. Our new CO, Group Captain Howie, came to the rescue by appointing me Station Entertainments Officer.

This was really a bit of a sinecure and I filled the post happily for the next three or four months. I was in complete charge of the recreation hall, and was expected to arrange shows, talent contests, bingo and all the things that were supposed to make life on the camp more agreeable.

One of the CO's ideas was that, at precisely eleven o'clock each morning, I should go down to the Operations Room and announce over the tannoy all the fun that was to take place that evening. The loudspeakers were placed all around the aerodrome, so that everybody could hear the good news. I decided that the bulletin should be preceded by the playing of the RAF March Past, but as this was in the days before tapes and cassettes, the only thing available was a 78 record, played on a portable, hand-wound gramophone. A/C2 Vicars solemnly held the lot in front of the microphone, and on a signal from me, moved majestically away to create a 'fade-out' effect. Then I went into my introduction: 'Good morning everybody. Here is your entertainment for today, and this is your Entertainments Officer reading it. Tonight in the Rec Hall . . .' Group Captain Howie had said to me firmly: 'No jokes, Edwards.' Weeks later I discovered that at exactly eleven o'clock he used to open his office window to monitor my performance.

Another aspect of my duties was to look after the casts

of the ENSA shows that visited us from time to time. This then was my first fleeting contact with 'show business', and a funny lot they were. Usually we were sent a concert party, full of ageing comedians and singers, with a smattering of fumbling jugglers and inept conjurors, but now and again we got a bit of culture in the shape of a play. These were the ones I found difficult to sell to the chaps. For one heavy play the bookings were so bad that I went to the CO and said, 'I'm afraid the hall's going to be pretty empty tonight, sir.' 'Use your brain, Edwards,' he roared. 'Get the janker-wallahs in.' The janker-wallahs, poor devils, had to sit mournfully through some classical three-act play and were not allowed to leave in the interval.

After the show it was my task to take the performers back to the Officers' Mess for refreshment. A few miserable sandwiches were passed round, and then I made my usual speech. 'Ladies and gentlemen, thank you for your splendid show'—(a hyprocrite at this early age)—'What would you like to drink? We have all the beer you want, or there is one bottle of gin—hands up for beer?' No reaction. 'Hands up for gin?' Every actor's hand shot into the air.

The only snag with the job was that I was forced to attend every one of the shows, and many times it was an ordeal. But I should not denigrate the artists, some of whom had come out of retirement to 'give the lads some fun'. Years later I was to be called upon to entertain the Forces myself, but that was in the heyday of 'Take It From Here' and 'Whacko!'. It happened that some trouble-maker of an MP stood up in the House of Commons and asked, 'Why aren't the stars entertaining the Lads?' And I soon found myself volunteering for a tour which took in Kenya, Aden and Cyprus.

There were five of us in the cast. Janet Brown—now famous for her impersonations of Mrs Thatcher; Maggie Mitchel, a Scots girl with a lovely voice; Clifford Stanton, who did brilliant impressions with rubber masks; Harry Jacobson, an accomplished pianist who had played for some of the great cabaret artists of the day—and myself.

By the time we reached Africa the worst of the Mau-Mau business was over, but there were still considerable mopping-up operations taking place, and plenty of troops to entertain. Our reception everywhere was rapturous, as we travelled extensively through the beautiful landscapes of Kenya.

We kicked off at the RAF station near Nairobi, where naturally I felt quite at home, but the rest of the tour was all army camps. There was a lot of road travelling and most of the stages were improvised affairs in Nissen huts or even tents. One night the audience were sitting in full battle kit, with rifles in their hands, when suddenly a bugle-call rang out, and they all leaped to their feet and ran out, leaving a handful of officers and admin. staff to watch the remainder of the show.

We flew from there to Aden where it was so hot and humid that I got through a whole bottle of gin one night and sweated it all out without getting the slightest bit tiddly. In that show, Maggie was singing the famous song 'Hey, There!'. She had just got to the line, 'Are you not seeing things too clear?' when the generator failed and all the lights went out. We finished with the aid of a hundred or so torches which the lads had obligingly been carrying with them. She was just as unlucky in Cyprus. We were doing our show on a platform erected at one end of a disused quarry. Several hundred airmen had climbed on to the corrugated iron roof of a latrine situated outside the arena—thus avoiding a small entry charge. At almost exactly the same place in poor Maggie's tear-jerking song the entire roof collapsed with a tremendous bang, and the chaps were all thrown to the ground, amid scenes of great confusion. That same night, we were on our way to Famagusta in a small RAF bus sandwiched between a tank and a heavily armoured jeep, and the terrorists threw a bomb at us from clump of bushes. It bounced across the road and exploded harmlessly in the ditch—but not before I had thrown myself on to the floor, with the girls on top of me! I needed copious quantities of alcohol to get me through the show that night. The organizer of the tour begged me not to mention the incident to the Press, but before midnight one of the London papers was on the telephone asking for the story and next morning my agent almost had a stroke.

201

At Down Ampney in 1944 we threw no bombs at our entertainers—though we often felt like it.

Much later during the BBC radio series 'Does The Team Think?' one questioner asked, 'What do members of the team think when they have things thrown at them?' After we had all reminisced about the various occasions when audiences had thrown pennies and other things at us from the gallery, I said to the young man: 'What prompted you to put this interesting question?' 'Well,' he replied, 'I was a member of the Forces in the convoy guarding you in Cyprus that memorable night when the terrorists threw a bomb at you.' 'Ah' I said, in my most pompous manner, 'I recall it well. I formed the conclusion that the enemy took me for somebody of importance.' Quick as a flash, Ted Ray interrupted, 'Lord Kitchener, probably!'

I included my trombone act in shows so often that Group Captain Howie said one day: 'Edwards, if you play that bloody thing again, I'll have you posted.' A few weeks later I staged a Hidden Talent contest, and asked him if he would be good enough to be one of the judges. He accepted with some reluctance. There were so few entries, and the show was obviously going to be so short, that at the end I brought out my faithful slush-pump yet again, and launched myself into the now familiar act. I'll never forget the Groupie sitting in the front row, purple-faced, waving his fist at me. But he relented, and allowed me to stay on.

It was another period of pretty heavy drinking. After all, my daytime duties were not onerous, and I had far too many evenings free to tank it up in the Mess, or go out on pub crawls round the villages of Gloucestershire. The wartime beer was pretty weak, and one had to consume vast quantities to become even moderately tiddly, so my bladder would often cry out for relief in the middle of the night. Our Nissen hut had no latrine attached to it, and often I would wake up in the pitch dark, and stumble about clumsily trying to find the door. Sometimes, in desperation, I would grope about for a flying-boot, and empty myself into that. Unfortunately I was not always able, in my state of extremis, to locate one of my own boots, and in the morning I several times heard the cry, 'Edwards, you bastard, you've pissed in my flying-boot!'

YOU'VE DONE ENOUGH

AT LONG LAST I felt bold enough to start, somewhat tentatively, a further attempt at a really presentable moustache. I was worried that the 'burning off' might have ruined my chances for ever, but how wrong I was! This time it really went away nicely, and I was soon sporting something that I could be proud of. There may be some parallel here with the 'burning off' that farmers do to stubble, or does that sound too far-fetched? The fact is that this model eventually blossomed into the one that I took out into civilian life, and I kept it, gradually expanding, for many years. Dick Bentley's jokes about it in 'Take It From Here' were to make our radio audiences aware of its existence, and on television later, in 'Whacko!', it was there for all to see. It became so long in the end that I had to start twirling it up with Pomade Hongroise, a wax that has been used by dandies over the centuries. Together with 'RAF' Hooper, the well-known cartoonist, I started 'The Handlebar Club', and I formulated this splendid rule for eligibility. The moustache must be 'a hirsute appendage, of reasonable proportions, with graspable extremities.' The length of it was not the criterion . . . it was quality we were after. I am sorry to say that I never did win the prize for the 'Prime Handlebar', but I kept on trying.

Then I was offered the part of John Jorrocks on BBC2, and Peter Dew somehow or other persuaded me so shave it all off (I must have been drunk to agree!). Once again I walked the streets naked. It was a ghastly experience, never to be repeated. My friends didn't know me, and on the polo ground at Cowdray someone said just before a match, 'Could we be introduced to the stranger? Oh, my God, Jimmy, it's you!!' As soon as the series was over I stopped shaving my upper lip, and then added sideboards for good measure. It's gone completely white these days, but, as I explain to the inquisitive, 'It bleached in the Australian sun.'

At last my time came to be drawn back into the war. On 3 April 1945, after one of my frequent medical checks, I was officially recategorized A2H BH UK Only. This meant that I was fit enough to fly as a captain of aircraft on operational duties, but not overseas. First of all, though, I had to find out if I still had the ability to fly. My great pal, Tim Beddow, now a squadron leader, and OC 'B' Flight, undertook the task of giving me a check-out flight. We went up together in a Dak, and after one hour and forty minutes of 'circuits and bumps' we both realized that I had not lost the knack, and accordingly I started on what was to be a couple of months of 'odds and sods' flying—trips hither and thither in England, taking people on leave, fetching beer and generally helping out so that fitter pilots could do the more important stuff. I was still pretty nervous, and did a lot of looking over my shoulder, but my confidence gradually returned. My left ear was fully healed but very tender, and I found the American-style earphones, standard in the Dak, very painful to wear. So I went to Stores and got one of the old-style Biggles helmets, which were made of soft leather, and had it adapted for the American plug. I caused a few raised eyebrows, but I carried it with me everywhere.

Soon I was back on to the Oxford as well. My friend IVJ came back from Italy, and after his disembarkation leave, I obligingly wangled a Dak out of Tim, and went and took him from Croydon to his new posting at Kirton-in-Lindsey, just outside Lincoln. Later he was to ask me another big favour. His old squadron was having a big booze-up at Tangmere in Sussex, so I took him there, spent the night and joined in the celebrations. This trip was in an Oxford, and they had a thick perspex roof over the pilot's head, which really magnified the effect of the sun on your head. We were having an unusual heatwave at the time, and I soon learned that the most effective head-gear was an old-fashioned straw boater. On the morning after the party I was taxiing out for take-off, in shirtsleeves and with my boater perched cheekily on my head, when a staff car came roaring out from the control tower to intercept me. I slammed on the brakes, and an Air Vice Marshal jumped out, ran to the aircraft, and opened the back door. It was the legendary 'Batchy' Atcheley, whom I had met at the party. He took one look at me, said, 'Carry on, old boy,' and slammed the door shut. He had thought that I was a civilian stealing one of his aircraft.

Strictly speaking, I should have been 'severely repri-manded' for flying in civilian clothes, but he wasn't the sort of chap to do that. In Fighter Command things were different.

None of these journeys contributed materially to the war effort, and were known in RAF jargon as 'Charley trips'. I was in the air almost every day doing one of these, and they make strange reading in my log-book. On 25 April 1945, I read, for example, that I flew from Down Ampney to Mendlesham (wherever that is!) and thence to Doncaster (where I probably dropped off Flight Sergeant Green, who had an antique shop in the town), and then we tootled off to Thornaby, Renfrew, Carlisle, Ringway (Manchester) and finally back to base—a total of roughly six hours in the air. Apparently we landed at Ringway because we were running short of fuel, for I added in my then quite legible hand-writing—'Big scare! Rockets, flares, blood-waggon, fire-tender—the works!!' I pain-stakingly noted all these aerodromes down in a list at the back of my log-book, and by the end of the war had landed at over 150 different places.

After a couple of months 'charleying' about the sky, I had a further medical check, and was pronounced fit enough to relaunch myself on the Continent. Soon I was flying freight and passengers to airstrips in France and Belgium, and even got as far as Copenhagen, where I noted 'first drink of SNAPS'—I enjoyed the stuff, but couldn't remember how to spell it. Often the return load was twenty or so stretcher case but it was about this time that we began to repatriate unfortunates who had been held as prisoners-of-war. Among those who had the privilege of being brought home courtesy of Jimair were Captain Lord Hopetoun and Captain the Earl of Haig, son of the great Field Marshal. Often I would invite one or two into the cockpit, and enjoy the looks of rapture on their faces when they caught their first glimpse of the white cliffs of Dover after so many years behind bars.

One evening we were lumbering across the English Channel carrying a load of miscellaneous freight which I hadn't even bothered to check, but which I assumed contained stores for the NAAFI and other inconsequential items, when my wireless operator (Bill Randall was now flying with Jim MacNeil, who had been elevated to Skipper), presented me with a message he had just received from Base. All it said, quite simply, was: 'Hostilities have ceased.' I stared at it in wonderment. It had never occurred to me that the war might one day end! After a long silence in the cockpit, I looked over my shoulder at the crates of junk in the aircraft. 'What do we do?' I said to the chaps. 'Open the doors and chuck this lot out?' There seemed to me no point in spending more effort and money taking stores to the battle-zone if we had already won the war. 'I'll ask,' said my W/Op, and a few minutes later came back with the cryptic message, 'Complete Mission', and so we went to Brussels and got plastered there.

So we had vanquished the Hun. Well, well, well. Who'd have thought it! But it wasn't just a matter of 'That's that. Now we can all get back to normal.' Far from it. Our work-load increased as we took more and more useless junk to Europe, and brought more and more casualties and prisoners-of-war back. And there were regular courier runs to do, linking up out of the way aerodromes with England, and delivering mail and newspapers to all three Services.

Then it was announced that we would have one day set aside to celebrate the victory. 'V-E Day' it was to be called, and Group Captain Howie set me, as Entertainments Officer, the solemn task of organizing 'the biggest piss-up that's ever been known', as he so graphically put it. 'First night, all ranks in the Officers' Mess; second night, all ranks in the airmen's canteen.' I set about my task with a will. As a transport squadron, we had a wonderful opportunity for stocking up the bar and the kitchen with the best of everything from the capitals of Europe, and during the next few days every captain who was flying anywhere interesting was charged by me with the duty of bringing back local goodies. Vast barrels of beer were fetched from our contacts in Doncaster and even Glasgow, so that by the time the doors opened on V-E Day the locals who had been invited by the CO were staggered by the display, and many actually thought that we lived in this luxury all the time. I had been up to Kirton-in-Lindsey in an Oxford to fetch IVJ so that he could join in the fun. Jouby happily authorized the trip as yet another 'Navigation exercise', and by midnight the floor was literally awash with beer. Some fool had broached a barrel without ensuring that there was a tap available, and the amber fluid gushed out as I exhorted all and sundry to bring their tea-mugs and catch as much of it as they could. Then, in an inspired moment, I went out into the nearby paddock and returned triumphantly leading a huge black carthorse mare, who splashed round the Mess until the owner, our local farmer, dragged her out again protesting that she was in foal and the excitement might well bring on a premature birth. But nothing mattered. At least, not to us. The carousing continued until the early hours, and next day we were at it again at lunchtime. At one stage our revered Station Commander toured the aerodrome sitting on the roof of his staff car, a bowler hat perched rakishly on his head, and a WAAF perched precariously on each knee. In the senior doctor's office, into which we had carried our pints on a purely social visit, the group captain picked up the phone to make a call. While he was speaking, I came across a pair of medical scissors and, giggling drunkenly, literally cut him off in mid-sentence. Nothing mattered.

Somehow I had to face up to the coming orgy in the Airmen's Mess. I consulted the venerable doctor. 'Here,' he said, 'take two of these, Edwards. They'll keep you going.'

Keep me going! Little did I know that the pills were benzedrine. At seven o'clock the next morning, when finally the all-ranks party ended, I was still so wide awake that I got out my twelve-bore and staggered out to shoot something. There was nothing about for me to slaughter, until, right outside the group captain's hut, an old rook hove into sight. In spite of my condition, I downed him with one barrel. As I picked my wretched victim up, the CO opened his window. 'What the bloody hell d'you think you're doing, Edwards?' he yelled. Grinning feebly, I held up the stricken bird. 'Just shot you your breakfast, sir,' I said, and tottered off to bed. I was due to fly that morning at eleven o'clock. Never have I been so glad of George. I put him in at about fifty feet.

At this stage, now that the Luftwaffe was no longer airborne, we were using quite a lot of their captured aerodromes, rather than the makeshift strips hurriedly put together by our troops. We found that the German Brylcream boys had certainly lived in style. Not only was the accommodation lavish, but there were certain installations which spoke volumes for their lifestyle. At Celle, for example, where I night-stopped more than once, the loo on the Officers' Mess revealed a very strange amenity. Along the wall was a line of what at first glance looked like washbasins. But above, at head-height there was a metal plunger: when you pressed this with your forehead, the basin was automatically flushed. In simple terms, they were puking machines, which our gallant adversaries apparently used when they had overloaded themselves with booze and wished to carry on with the debauch. A trick they pinched off the Romans?

I had lunch in Leipzig one day, and noted in my log-book, 'German Sausage and Lager . . . Lovely!' That same night I stopped in Pilsen in Czechoslovakia, and a memorable occasion it was indeed. As we assembled in the Mess for the evening session, we were addressed by a grave-voiced wing commander.

'Gentlemen,' he began solemnly, 'we have just been informed that in two weeks' time the line of demarcation is to be altered, and this aerodrome will be in Russian territory. Also we have only today discovered Hermann Goering's private stock of French champagne. Gentlemen . . . it must be drunk before the Ruskies arrive.'

We needed no second bidding, and set about our task with unmatched zeal. It's the only time in my life I have woken up in the morning underneath a grand piano with my hand on the pedals.

I seemed to be able to recover from these debauches quite easily, and my confidence as a pilot was now fully restored. You might say that I was a flying advertisement for Alka Seltzer. I was in the air almost every day, but the trips did not always take me to Europe. There were still all the mundane tasks to perform, like testing aircraft when they had been serviced or giving ATC cadets air experience. The tests were quite fun, even though there was always the lurking thought that something might have been left undone, or some nut or bolt improperly adjusted. To make certain that the groundcrew had done their stuff properly, the corporal in charge was by custom obliged to accompany us on these trips, and the sight of his ashen face as he stood behind the two pilots on take-off always amused me. A casual remark such as, 'Starboard engine seems to be running a bit rough,' would drain the blood from his face.

In Frankfurt I visited Supreme Headquarters Allied Expeditionary Force (SHAEF) a couple of times and logged my first experience of southern fried chicken with some satisfaction. There were frequent trips to Brussels, including one in which my load was £28,000 worth of Belgian currency. Then I was sent on detachment to Northolt, where we concentrated entirely on passenger work. More often than not it was simply a case of taking ATS girls to and fro on leave, it being deemed unwise to shove them on to troop trains and leave them to the tender mercies of the soldiery. Naturally, one took the opportunity to show off to the prettier ones. 'Would you care to come up into the cockpit, my dear?' 'Oh yes, sir. I'd love to.' 'Get into the second pilot's seat, my dear. He'd like to go back and visit your friends.' 'Ooh, I say! What a lot of instruments! I don't know how you understand them all!'

'Oh, it's nothing really. Piece of cake in fact.' And so on.

There were lots of regular flights to do as well—'Courier runs', they were called. A favourite was Northolt-Paris-Rennes - Bordeaux - Toulouse - Marseilles - Lyons - Paris - Northolt—picking up passengers and delivering mail right round France. This run was supposed to take only a couple of days, but I managed to stretch it on one occasion at the suggestion of one of my passengers. He was a flight lieutenant in the Intelligence Branch I think, and spoke fluent French. As we approached Toulouse he said casually as he stood in the cockpit: 'I suppose you know Toulouse is noted for having the finest brothels in the country?' 'Really!' I replied, not wanting to show too much eagerness. 'We're not scheduled to night-stop, you know.' 'Pity,' says Flight Lieutenant Ball (I still remember the villain's name—nicknamed 'Tess', of course), 'I hear they have a wonderful reputation. Shame to miss the opportunity. You'll think of something.'

So, after we'd landed, I said casually to the flight sergeant in charge of the groundcrew, 'Don't like the sound of the starboard engine. I think we'd better spend the night while you have a look at it.' I gave him a wink, and he grinned as he replied, 'I understand perfectly sir. We'll have a look at it straight away.' Out came a ladder, and off came the cowling, and off we went into the town on our wicked quest. 'But how do we actually find a brothel if you've never been here before?' I asked in my innocence. 'Oh,' says Tess casually, 'we'll simply ask a policeman. They always know.' In a few minutes we spied a gendarme, whistle in mouth, directing the traffic with raucous panache. Tess leaped out of the truck and was quickly in gesticulatory conversation with the gallant Gaul. He was soon back, having been given the address. We found the place easily enough, the door that discreet inch ajar, and the girls were on parade in no time. I chose mine with some diffidence, never having visited such a place before, and followed her upstairs with mounting excitement. This was going to be quite an experience! But my ardour was dashed when she got out a chipped enamel basin and proceeded to fill it with warm water and mix the permanganate of potash. The previous time I had used it was for a bad case of athlete's foot! End of visit to 'Les Violets de Toulouse'!

This period at Northholt turned out to be unexpectedly useful in nudging me towards my subsequent career. I have often said, in my rambling, shambling, after-lunch speeches, that in our profession there are only three essentials. A certain amount of talent, of course. A stroke or two of luck. And stamina. My stroke of luck at this stage was that Tim Beddow's sister, Miranda, lived in Ruislip, just a mile or two from Northolt, and she worked for the BBC.

One night, at an Officers' Mess Party, she suddenly said to me, 'Why don't you do a broadcast about your experiences at Arnhem?' Flown with wine as I no doubt was, I immediately accepted the idea, and next day started work on what eventually became a fifteen-minute broadcast entitled 'Treble-Four: The Story of a Glider-Tug'. It was put out after the 1 o'clock news one day whilst I was on leave in Barnes. Listening to it now, one is struck by the change that has taken place in my voice. Then it was clipped, and British, and terribly self-conscious, and much higher in tone. I don't let many people hear the record. But it served its purpose, and I still have in my possession a letter from the then RAF Director of Public Relations thanking me for doing it. My mother was delighted by it too, and I went on a typical Barnes pub-crawl that night with a certain pride. This was short-lived, however. In the Hare and Hounds in East Sheen there was usually quite a collection of RAF types, and that evening I ordered my first pint wondering how I could bring the subject round to The Big Broadcast. Thank goodness I didn't open my mouth, for just behind me I heard an obvious Bomber Command type holding forth on the subject. 'Did you hear that clot on the BBC at lunchtime today?' he boomed. 'What an idiot. Ten thousand feet over enemy territory with George in. Serves him bloody well right.' I drank my pint and slunk away. But at least I had made my first nationwide broadcast in England.

Now my happy two-year association with 271 Squadron was to end. The war against Hitler had been over for some months, and the conflict against Japan began to loom on our horizon. On return to Down Ampney, I was told that the whole unit had been instructed to prepare to fly to the Far East, but my restricted medical category precluded my going with them.

'This time, Jim,' said Jouby, 'I shall have to post you.' I was having a thorough medical check-up at the Air Ministry every six months, but, although I was considered fit enough to dash all over Europe by night and day, the medicos would not sign me out as fit for anywhere else. Quite how or why I was selected to join 24 Squadron, who flew VIPSs out of Hendon, I never found out. But I suppose I should have been flattered. Whatever the reason, on 5 August 1945, Lieutenant Colonel Joubert signed me out as an 'Above Average Transport Pilot', and added, as further consolation, 'a good all-weather pilot.' I had done something like 600 hours with 271, and look back on those years as the happiest in my RAF career. Perhaps 'fulfilling' would be a better word, because for the first time since the whole thing began, I saw the war effort at close quarters, and what's more, actually took part in it. We were a happy station, and I played my part in that as well. We were intensely proud that a member of our squadron was awarded a posthumous VC. He was Flight Lieutenant 'Lumme' Lord, who was killed on the same day that I was shot down. He was making a third pass over Arnhem to drop supplies, with one engine on fire, when the whole thing blew up.

24 Squadron at Hendon was a totally different cup of tea. When carrying passengers we were required to take to the air wearing best blue. Gone were the days of the scruffy battledress and rakish cap with a split peak and whitewash. Gone was 'walk round it once and kick the tyres'. Gone, too, were split-arse approaches and carefree landings. And there was so little accommodation available in the Mess that I was asked to billet myself at home in Barnes. This was fine on non-working days, but when my presence was required it meant chugging round the North Circular

Road, early enough to be on parade at 8 a.m. And when I say 'parade', that's exactly what it was. No breezing into the flight office and asking cheerily, 'What's on today, chaps?' We all formed up on the tarmac and did all that stuff about 'Officers . . . outwards TURN!' At Down Ampney we'd gone a bit rusty on all that, and I was soon in trouble. Often I was simply too late for the show. Or I'd arrive with seconds to go and be told it was 'Greatcoats today, Edwards!' and be sent off the parade-ground. I was only with them for five months, but I never got promoted to the VIP Flight.

As for the flying, I was immediately sent up to do boring navigational and radio range exercises, and I got so cheesed off with being regarded as a bit of an amateur that, within a month, I applied, in a somewhat stilted but none the less forthright letter, for a posting back to my old squadron, but I have no record of any reply! In fact, the CO's response was to send me off to Snaith to do yet another course on the radio range. I still hadn't had my check-out as a captain when the first post-war 'RAF-DAY' came along on 15 September. At least there was some excitement here. A huge crowd of people turned up, and, as I was known to have a certain amount of experience with a microphone, I was sent up in a Dak to give a running commentary from the cockpit which was relayed through the loudspeakers on the ground. Even in those days, the aerodrome at Hendon was in a very built-up area—in bad weather the standard procedure for finding the runways was to 'turn left over the Co-op'—but we managed a couple of extremely low-level beat-ups over the heads of the spectators, with me gabbling away excitedly, describing what the pilot was doing. This air display was a very sedate affair when compared with today's offerings. I went recently to fly in a Dak at a show at the USAF base at Mildenhall, and was forced to endure three hours of the screeching and roaring of jets, some of which flew over the runway at some hideous speed, fifty feet up—and UPSIDE DOWN!! I'm glad we didn't try that in the Dak!

Eventually I was deemed capable enough to have my own crew, and the trips that we began to do were interesting enough.

I always had to arrive at Hendon carrying night-stop equipment, because you never knew what they were going to come up with next. One day it would be a humdrum flight to Belfast and back. The next day they might—never mind 'might', they did—tell me to take a load of battledress uniforms to Cairo. Now that was an epic trip, and I made the most of it. We flew via Marseilles, Malta, and El Adem, sight-seeing all the way. We stayed two nights in Cairo (I don't like the sound of the starboard engine, Flight Sergeant'). Sight-seeing around the city, I was accosted by a local trying to sell me a fez. He had a whole pyramid of them in his hand, and, forewarned by chaps who had spent more time abroad than me, I decided to haggle with him. I can't remember how much he asked, but I know I very daringly offered him exactly half. To my amazement, he took the money . . . and gave me the whole blessed lot!

On the return journey, I wangled a seat for my sister Aline, who had been out there for two years in Queen Alexandra's Nursing Corps. She had sent her heavy baggage on via brother Hughie's ship, which had passed through the Canal at a convenient moment.

24 Squadron is stationed at Lyneham nowadays, and not long ago, when I was doing a show at Swindon, the CO asked me to pay them a visit. In the adjutant's office they had dug out the records, and there it was, in longhand . . . 'F/Lt Edwards airborne Sept 29th 1945 for Cairo', etc., etc. Then the damning phrase: 'Returned eight days later.' Well! Both wars were over by now, and I could feel no urgency about things. Once I had a very jolly three-day jaunt round France and Germany carrying a party of twenty Armament Officers. They wanted to inspect the damage that Bomber Command had done, and my job was to make low and slow orbits of such places as Dunkirk, Ostend, Cologne and Essen. I was as interested as they were, but from a different point of view. I recall another fun jaunt, when I had to take a spare engine for an aircraft that had force-landed at Lisbon. I managed to squeeze three nights on the booze in that lovely city into the schedule. The CO wasn't too pleased with this escapade, and I found myself

relegated to the Hendon-to-Belfast run more and more often. I still hold the record for cancelling that trip—four days running. I expect that's in the records as well.

It wasn't all flying, however. There was a very keen flight lieutenant who ran the entertainments side of things, and I soon teamed up with him. He wanted to produce a pantomime, and, although I don't recall what part I played, it was inevitable that the King or the Mayor, or whoever I was, would play the trombone at one stage in the proceedings. This chap was also very friendly with Alan Dent, who at that time was theatre critic on the *News Chronicle*, and who came to see the show. He was so impressed that the next day he included this very ordinary amateur production in his column and said, in effect, that we were funnier than the Grazy Gang, who were doing their own panto at the Victoria Palace at the time.

I arranged to meet Mr Dent in a pub in the West End, and asked him point-blank whether he thought I could make a success in show-business. He hummed and ha'ed over his pint, and then said, 'I'm afraid I can't answer that. I'd hate to feel that I was responsible for you taking it up if you turned out to be a failure.' Nothing much to go on there. My very last flight as captain of a Dakota came on 17 December 1945, when I brought twelve passengers back from Belfast, one of whom, I noted, was Earl Granville. I had no idea that this was destined to be the end of my RAF flying career, and returned home to Barnes to celebrate a few days' leave in typical Edwards style, mostly in the Market Gardener. I was scheduled for one of my regular medicals on 27 December and went up to the Air Ministry with an all embracing hangover. After a few normal tests, the wing commander asked me casually, 'Do you still enjoy flying?' 'Sir,' I replied, in my most jaundiced fashion, 'I don't really care if I never fly again.' He wanted the truth, and that was the truth—at that particular moment. 'My word,' he said, in some alarm, 'you'd better go upstairs and see our psychiatrist.' I buttoned up my tunic and duly presented myself in front of a grey-haired, avuncular group captain, who proceeded to cover several sheets of foolscap with my answers to his stupid questions. At least,

I thought they were stupid. I don't remember them all, but I know that the very first one was, 'Do you feel tensed up at the wheel before take-off?' which I answered with a very strong affirmative. He followed this flatulence with more idiocies, and ended up with, 'Do you feel a sense of relief after a landing?' Well, of course I did. Who doesn't? He paused, put down his pen, stood up and said, with a hint of emotion: 'My boy, you've done enough,' and shook me warmly by the hand. He then sat down and wrote, 'Categorized A4H Bh (UK Only) by No. 1 Central Medical Board.' I knew at once what those hieroglyphics meant—I was unfit for any form of flying. Grounded, in fact.

Back at Hendon the wing commander was astounded. 'Last week, Edwards, you left here perfectly fit. Today, you come back totally grounded.' He boggled. 'Edwards,' he stuttered at last, 'whatever happened at that medical?' 'I don't know, sir,' I replied, rather too casually for his liking, 'must have been something I said.'

I must add that some time during this period we had celebrated VE Day in typical RAF fashion. Our rejoicing in the total end of the war was tempered by sad news that filtered through from Down Ampney. During the party there, Lieutenant Colonel Joubert (Jouby to us), now holder of the DSO and AFC, had made his own private celebratory rocket out of a couple of Very cartridges stuffed into a length of drain-piping, and, whilst trying to set light to it, had blown himself to smithereens.

WHAT NEXT?

IT'S HARD TO know how 24 Squadron got on without me, but they managed somehow. In fact, flying VC10s from Lyneham, they became some of the unsung heroes of the Falklands war, putting in an immense number of hours to and from Ascension Island. Often, when I see some politician or potentate on TV waving a regal arm as he walks down the steps of a VC10, I try to catch a glimpse of the squadron number painted on the side, but the cameras never focus on it.

My flying days may have been over, but my RAF career was not quite at an end. Like so many heroic stories, it did end three months later, not with a bang, but a whimper. I was given a 'release number' and they had to find something for me to do while I waited for it to come up. It was going to be several months, and they didn't want me kicking my heels at home on full pay, so I was sent down to Blackbushe, near Camberley, and put in charge of a small flight of Ansons whose sole job was to take newspapers to the SHAEF HQ every morning. It was good to see the old 'Annie' again, but I was not allowed to go up in them. I had to occupy myself with what are laughingly called 'administrative duties'. In other words, I sat in my office and tried to look important. It soon became clear to me that there was 'an atmosphere'. The young flying officer who had been running the show until my arrival clearly resented me and made his feelings obvious in many different ways, so I started spending more and more time at the bar in the Mess, and less and less behind my desk. This suited me so well that eventually I reasoned that I might just as well be buying my booze in the pub at home as in a not very congenial Mess, where I knew nobody, and so slipped quietly home in the faithful Austin 7, with the injunction, 'Phone me if there are any problems.' The whole scheme worked splendidly. The young F/O was delighted to take over the reins again, and made sure that nobody noticed my absence, and I drank merrily and played darts in the Market Gardener.

I also went into town occasionally to see a show, and it was at the Prince of Wales Theatre that I first saw a comedian whom I immediately admired. This was the great Sid Field, who, after nearly twenty-five years on the boards, had suddenly been 'discovered', and had become the darling of the West End. In those days you could get a standing-only ticket for five bob, and it was well worth it. Then, one Sunday lunchtime, deserting the old Gardener for once, I strolled across Barnes Common to take a pint in the Railway Arms, now known as The Red Rover. There, to my surprise, I saw my idol, surrounded by sycophantic friends and downing Scotch at a fair rate. I went in there on several occasions after that just to catch a glimpse of him, and I also popped into the Prince of Wales Theatre more often. How I laughed at his portrayal of 'Slasher' Green and his classic golfing sketch, but I began to get a bit bored with the lavish scenes in between the comedy, and took to popping into the stalls bar when they were on to have a quickie. Lo and behold, one evening when I had sneaked away like this, into the bar comes Sid and orders a Scotch. I was, of course, still in uniform, and he instantly recognized me. 'Haven't I seen you in the Railway?' he asked, and I blushingly admitted that I lived only a few hundred yards from it. 'Well,' said the great man, 'I live in East Sheen myself. How are you getting home tonight?' 'I usually go by bus.' 'Nonsense,' said Sid, 'I'll give you a lift home. Come round to the stage door after the show.' And so came my next stroke of luck. I got to know Sid Field in a nodding sort of way, and we often quaffed a glass together. Then, another coincidence. Somewhere or other I bumped into F/O Day, who had been in charge of entertainment when I had first gone to Down Ampney. 'Would you like to do your act at the Stage Door Canteen?' he asked. 'I can arrange it.'

The Stage Door Canteen was in Piccadilly next to Simpson's, and I had often been in there to have a drink and watch the show, which usually contained one or two stars, but the idea of appearing there myself had never occurred to me. 'Well,' I said . . . 'Go on,' said the enthusiastic Johnny Day. 'You ought to get into showbusiness, anyway.' I agreed, somewhat half-heartedly, and went up there and fixed a date. On the next Sunday I approached Sid Field in the saloon bar at the Railway. 'I am thinking of coming into your business,' I said tentatively. 'What do you reckon?' His reply came in that hilarious pseudo-posh voice he affected on the stage, 'You must be mad, my boy!'

'No, seriously,' I said, 'I'm appearing at the Stage Door Canteen next week.'

'Well,' said Sid, 'if you really mean it, the least I can do is get my agent to go and see you. You never know, do you?'

And he was as good as his word. I won't say I was a riot, but at least they didn't throw things at me, and as I was putting away my trombone, a thickset chap called Jack Adams presented his card and said he would try and get me an audition at the Windmill Theatre, which in those days was still going strong with its show called Revudeville, which had been going on all through the war.

Vivian Van Damm, who ran this theatre for Mrs Henderson, the owner, was only too keen to give auditions. His nude show needed occasional light relief, and there was a new programme every six weeks. I changed from uniform into my comic professor's outfit, and went up to the rehearsal room with my minute collection of musical parts. The great man lit an enormous cigar, leaned his elbow on top of the upright piano and said, 'Go ahead, my boy. You'll find I'm very easily amused.' After I had stumbled through my mish-mash of mirth, merriment, and music in complete silence, he slowly took the cigar from his mouth. 'Yes,' he said slowly, 'there's the makings of an act there somewhere.' Pause. 'Tell me, my boy, what are you going to do about that ridiculous moustache?' 'Oh, Mr Van Damm,' I faltered, 'I'll shave it off if you like.' 'No, no don't do that,' (there was a twinkle in his eye which later on I grew to recognize), 'it's the only funny thing in the act.'

After negotiations with Jack Adams which must have lasted all of three minutes, he signed me up for a six-week stint, six shows a day, six days a week, £20 a week. The snag was that I was still a serving member of His Majesty's Forces. The fact that I was doing most of my serving behind Albert's bar was beside the point. I had to wait for my discharge. It came, at last, on 4 March 1946, when I presented myself at a vast demob clothing store at Wembley. The corporal behind the counter didn't even bother to remove his tape-measure from round his neck. He eyed me up and down sarcastically and shouted over his shoulder to his cohort, 'Forty-four, portly!' and I was out once more into the mad world of civvy street.

And what a different civilian from the one who had climbed aboard that train to Blackpool. Gone the corduroy trousers and spotted bow tie. Gone the *Oxford Book of English Verse*, gone the ambition to teach and to write poetry, and the diffident introvert who didn't get on easily with people. Instead, we had the hard-drinking, hard-swearing, jocular Jim, ready to mix with anybody, and ready to do almost anything for money!

I was in showbusiness now. I'd already had two strokes of good luck; now, so early in my career, I was to experience one of the hazards of the profession—disappointment. I hadn't been home very long, and was still ill at ease in my brand-new three-piece suit, when Jack Adams phoned to say that the Windmill had postponed my engagement for six months. This was a great set-back before I had even started forward, but I took it like a man. I walked resolutely in Richmond Park every morning, and drank just as resolutely in the Market Gardener every night. My gratuity—a Rockerfellerian sum of £98—began to dwindle down my throat, but I clung on grimly. What else could I do? Cambridge had already declined to have me back, as I had my MA degree, and they were desperately full up with people of far greater ability than me. Nobody knew me in showbusiness. I just had to hang on. It was a bleak time. Rather Blackpool than this.

My four brothers returned one by one from their various service careers, each fresh arrival promoting a further debauch, and on one memorable night all five of us set the Market Gardener alight, and switched road signs round vandalistically on the way home.

My mother found it difficult to grasp the fact that I was going on the stage. 'I do hope, James,' she said sternly, 'that you will never lend yourself to anything suggestive.' Never lend, only sell, I thought to myself. I think my mother had only the vaguest idea of what showbusiness was all about, probably subscribing to the widely-held view that all actors were rogues and vagabonds. I suspect that the subject of my new profession was carefully avoided at the regular tea-parties and bridge evenings that took place in and around Woodlands Road in Barnes. She quite liked 'Take It From Here' later on, and when we put on a stage version at the Prince of Wales Theatre, her favourite act on the bill was Bob and Alf Pearson—'Very lively, and so well-dressed.' Her views about the whole matter were changed, however, when I was invited to entertain at a Christmas party at Buckingham Palace and took her along as my guest. She sat immediately behind the King and Queen, and was thrilled by the whole thing. 'I was so close to the Queen,' she said afterwards, 'that I could have touched her.'

'I'm glad you didn't, Mummy, or you'd have ended up in the Tower.'

But the great day eventually came. I donned my suit, my spats, my bicycle-clips, grasped my trombone, and went on to that tiny stage . . . and nothing happened. Well, it never did at the Windmill. Lots of ex-Service comedians had the same hard lesson. The audience was made up entirely of lascivious incipient perverts, and warped old men . . . and they don't laugh all that much. The first show was at about twenty minutes after midday, and after about an hour and forty minutes there was a short break before we did it again. Very often they would sit through two or even three performances, and there were occasionally those who sat in the front row from start to finish. I hated it, but did well enough for the Old Man—as I had learned everyone called Van Damm—to sign me up for another spell, and I was pleased enough with those four beautiful crinkly white fivers that I received each week. I had never handled one before, and I hid them about my person like a miser.

I paid my mother some rent, I journeyed between Barnes and Piccadilly by bus and underground train, and still had enough for beer in 'Daddy' Allen's club across the road in Windmill Street. Here I met several other comedians, also newly demobbed. Harry Secombe, Spike Milligan, Michael Bentine, and Peter Sellers were all looking for work, and had not even thought of 'The Goon Show'. They all, in turn, appeared at the Mill eventually. I was miserable there. No laughs, and a long winding staircase up to the dressing-room, which I shared with about six others.

Then came another stroke of luck. In the *Daily Telegraph* I read in the Peterborough column a small piece about a show which was about to open at the Stoll Theatre in Kingsway. It was to be a revue which some RAF chaps had put on at one of the prisoner-of-war camps in Germany, and the material was largely written by a Flight Lieutenant David Porter. I couldn't believe by eyes, having been quite satisfied in my mind since those days in Algiers that David was a gonner. It couldn't be the same person. I phoned the Stage Door at the Stoll, and again luck was on my side. David was just leaving as I rang. 'Is that the David Porter from North Battleford and Moncton?' I asked. 'Why ever not?' came back that well-remembered voice. 'But I was told you'd been shot down.' 'So I was, but I baled out and have been in Stalag Luft Six ever since.'

'We must meet,' I shouted in my excitement. Then: 'What are you doing with yourself, David?' 'Oh, I'm back at my old job at the BBC. Light entertainment department. What are you doing?' 'I'm in showbusiness too. Perhaps you can help me.' And that's what happened. I met David one day in The George, near Broadcasting House, and we had a pint with Gordon Crier, who, wonder of wonders, was running a radio show for ex-Servicemen called 'They're In . . . Because They're Out'.

Over a second pint, and with David's recommendation to urge him on, 'Gordie' booked me at once without an audition. At the rehearsal in the Aeolian Hall in Bond Street my corny old trombone was accompanied by George Melachrino and his fifty-seven-piece orchestra, and, as I finished the run-through, the musicians gave me a little round of applause, the string section rattling their bows on their instruments. A strange, almost indescribable, thrill ran up the burnt left side of my face, as still happens today in occasional moments of emotion or premonition.

Gordie was at the door as I left after the broadcast. He tapped my trombone-case with his finger. 'You want to hang on to that,' he said. 'You're going to make a lot of money with it.'

I had had my strokes of luck. Now I was going to need the stamina.

Postscript

I HAVE ONLY had my hands on the controls of a Dak a couple of times since the war. In about 1980, touring Australia with Eric Sykes in *Big Bad Mouse*, as we landed at Cairns, in Northern Queensland, I noticed about five of the darlings lined up on the tarmac. Painted on the fuselage was the legend 'Bush Pilots' Airline', and I lost no time in contacting the owner. I found that they specialized in leisurely eight-day sight-seeing trips around the Great Barrier Reef, landing and spending the night on various islands. They called them 'Gooney-bird' flights, the Aussie nickname for the DC3, but they also did regular freight runs to inland aboriginal settlements.

I managed to wangle myself on to one of these trips, and it was the greatest day of the whole tour. We hadn't been airborne long before the captain invited me to take over ('No passengers to scare the pants off, Jim!'), and I was soon in my element. Then: 'I see you haven't lost yer touch, Jim.' (I swelled with pride.) 'Take 'er down to five hundred feet, follow the river, and look for crocodiles.' It was an hour or so of sheer bliss for me. You never forget the feel of a Dak. I swooped along, totally relaxed, following the line of the river, the co-pilot constantly urging me to 'get 'er down lower, Jim'. We found our destination far too soon for my liking, but I was none the less relieved that the pilot wasn't mad enough to allow me to attempt the landing.

Back at Cairns, in the manager's office, I found an aspiring second pilot being put through some sort of examination. 'If he doesn't pass,' I said jovially, 'you might consider me for the job.'

'Sorry, Jim,' said the manager, 'you were really comparatively inexperienced when you mucked about in

223

these. We don't take anybody on even for co-pilot unless he's done two thousand hours.'

My miserable sum-total for the entire war had been only 1,620 hours.

Then came 1984, and I realized that it was forty years since I had taken my glider across the Channel to the River Orne. I knew that there were several Daks flying from the island of Jersey, owned by an outfit called 'Air Atlantique', and I decided that this was an anniversary not to be missed. 'Jim must be there,' I thought, 'whatever the cost.' Accordingly, in February of that year I chartered one, paid the deposit, and sauntered off to Western Australia for a holiday.

When I came back in May it seemed that the whole world had got wind of my plans, and the Queen, President Reagan, and M. Mitterand had all decided to go to the beaches to see me fly past. Greatly flattered, I gathered together some more members of 271, including Bill Randall, Bob Rees, and Jouby's navigator, David Grant, and we set off from Eastleigh, near Southampton, at four in the afternoon. To my astonishment, there were seats for thirty-five of us, because they had cut out completely the seats for the wireless-op and navigator, and moved the partition forward. So we included some chaps who called themselves 'enthusiasts', and they were all there, festooned with cameras, and calling for autographs. As we approached the French coast, I asked the captain if I could occupy his seat, and he was game enough to agree. Soon I had the wheel in my hands, and the old thrill came back.

And so it was that, exactly forty years after D-Day, I was flying a Dakota over the River Orne. The difference was that we were at six thousand feet, because a nervous French air-traffic controller had sent us up there to keep out of the way of the Queen's helicopter. So I never saw her wave. There was another difference. We had no glider behind us. Oh . . . and there was no eggs and bacon when we got back.

As I write this, we have just planned a trip to Arnhem, so that, about the time this book is being published. I shall be inspecting the exact spot where Treble Four went up in flames.